EXPERIENCING MAHLER

The Listener's Companion

Kenneth LaFave, Series Editor

Titles in **The Listener's Companion** provide readers with a deeper understanding of key musical genres and the work of major artists and composers. Aimed at nonspecialists, each volume explains in clear and accessible language how to listen to works from particular artists, composers, and genres. Looking at both the context in which the music first appeared and has since been heard, authors explore with readers the environments in which key musical works were written and performed.

Experiencing Alice Cooper: A Listener's Companion, by Ian Chapman
Experiencing the Beatles: A Listener's Companion, by Brooke Halpin
Experiencing Beethoven: A Listener's Companion, by Geoffrey Block
Experiencing Berlioz: A Listener's Companion, by Melinda O'Neal
Experiencing Bessie Smith: A Listener's Companion, by John Clark
Experiencing Big Band Jazz: A Listener's Companion, by Jeff Sultanof
Experiencing Billy Joel: A Listener's Companion, by Thomas MacFarlane
Experiencing Black Sabbath: A Listener's Companion, by Nolan Stolz
Experiencing Broadway Music: A Listener's Companion, by Kathryn Sherrell
Experiencing Carl Maria von Weber: A Listener's Companion, by Joseph E. Morgan
Experiencing Chick Corea: A Listener's Companion, by Monika Herzig
Experiencing Chopin: A Listener's Companion, by Christine Gengaro
Experiencing David Bowie: A Listener's Companion, by Ian Chapman
Experiencing Debussy: A Listener's Companion, by Teresa Davidian
Experiencing Film Music: A Listener's Companion, by Kenneth LaFave
Experiencing Herbie Hancock: A Listener's Companion, by Eric Wendell
Experiencing Jazz: A Listener's Companion, by Michael Stephans
Experiencing Jewish Music in America: A Listener's Companion, by Tina Frühauf
Experiencing Led Zeppelin: A Listener's Companion, by Gregg Akkerman
Experiencing Leonard Bernstein: A Listener's Companion, by Kenneth LaFave
Experiencing Mahler: A Listener's Companion, by Arved Ashby
Experiencing Mozart: A Listener's Companion, by David Schroeder
Experiencing Ornette Coleman: A Listener's Companion, by Michael Stephans
Experiencing Peter Gabriel: A Listener's Companion, by Durrell Bowman
Experiencing Progressive Rock: A Listener's Companion, by Robert G. H. Burns
Experiencing the Rolling Stones: A Listener's Companion, by David Malvinni
Experiencing Rush: A Listener's Companion, by Durrell Bowman
Experiencing Schumann: A Listener's Companion, by Donald Sanders
Experiencing Stravinsky: A Listener's Companion, by Robin Maconie
Experiencing Tchaikovsky: A Listener's Companion, by David Schroeder
Experiencing Verdi: A Listener's Companion, by Donald Sanders
Experiencing the Violin Concerto: A Listener's Companion, by Franco Sciannameo

EXPERIENCING MAHLER

A Listener's Companion

Arved Ashby

ROWMAN & LITTLEFIELD
Lanham • Boulder • New York • London

Published by Rowman & Littlefield
An imprint of The Rowman & Littlefield Publishing Group, Inc.
4501 Forbes Boulevard, Suite 200, Lanham, Maryland 20706
www.rowman.com

86-90 Paul Street, London EC2A 4NE

British Library Cataloguing in Publication Information Available

Library of Congress Cataloging-in-Publication Data

Names: Ashby, Arved Mark, 1964– author.
Title: Experiencing Mahler : a listener's companion / Arved Ashby.
Description: Lanham : Rowman & Littlefield Publishing Group, 2020. | Series: Listener's companion | Includes bibliographical references and index. | Summary: "Arved Ashby takes readers into the seeming chaos of Mahler's work to investigate the elements which make each piece an experiential adventure. The book surveys Mahler's symphonies and song cycles in detail, introducing them as intensely vivid, truthful, and lived and felt experiences"—Provided by publisher.
Identifiers: LCCN 2019043173 (print) | LCCN 2019043174 (ebook) | ISBN 9781538198865 (paper)
Subjects: LCSH: Mahler, Gustav, 1860–1911--Criticism and interpretation. | Mahler, Gustav, 1860–1911. Symphonies. | Mahler, Gustav, 1860–1911. Song cycles.
Classification: LCC ML410.M23 A83 2020 (print) | LCC ML410.M23 (ebook) | DDC 780.92—dc23
LC record available at https://lccn.loc.gov/2019043173
LC ebook record available at https://lccn.loc.gov/2019043174

∞™ The paper used in this publication meets the minimum requirements of American National Standard for Information Sciences—Permanence of Paper for Printed Library Materials, ANSI/NISO Z39.48-1992.

CONTENTS

SERIES EDITOR'S FOREWORD

The goal of the Listener's Companion series is to give readers a deeper understanding of pivotal musical genres and the creative work of its iconic composers and performers. This is accomplished in an inclusive manner that does not necessitate extensive music training or elitist shoulder rubbing. Authors of the series place the reader in specific listening experiences in which the music is examined in its historical context with regard to both compositional and societal parameters. By positioning the reader in the real or supposed environment of the music's creation, the author provides for a deeper enjoyment and appreciation of the art form. Series authors, often drawing on their own expertise as both performers and scholars, deliver to readers a broad understanding of major musical genres and the achievements of artists within those genres as lived listening experiences.

Peeking behind a creative artist's work is a dangerous thing. It is also the only way we can begin to understand why a piece of music—or a poem or a painting—moves us the way it does. A work of art needs no explanation to touch us; indeed, analysis can get in the way. But to know why it moved us requires grasping many subordinate elements. Some of these are purely aesthetic: form, genre, materials, the historical traditions and contemporary environment surrounding the work. Others are more speculative. What light can be shed on the work by the artist's state of mind? What clues exist in the artist's letters and personal exchanges at the time the work was created? What role is played by the artist's sense of historical place, or the lack thereof? Who were the artist's influences? All these factors and more directly affect the artist's choices, and those choices make the work. Examining them is not biography, but genealogy (though biographical elements will always be in play). Such is the purpose of the Listener's Companion series: to illuminate the origins of an artist's music by tracing the roots of its creation and making them clear for the average reader.

Arved Ashby has taken on the task of illuminating the origins of music composed by one of the most complex musicians of any era, Gustav Mahler. Mahler straddled the nineteenth and twentieth centuries like no other composer. He brought to final ripeness the symphony, a form that had undergone amazing maturation in the 150 years or so since its beginnings in opera overtures and courtly dance music. From that standpoint, his music culminated the nineteenth century. But in its irony, its stretching of formal expectations, and above all its sense that the very tonal system it employed was approaching fruition and exhaustion, Mahler's music belongs to the twentieth century.

In energetic prose, Ashby guides us through Mahler's ten numbered symphonies and numerous songs, an astonishing output for even a full-time composer given three score and ten, but something approaching miracle from a "summer composer," whose seasonal vocation was conducting the major orchestras and opera houses of Europe and the United States, and whose sickly life granted him only five decades. Ashby's recurring themes include the influence of nature on the composer's work, Maher's awareness of music history and its perilous future, and Mahler's consistent aim at shaping "symphonic journeying," which in the early symphonies takes the form of simple storytelling. He creatively draws on the insights of major Mahler interpreters, on the work of previous Mahler scholars, and on his own perceptions of Mahler's style and method to present a lucid vision of this indispensable catalog, at one juncture even writing a speculative lyric to one of the Third Symphony's melodies to make a point about the tune's shape.

The listener for whom Mahler is a new enthusiasm will find in this book a door to understanding the whys and wherefores of the composer's oeuvre. The veteran listener to Mahler will find new facts, fresh perspectives, and pertinent questions. The seemingly naïve Fourth Symphony may not be so naïve, after all. The key to what Leonard Bernstein called the "parodistic" elements of the Seventh Symphony may lie in "defamiliarization," the process of rendering the familiar unfamiliar by calling attention to its more obvious traits. What can be gained by hearing the first movement of the Ninth Symphony, not as sonata-allegro, but as a set of variations on two themes, "one songful and the other anxiously frantic"—an opposition that might well sum up Mahler's grounding aesthetic? And what reason might be given for the passage from utter darkness to sky-blue exuberance in the Fifth Symphony?

Like the output of any other major composer, and maybe more than most, Mahler's music prompts thoughts about how the notes on the page relate to the artistic experience as it presents itself to open ears and minds. To that end, Ashby spends considerable ink examining the composer's complex, post-Wagnerian harmonies, but does so in a way that will not put off the listener who lacks a musical education. If you have heard even a bit of Mahler in a non-concert context—the Adagietto of Symphony no. 5 in the film *Death in Venice*, perhaps, or the opening of Symphony no. 1 in the last episode of the TV series *Boardwalk Empire*—chances are you were captivated and eager to explore the composer's vast, amazing canon. To do that, gather some recordings and read this book. All you need are a love of music and the willingness to learn.

Kenneth LaFave

INTRODUCTION

> When I first started listening to Mahler, I used to wonder if he wasn't just fundamentally mistaken about how to go about creating music. I sometimes feel that way even now. Why is he doing *this* in *this* part of the composition?
>
> —Haruki Murakami (*Absolutely on Music*, 2011)

> Must I have a correct understanding of what I have lived and felt? And I believe I have felt your symphony. I shared in the battling for illusion; I suffered the pangs of disillusionment; I saw the forces of evil and good wrestling with each other; I saw a man in torment struggling towards inward harmony; I divined a personality, a drama, and *truthfulness*, the most uncompromising truthfulness.
>
> —Arnold Schoenberg (in a letter to Mahler after hearing the Third Symphony, 1904)

The "experiencing" title fits my subject, since Mahler's music speaks to the highs and lows of life more than it deals in learned abstractions or reassuring conventions. As critic and musicologist Paul Bekker put it in his 1921 book *Gustav Mahlers Sinfonien* (*Gustav Mahler's Symphonies*), this composer "was filled with a burning desire to break through the layers of distorting educated intellect that lay above the pure humanity of the natural being." In turning away from abstractions, like foreseeable structures or consistency of style, his music often seems to give up musicality for harsh reality: it speaks explicitly, in terms so strong and raw they can alarm us even in the twenty-first century, as if the ink were still wet on the page.

Mahler's pieces seem to ask, as a basic rationale, "Since when has music been something one is supposed to *understand*?" As Arnold Schoenberg suggests in the letter quoted above, experience is different from understanding, let alone "correct" understanding. Schoenberg opened his letter on Mahler's Third by saying music terminology could hardly account for the piece as he experienced it: the composition left him able "[to] speak only as one human being to another." It says something about the Third Symphony's power that it discouraged even a composer, teacher, theorist, and outspoken polemicist like Schoenberg from using the rationalist's usual terms of understanding, leading him instead to try and explain "the feelings an experience arouses in me."

We could talk about listeners becoming immersed in Mahler—plunged into a music that is too irrefusable to be understood. Immersion suggests an all-enveloping experience where the intellect plays no role. Mahler's listeners can have the strangely pleasant feeling of fighting for survival against overwhelming, sublime forces. Richard Wagner, probably Mahler's key musical influence, talked about music in such terms: he spoke of melody being set into motion by rhythm, becoming a musical equivalent to wind-swept waves, and "in such a sea a person immerses himself" ("*in dieses Meer taucht sich der Mensch*"). Water goes where it wants to, and it's this kind of tidal dynamic that Haruki Murakami points out when he refers to Mahler's "fundamentally mistaken" structures. We could even say that Mahler's expressive power comes from his refusal to do things "properly." The tried-and-trusted conventions of sonata form were synonymous with musical rule-following, and symphonists as diverse as Charles Gounod, Vasily Kalinnikov, and the younger Antonin Dvorak showed how "proper" formal scaffoldings could serve the moment-to-moment dynamics of well-mannered expression in the late nineteenth century.

Sitting down to hear the first movement of a symphony, listeners of the time would have expected a sonata form—a musical structure involving three contrasting thematic areas that play out across the three traditional functional sections of (1) *exposition* of themes, (2) intricate and often ingenious *development* of said themes, and then (3) recognizable *recapitulation* of those themes. Traditionally speaking, the symphonic composer underlined such structural junctures as points of emotional tension, drama, or completion: the point of recapitulation, for instance, often becomes a moment of triumph or satisfied re-arrival. In overall terms, the emotional-dramatic progression of a movement tended to be plausibly mapped upon the formal structure. Mahler did things differently. The philosopher and social critic Theodor Wiesengrund Adorno, working from ideas set forth by Paul Bekker, even came up with experiential terms for Mahler's "mistaken" formal practices. He talked about some of Mahler's forms in terms of structural breakthrough (*Durchbruch*), suspension (*Suspension*), and fulfillment (*Erfüllung*). These are nonanalytical terms, suggesting psychology or philosophy rather than music. In using them, Adorno focused not on standard patterns of repetition, but on willful musical events that take on far-reaching implications.

Mahler himself famously said that "the symphony must be like the world; it must contain everything." His statement is revealing in so many ways. Worlds are usually created by gods rather than musicians, and Mahler is an example of high-handed creation doing exactly what it wants and succeeding or failing on that account. As the philosopher-essayist Ralph Waldo Emerson put it, "To believe your own thought, that is genius." Such self-importance is part of Richard Wagner's and Friedrich Nietzsche's influences on Mahler, resulting in a culture of mad indulgence that carries on to composer-cranks as musically different as Harry Partch, Karlheinz Stockhausen, and Michael Tippett. And yet Mahler didn't cloak his self-importance and impropriety in ill-defined and doctrinaire notions of "modern music." Maybe his most audacious musical act of all was to tempt comparison with classical forbears by writing minuets (as in his Second and Third Symphonies) and, as a way of rebelling sometimes against his own loyalty to "the natural being," writing some sonata-form movements that are almost cheeky in their straightforwardness (as in the Fourth and Sixth Symphonies).

It should be clear from these observations that Mahler is a daunting topic, all the more so because piles of books have been devoted to him. Nonacademics will find certain volumes from these bulging library shelves more helpful than others. The definitive life account is Henry-Louis de la Grange's multivolume biography, but Peter Franklin's much more concise and still beautifully written *Life of Mahler* will be more useful for nonspecialists. For a straightforward life-and-works, I suggest Michael Kennedy's *Mahler* or Kurt Blaukopf's volume *Gustav Mahler*, published in English translation in 1973. For a synoptic account of the music, Constantin Floros's *Gustav Mahler: The Symphonies* is a go-to volume, though the English translation is at times questionable. Paul Bekker's richly insightful and engaging book *Gustav Mahler's Symphonies*, published in 1921 and recently translated from the German, offers the perceptions of a musician and critic of Mahler's own time.

My own book is no biography, nor is it a life-and-works study. I intend it as a broad introduction to Mahler's music and ideas, with an emphasis on "bring[ing] readers closer to the musical work as a living listening experience"—as blurbs for the Listener's Companion series would have it. My aim has been to bring readers closer to Mahler's compositions by simplifying discussion of his structures and his compositional aims, and by usefully uncovering avenues of experience. I have tried to open his daunting world of musical abandon for the reader by giving some points of access, some "ways in." There's nothing systematic or especially original about my similes, insights, historical comparisons, and semantical discussions. Apart maybe from the references to musical events and ordering, I'm not sure if any of these approaches can be replicated in someone else's experience. But then Mahler forces us to realize one of the basic truisms about music more broadly: that musical meaning can't be nailed down by any one interpreter.

To connect with this music is an ongoing, conversational effort, a fulfilling task for a lifetime. Even in those cases where Mahler himself gave detailed subtitles, storylines, and programs to his symphonies, the musical significances begin rather than end there. And so I hope my readings won't be taken literally, but will instead provoke similar or dissimilar reactions of your own. When I say, for instance, that a panic attack is suggested in the first of the *Kindertotenlieder*, that the climax of the first movement of the Fourth Symphony explodes like a child's tantrum, and that the repeated stopped-horn rasps in the first movement of the Ninth Symphony sound like pleas for mercy, I don't mean to be taken literally. These are suggestions rather than conclusions: they are potential footholds, similes for passages that could just as easily lend themselves to other interpretations.

READING MAHLER

Talking about Mahler in terms of listener experience can help counter the trend toward urban myth and the deluge of highly specialized research. As examples of the former, we have the racy anecdotes surrounding Mahler's wife, Alma—for instance, from Oliver Hilmes's book *Malevolent Muse*. As instances of the latter, we have local details of Gustav's instrumentation, or—as surfaced in a recent musicology conference—the practice of Alma's gynecologist. As approached through such avenues, Mahler has become one of the most heavily discussed topics in all music. One North American search engine lists 272 books published on him. Since most of these have appeared in an increasing torrent over the past forty years, the cascade of publications amounts to an average of two Mahler books per year over the past four decades.

For readers of English, Mahler studies really began in earnest with Henry-Louis de la Grange's mammoth, groundbreaking biography, published between 1973 and 2008 though of course researched decades earlier. Before La Grange, there was Natalie Bauer-Lechner's *Recollections of Gustav Mahler*: a charming and very readable memoir of the composer stretching from the gestation of the First Symphony to his marriage. Then came Alma Mahler's two engrossing books involving her husband, *Gustav Mahler: Memories and Letters* (1940), and *And the Bridge Is Love: Memories of a Lifetime* (1958). Here, she proposed that the symphonies were in essence musical autobiographies when they weren't foretellings of the future (the finale of the Sixth Symphony presenting "three blows of fate, the last of which fells [the author] as a tree is felled"). Alma also helped inscribe Gustav's death preoccupation into the historical record, as she did the traditional explanation of it as the composer's reaction to the early demise of so many of his siblings. And then, in a musical-creational narrative that sounds authored in itself, the specter of extinction comes full circle when the composer is said to have written his last works under the shadow of his own imminent death. This moving "twilight of a composer" scenario, rendered indelible by Alma, was first offered by Richard Specht (in his 1913 book *Gustav Mahler*) and then corroborated by Bruno Walter in his own warm and enjoyable little volume *Gustav Mahler* (first published in 1936).

Over the decades, Mahler's many inquisitors have concentrated on biography and structural-theoretical discussions. These preoccupations with the same kinds of meanings are blinkered and misleading—though it's understandable that people should be interested in his life, just as it's forgivable that people should want his life to be as complex and interesting as his compositions. But to think of Mahler's works as diaries or as compositional "pounds of flesh"—as musically illustrated autobiography, à la Richard Strauss's *Ein Heldenleben* and *Sinfonia Domestica*—is to confuse the composer's experience with our experience, and to limit ourselves as listeners. Likewise, to confine Mahler's musical meanings to reductive discussions of "absolute music" abstraction versus "program music" illustration—discussions that continue to this day—is to stymie the listener in his or her own quest for musical experience.

A WORD ON MUSIC TIMINGS

The goal is to focus as directly as possible on experiences and meanings in Mahler's very long instrumental spans, and to do so without getting mired in the structural terminology (for instance, *third theme group*, *retransition*, *recapitulation*, *coda*) that we had best avoid as remnants of "the educated intellect." To accomplish this, I cue my discussions to specific, moment-to-moment points in the music. I do this by placing specific time stamps in the main text—times taken from Leonard Bernstein's historic and readily available cycle on Columbia (recorded 1960–1967, now on Sony Classical). It should be mentioned that Bernstein recorded the Second Symphony twice for that label; my timings are from his 1963 version with the New York Philharmonic, not the London Symphony rendition from a decade later. In the case of the *Lieder eines fahrenden Gesellen*, *Kindertotenlieder*, and *Rückert Lieder*, I've taken my time stamps from the 1988 and 1990 recordings that Bernstein made with Thomas Hampson and the Vienna Philharmonic on Deutsche Grammophon. With the Deryck Cooke edition of the Tenth Symphony, a work that Bernstein did not conduct, I take my timings from Riccardo Chailly's 1986 Berlin recording on Decca. The hope is that the reader will use these timings in my text to connect with specific points in the music, and will then pass those observations on to other recorded interpretations—for example, those listed in my discography. To readers looking for interpretations more objective than Bernstein's and for more consistent and reliable orchestral playing, I'd recommend Claudio Abbado, and Bernard Haitink with the Concertgebouw Orchestra.

ACKNOWLEDGMENTS

Debts of gratitude are owed to Amy Bauer, Eric Davis, Beth and James Himsworth, Kathy and Andy Steinman, and especially Jiung Yoon for his forbearance. I'm thankful to Bennett Graff for the original invitation to contribute to this series. At Rowman & Littlefield, Natalie Mandziuk and Kenneth LaFave deserve many thanks for their very patient support of this project as acquisitions editor and series editor, respectively. Thomas Peattie was selfless with his untiring supplies of encouragement, good cheer, and intimate knowledge of things Mahlerian, but all errors and omissions remain my own.

TIMELINE

1860 7 July, born to Marie and Bernhard Mahler, Kalischt near Iglau, Bohemia (now Kaliště near Jihlava, Czech Republic); family moves to Iglau later that year.

1866 Composes one of his first pieces, "Polka with Introductory Funeral March" (now lost).

1870 Gives first piano recital.

1875 Enters Vienna Conservatory, where he enrolls for three years; studies piano and majors in composition.

1876 Writes and premieres his first composition that survives, the opening movement of Piano Quartet in A Minor (first modern performance given in New York, 1964).

1877 Enrolls in University of Vienna concurrently with his last conservatory year; joins the student Academic Wagner Society, which devotes itself to the philosophies of Nietzsche, Wagner, and socialist thinkers; gives up ambitions of becoming a professional pianist.

1880 First music publication: a two-piano arrangement of Bruckner's Symphony no. 3, prepared with his friend Rudolph Krzyzanowski at the composer's request.

1880 Takes his first conducting job leading a small summer operetta company at Bad Hall, upper Austria; opts for this only after running out of employment options, but finds himself suited to it.

1881 Submits his ambitious dramatic cantata *Das klagende Lied* for the Beethoven Prize in composition, a competition sponsored by the Vienna Conservatory and judged by Brahms; it fails to win an award.

1881 Conducts his first opera, Verdi's *Il Trovatore*, at the Landestheater in Laibach (now Ljubljana, Slovenia).

1883 Becomes music director at the Königliche Schauspiele, Kassel.

1883–1885 While director at Kassel, writes the *Lieder eines fahrenden Gesellen* (*Songs of a Wayfarer*), settings of his own love poems to house soprano Johanna Richter; on departing, Mahler spites his higher-up by conducting a triumphant local performance of Mendelssohn's *St. Paul*, an oratorio the superior had been planning on conducting himself.

1886 Becomes assistant to the eminent conductor Arthur Nikisch at the Neues Stadttheater in Leipzig; takes over performances of Wagner's *Die Walküre* and *Siegfried* when Nikisch falls ill in January 1887, and gets rave reviews.

1887 Enters a long and mutually beneficial friendship with Richard Strauss.

1888 Conducts his free completion of Carl Maria von Weber's unfinished opera *Die drei Pintos* in Leipzig, to high acclaim; having fallen in love with the wife of Weber's grandson, he is inspired to write tone poems that will become his First and Second Symphonies; quits the Leipzig position in May.

1888–1891 Serves as music director of the Royal Hungarian Opera, Budapest, where he performs operas in Hungarian translation and increases box office returns; Johannes Brahms is impressed by his Budapest *Don Giovanni*, and the two become friends.

1889 His parents and sister Leopoldine die, leaving Mahler the breadwinner for six siblings; he becomes close with his younger sister Justine. Premieres Symphony no. 1 in Budapest, to hostile reviews.

1890 Enters eleven-year friendship with violist Natalie Bauer-Lechner, who becomes his confidante and later on possibly his lover; Bauer-Lechner later authored the invaluable book *Erinnerungen an Gustav Mahler* (posthumously published in 1923, and in translation as *Recollections of Gustav Mahler*, 1980).

1891–1897 Serves as chief conductor at the Stadttheater, Hamburg, where he conducts his first *Tristan und Isolde* and earns Tchaikovsky's praise leading the German premiere of *Yevgeny Onegin*.

1892 Falls victim to Hamburg cholera epidemic, but returns to work after only ten days; publishes the *Lieder und Gesänge* for voice and piano.

1894 Death of his eminent conducting mentor Hans von Bülow, whereupon Mahler takes over von Bülow's philharmonic subscription concerts and is moved to finish his own Symphony no. 2 (*Resurrection*); meets Bruno Walter, a young conductor and composer from Berlin, and takes him under wing.

1895 Richard Strauss invites Mahler to conduct the three instrumental movements of his Symphony no. 2 with the Berlin Philharmonic; nine months later, Mahler premieres the complete symphony in Berlin before an enthusiastic audience.

1896 Completes Symphony no. 3 at his summer retreat at Steinbach am Attersee, upper Austria.

1897 Publishes Symphony no. 2, his first multimovement work to make it into print.

1897–1907 Converts to Roman Catholicism in preparation for becoming director of the Vienna Court Opera; during his ten-year tenure he raises artistic standards and box office revenues, but also inspires controversy and hostility among musicians and the public.

1898–1901 Leads three seasons of Vienna Philharmonic subscription concerts; in June 1890, their first tour abroad ends with the orchestra stranded in Paris without funds.

1899 Publishes Symphony no. 1 and *Des Knaben Wunderhorn*, twelve songs for voice and orchestra.

1899–1900 Writes Symphony no. 4, completing it at the Wörthersee in Carinthia.

1901 Begins collaborations at the Court Opera with brilliant stage director Alfred Roller; declares "death to programs!" in a letter to a friend; suffers a severe rectal hemorrhage, necessitating emergency surgery and a long convalescence; builds a summer villa at Maiernigg on the Wörthersee, Carinthia.

1901–1902 Composes five songs to Friedrich Rückert texts; loosely assembled, these become known as his *Rückert Lieder*.

1901–1902 Composes Symphony no. 5, completing it at Maiernigg.

1901–1904 Sets five poems from Rückert's *Kindertotenlieder* for voice and orchestra, publishes them as his only integral song cycle.

1902 Marries twenty-two-year-old Alma Schindler on 9 March, after a four-month courtship.

1902 First complete performance of Symphony no. 3 in Krefeld, near Düsseldorf, stirs interest in his earlier works.

1902 First daughter Maria born, 3 November.

1903–1904 Composes Symphony no. 6, completing it at Maiernigg.

1904 Second daughter Anna born, 15 June.

1904–1905 Composes Symphony no. 7, completing it at Maiernigg.

1906 Conducts premiere of Symphony no. 6 in Essen, to general confusion, on 27 May; composes Symphony no. 8 at high speed, completing it at Maiernigg.

1907 Resigns from Vienna Court Opera and signs contract with the Metropolitan Opera, New York; Maria Mahler dies, 5 July, prompting Mahler family to vacate the Maiernigg home.

1908 Composes *Das Lied von der Erde*, completing it at Toblach in the South Tyrol.

1908–1909 Composes Symphony no. 9, completing it at Toblach.

1908–1909 Director of the Metropolitan Opera, New York; debuts with Alfred Roller's acclaimed production of *Tristan und Isolde*.

1909–1911 Resigns directorship of the Metropolitan, becomes director of the newly reformed New York Philharmonic Society.

1909 Conducts his first performance of a Mahler work in the United States: Symphony no. 1 with the New York Philharmonic, 16 December.

1910 Begins composing Symphony no. 10; discovers Alma's affair with the young Walter Gropius; in August meets Sigmund Freud in Leiden, Holland, and undergoes four hours of psychoanalysis; remorseful over suppressing his wife's compositional ambitions, Mahler has Universal Edition issue five of Alma's songs under the title *Fünf Lieder*.

1910 Premieres Symphony no. 8 on 12 September in Munich to high acclaim, marking the apex of his compositional career and status as a public figure.

1911 Further revises Symphonies nos. 5 and 9; afflicted with a streptococcus infection and suffering a high fever, he conducts the New York Philharmonic in his final concert, an Italian program with Ferrucio Busoni and Arturo Toscanini in the audience, 21 February.

1911 Arrives in Paris 18 April to consult with a bacteriologist; dies in Vienna 18 May; buried 21 May in Grinzing, suburb of Vienna, beside daughter Maria.

1

SYMPHONY NO. 1

The Journey Begins

Mahler began the First Symphony in 1887 and his Second the following year, and nurtured these large-scale projects while working as conductor at the Leipzig Stadttheater. The twenty-seven-year-old musician had high ambitions as both conductor and composer, though just eight years out of the Vienna Conservatory and not yet employed as music director of an opera house. He was playing the field audaciously as a conductor: pitting directors against each other, forcing cancellation of his contracts, and negotiating municipal opera house politics in ways that promised to leave him unemployed rather than highly stationed. In her memoir of Mahler, friend Natalie Bauer-Lechner remembered seeing him in such a self-induced crisis right after the Leipzig position: "He looked miserable, was physically very run-down and—as always when he had no position—was oppressed by the darkest misgivings, as if he would never find employment again." This musician from the provinces was clearly a man of extremes, hypersensitive yet outrageously ambitious.

All of Mahler's symphonies are autobiographical insofar as they embody these grandiose, bold, and self-tortured aspects of his character. But the first two are especially self-focused and vividly reflect their author's youthfulness: every bar sounds like a young man's work, driven to excess, dew-laden one moment and chest-beating the next. Just as Mahler was developing a split personality between performing and composing, his compositional energies were dividing between instrumental works and vocal music. In both cases, the one side informed and motivated the other. With his first four symphonies, he incorporated extended passages from his own songs into his instrumental compositions. This practice, along with programmatic aspects, was a way to bridge divisions between "abstract" and illustrative music, and in doing so helped revitalize the Austro-German symphony at a time—after Brahms's fourth and last example—when younger musicians considered it a hidebound genre.

Mahler developed ways to incorporate songs in symphonic movements, especially in his first two symphonies. When he simply gave the vocal line of a song to an instrument in the orchestra, these passages became importations of real-world emotional, descriptive, or narrative significance into the wordless, nonspecific domain of instrumental music. But this was just one way Mahler played with the question of where and how specific meaning can be construed in the abstract, wordless realm of orchestral writing. As the fourth movement of the Second Symphony, he simply included his *Lied* "Urlicht" ("Primal Light") with no changes. For the first movement of the First, he took his earlier song "Ging heut' Morgen übers Feld" ("I Walked Out This Morning onto the Meadow"), added new material, shuffled its constituent parts, and further composed it out. In this way, the new fifteen-minute musical span became an elaboration on the song's original text about welcoming the morning. Mahler's first several symphonies also cultivate a general lyricism of style that can make instruments of the orchestra seem as if they are just about to break out into song, or even into the unpatterned directness of speech.

While Mahler's mastery on the conductor's rostrum was recognized early on, the critics soon made it clear he wouldn't be making a living from his compositions. "A crude din deliberately presented as a parody." "Grotesque cacophony." "A stylistic absurdity." "Alien to music." "A total failure." So read some of the critics' reactions to his First Symphony when he led its Vienna premiere in November 1900. But what flustered early audiences was the same quality that actually attracts today's listeners: namely, the young composer's queer intensity of expression, as couched in the highbrow genre of the symphony with all its rhetorical weight and cultural cachet. Viennese audiences of 1900—listeners acculturated in the instrumental music of Haydn, Mozart,

Beethoven, and Brahms—heard such intensity as loud inauthenticity, as emotional violence. And they believed such brutality was out of place in the symphony, a traditionalist's genre that was defined by cumulative impact, continuity of thought, and historical convention. Those were the ways instrumental concert music had of being meaningful, and more conservative listeners—those sharing critic Eduard Hanslick's distaste for the "emotional bombast" of Richard Wagner and Franz Liszt—drew a distinction between "purely" symphonic music and those "artificial" musical strivings for effect that had no place outside the theater.

Listeners of the time couldn't understand Mahler's jumbled extravagances without help from extramusical rationales—which they'd expect to come from literature and history. In writing the symphonic poems *Les Préludes* and *Tasso: Lamento e Trionfo*, Liszt had devised new instrumental music structures under the banner of poets Alphonse de Lamartine and Torquato Tasso, respectively. Mahler's orchestral virtuosity, admired even by his naysayers, ended up making listeners want explanation all the more. After he abandoned programs in 1901, his audiences felt shortchanged by such overtly theatrical orchestral pieces with no programmatic "keys" to unlock them. For these various reasons, audiences considered Mahler's First Symphony a challenge, an affront, or even a joke. The first critic I quote above suspected parody, and he wasn't alone in hearing contempt in Mahler's intensity, contrasts between mania and disaffection, and love of effects. Parody had a home in the theater, critics argued, but in the august history of the symphony—a native Viennese genre promulgated most recently by Brahms, a composer without a satirical bone in his body—it was absolute poison.

NATURE'S AWAKENING BECOMES A SYMPHONIC BEGINNING

In its four-movement layout, the First Symphony pays a debt to the classical symphonic setup of first movement, scherzo, slow movement, and summational finale. But in the event, Mahler's four movements seem an assemblage of music from unrelated sources. We have a first movement tracing a dawn-to-noon onrush of light and energy, then a dance bursting with bumpkinish *joie de vivre*, followed by a sardonic funeral march that begins and ends with a distorted minor-mode version of the children's song "Frère Jacques," and lastly an all-encompassing finale that begins with a piercing cry of pain and ends with roof-raising affirmation.

1. *Langsam, schleppend. Immer sehr gemächlich* (Slow, dragging. Always very leisurely) (15 minutes)
2. *Kräftig bewegt, doch nicht zu schnell. Recht gemächlich* (Strongly animated, but not too fast. Quite leisurely) (8 minutes)
3. *Feierlich und gemessen, ohne zu schleppen – Sehr einfach und schlicht wie eine Volksweise – Wieder etwas bewegter, wie im Anfang* (Solemn and measured, without dragging—Very simple and plain like a folk song—Somewhat more animated again, as at the beginning) (10 minutes)
4. *Stürmisch bewegt – Energisch* (Stormily animated—Vigorously) (19 minutes)

Some of Mahler's critics, astute even when annoyed, asked what these four movements could possibly have to do with one another. "Is it a weasel, a cloud, or a camel?" one writer asked of the piece, referring to the scene in Shakespeare where Hamlet baits a fool by interpreting and reinterpreting a cloud formation. Another Mahler critic wondered why the finale of a symphony about nature and dancing and mordant irony should open with a darkly explosive "end of the world" scenario. Yet another critic heard such conflicts not only between movements but within them, asking why the symphony was allowed to move on impulse from pastoral innocence to insanity, and then back again.

Those turn-of-the-century listeners who heard dilemmas in Mahler's early music failed to see how Beethoven had devised similar quandaries almost a century earlier. Beethoven's pieces were holy writ through the nineteenth century. And yet—to give just one example of a Beethoven transgression—the funeral march of the *Eroica* Symphony gave critics pause for much the same reason the sardonic third-movement funeral march of Mahler's First caused concern eighty years later: it didn't fit with the symphony's heroism program, or even ended up contradicting it. In Beethoven's case, commentators struggled—heroically, one might say—to find a programmatic explanation for the funeral march. For instance: this is where the hero ruefully surveys the carnage of the battlefield; or, as Richard Wagner claimed while portraying Beethoven's works as autobiographical, this is where the composer rounds out his broad portrayal of heroism with personal impressions of heartbreak and loss. In both these interpretations, the gloominess becomes a point of contrast that makes the heroism all the more heroic. Mahler himself offered the same simile to Bauer-Lechner when he related his third movement to a scenario where "a funeral procession passes by our hero, and the misery, the whole distress of the world, with its cutting contrasts and horrible irony, grasps him." In a letter he wrote to Bruno Walter while preparing the First Symphony for performance in New York, he situated his funeral march as a jumping-off point for the finale's rage against God: "The Funeral March and the storm that follows are a flaming indictment of the Creator!" But Mahler revealed his ultimate disinterest in such interpretive exercises, or even his belief in the wholesale incompatibility of words and music, when he later offered Bauer-Lechner a droll account of the same funeral march: "Now he (my hero) has found a hair in his soup, and his meal is spoiled."

Instead of jumping right into a musical argument involving themes and maneuvering around themes, as we would expect at the start of a Mozart or a Brahms symphony, Mahler begins his first movement with a steady A pitch that steals in quietly across a full seven octaves of the orchestra—a span as wide as the highest and lowest notes of the piano. His start is not like the slow, attention-getting introduction of Haydn's later symphonies, or like the quiet setting of a pulse, as we often get in Bruckner. Beethoven had supplied a precedent for such a feeling-out-the-space symphonic opening with his Fourth Symphony, but Mahler sustains the expectant tension far longer. Mahler's sustained A is less a musical gesture than a psychoacoustic gambit, a hushed underscoring of the listener's anticipation and range of hearing. It is a staking-out of an aural space. It is less like a symphonic opening than the keening of summer cicadas ("wie in Naturlaut," or "like a sound of nature," the composer indicates in the score) or the nervous, high-pitched hum of human expectation. Mahler's opening A is odd simply in terms of its sound. Returning to the passage after the Budapest premiere, he rewrote the note as a harmonic for the violins. This means the players touch the string so as to eliminate a strong fundamental pitch, creating instead a kind of "phantom" A: the note is glassy and disembodied, and harder to pinpoint in terms of pitch than a normal note. Contrary to the thudding and portentous C minor chord that begins Brahms's own First Symphony—for example—Mahler's specter A takes a half second to sound and then only appears as a darker shade of silence. It's a self-questioning, incantatory equivocation that will be counteracted by the huge, roof-raising coda at the end of the finale—creating a typically Mahlerian epic journey from the symphony's beginning to its end.

Mahler himself described the slow introduction, in a program note he later squelched, as the "awakening of nature from a long winter's sleep." Descending fourth intervals drop tentatively, a sort-of musical argument slowly precipitating, like droplets from the quietly buzzing woodland humidity. When distant trumpet fanfares emerge, different depths of life and motion start coming into focus. With the clear sound of a cuckoo in the clarinet (at 1:49), splashes of real life start to invade the rousing consciousness. Nature's awakening is marked by arrival at a relaxed D major, and then (starting at 3:29) a cheery, striding melody in the cellos that Mahler stole from one of his own earlier *Des Knaben Wunderhorn* songs: "I walked out this morning onto the meadow," the lyrics of the song reminisce, "the dew still hung on the grass." This jaunt toward daylight is retreated several times, allowing it to grow more brassy and enthusiastic each time it resumes. The hopefulness really begins to swell when the melody arrives at the song protagonist's morning greeting, "Hello! It's a fine world, isn't it?" We can hear the contour of the inquiring, pressing words "schöne Welt, schöne Welt!" ("a fine world, a fine world") traced in the high woodwinds at 4:46. Looking back at the exposition section, we see that Mahler has given us a long, unbroken, 156-bar crescendo of optimism and liveliness, modeled in large part on the emotional trajectory of the original song, "I Walked Out This Morning onto the Meadow."

The early-day optimism is suspended when the high string harmonic A returns (at 7:27, after the repeat of the exposition section), the orchestral texture thins out, and the dynamic returns to a hushed *pianissimo*. The cellos start (at 7:27) quietly obsessing over falling fifth and sixth intervals pulled from the "I Walked Out This Morning" tune, and from which the strings will slowly eke out a new variant of that melody. A mysterious, portentous low F appears in the double basses and tuba (at 8:29), initiating a darker section marked by a steady quarter-note processional rhythm (starting in the harp at 9:03). Under a return of nature's falling-fifth glimmers, the low F drops down through E-flat to the tonic pitch D. At this point (10:10) the movement makes its first arrival at a stable and clear D major, the bass line finally starts to function like one instead of being frozen in pedal points, and the movement has permission to start moving forward with a real argument. Another detour arises starting at 11:17, when the full strings get to state the melody derived from the "I Walked Out This Morning" song.

We are now being pulled away from the home tonic of D major, in the attempt to make us want it all the more strongly. A harmonic twist on the detour starting at 11:36 pulls us away momentarily from the circle of influence of D major—though only for the final purpose of making its return all the more emphatic. An oblique transition back toward that harmony begins at 12:10, the falling fifth and falling sixth brought to the fore. Strangely obsessive repetitions of the falling octave, initiating prolongation of a D-flat chord (starting 12:37), swell and subside like a tortured young artist's heartaches. The throbbing moves to an E-flat harmony and presides over a slow crescendo to the most decisive cadence yet on the tonic D major (at 13:37). The horns celebrate our arrival with three exuberant whoops. The "I Walked Out This Morning" theme returns, stated for the first time in full phrase and in full orchestration. As a coda, we get an accelerando that presses all the way to the end, the young, morn-walking wayfarer's love of life and the day now almost uncontainable. But even when the quickest tempo does arrive, the last, long-awaited, clinching cadence to a triumphant D major is blocked by cheeky pauses (first at 14:55) that imbue the close of the movement with Haydnesque mischief. Mahler must have known the "are we finished or are we not?" ending of the old master's String Quartet in E-flat Major, op. 33, no. 2, Haydn's so-called Joke Quartet.

In its basic outline, Mahler's first movement moves simply if also sometimes hesitatingly from the opening dormant landscape to an exultant, sun-drenched scene. This is a remarkable structure, intuitively crafted not as a sonata form but more as a gradually awakening crescendo and a finding-its-way-into and then finding-its-way-back-to the original tonic. Anyone listening for a traditional sonata structure will be thwarted by the lack of a contrasting second theme, or even a recapitulation marking a distinct return to themes once known and now to be re-recognized. But here again, it was Beethoven who set the precedent. Like the opening movement of Mahler's First, the Allegro con brio movement of the *Eroica* Symphony traces a unilinear trajectory from first bar to last, a dramatic "realization of a theme" that brooks only momentary obstacles in its path to victorious fulfillment.

DANCING AND LAMENTING

For the original second movement to his symphony, Mahler appropriated an excerpt from some theatrical incidental music he had written in 1884. He titled this charming movement "Blumine" ("Flower Piece") after a chapter by the novelist Jean Paul Richter, who he said at one time was his inspiration for the whole symphony. Mahler dropped "Blumine" after his third performance of the symphony, and thereby made the work less fragmented and more symphonic as a whole—more straightforward in its overall trajectory from hesitating start to exultant finish. Mahler published the First Symphony in 1899, as a work in four movements without "Blumine." A copyist's manuscript of the jettisoned movement was discovered only in 1966, and it is now occasionally incorporated in performances of a five- rather than four-movement First Symphony, which makes the work a different sort of animal. "Blumine" could be the most beguiling thing Mahler ever wrote, his simplest and least anxious creation, and it still gives hope that someday more early scores will be uncovered. (We know he wrote several symphonies in his late teens and early twenties, works—now lost—that were last seen in Dresden archives.) "Blumine," in its wide-eyed naïveté, is a clear precursor to the nostalgic inner movements of the Second and Third Symphonies, but it is also shorter and more clear-cut in its form. Its delicate, folkish charm falls just short of understated tragedy, and—contrary to a common criticism—is really too pristine to be heard as sentimental. This early music obviously predates the various revisions Mahler made to the First Symphony, the last of them as late as 1906: it is written for a smaller orchestra than one hears in the rest of the symphony after the revisions, and the solo trumpet gently guides the ear with its gleaming and naïve presence. (Certainly, to go from this solo to the trumpet in the *Trauermarsch* introduction to the Fifth Symphony is to hear a seismic change in worldview, a fall from innocence to the deepest depths of chastened experience.)

The second movement of the First Symphony as published—third in the first performances, and second in the revised sequence—is a triple-time dance piece that music historians often compare to a waltz but that, with its sturdy and carefree character, has more in common with the rustic Austrian *Ländler*. Listen for heavy footfalls, yodeling upbeats, and enough lusty repetition in string and wind parts to suggest amateur performance. Listen also for the lyrical trio section (starting at 3:49) that counters all the clomping with a quiet, folklike lyricism, perhaps touched by Bruckner's scherzo movements. Mahler gives this melody a rather startling number of performance instructions: "very tenderly but expressively"; "not rushed"; and, in terms of tempo, "quite leisurely." The directions demonstrate just how complex it can be to create something simple. Ending this movement is a heady coda section (starting at 7:40) that is so exuberant as to become breathless: he marks it "moving forward," meaning it should rush ahead to the very close. Why should a peasant-stock *Ländler*, or even a more conventional symphonic scherzo, become almost giddy in such a way? Even out in the provinces, Mahler's stylizations have a certain larger-than-life quality: these are fairly cinematic peasants, and they seem to be dancing for the tourist trade.

As the third of his four movements, Mahler wrote a funeral march. While his audiences tolerated the first movement of the symphony and applauded the second, the march caused a scandal. (Bruno Walter, soon to become Mahler's assistant in Hamburg and then a lifelong friend, got wind of the march before he met its composer and before he had a chance actually to hear the music: "I marveled at the courage of the unknown composer of the March, and ardently desired to know the man responsible for so extravagant a work.") Coming from the previous movement's ritual of peasant merrymaking, early audiences were appalled at being plunged into a ritual of lament. To make matters worse, Mahler's funeral march usurped the songlike slow movement that Austro-German symphonic tradition would have encouraged listeners to expect. He then rubbed salt into his audiences' wounded expectations by basing his morbid procession on the children's round "Frère Jacques" (sung in German with the text "Bruder Jakob, Bruder Jakob, Schläfst du noch?" and in English with the words "Are you sleeping, are you sleeping, Brother John?"). He exacerbated the *grotesquerie* by introducing the melody on the solo double bass. The original song exhorts Friar John, the monastery's bell-ringer, to wake up and sound the call to Matins prayers. Why did Mahler choose this song? The words must have been important. When the tune is moved from major to minor and set as a funeral march, the phrase "Are you sleeping?" takes on a rather different meaning. Musicologists Francesca Draughon and Raymond Knapp, in the online journal *Echo*, suggest that identity politics might have led Mahler to use "Bruder Jakob." He was born a Jew in a Catholic monarchy, and—according to Draughon and Knapp—he would have grown up knowing "Bruder Jakob" as a Christian taunt. The taunt became even more pointed when the tune was sung in minor, though that might just have been general practice in singing the song in the late nineteenth century. The more familiar explanation for Mahler's use of the march relates to a famous engraving of a satirical woodland funeral scene. Mahler said he was moved to write his funeral march when he recalled Moritz von Schwind's absurdist image of the animals of the forest tearfully escorting the casket of the huntsman, their former nemesis, to his final resting place.

Mahler added yet another layer to this movement by using a song from his *Lieder eines fahrenden Gesellen* (Songs of a Wayfarer). Putting in an illustrative appearance is "Die zwei blauen Augen" ("The Two Blue Eyes"), a song-cum-cortège that recounts the despair and death of a heartbroken lover. The lovesick young man sets out as a wanderer to escape his beloved's haunting gaze and finally finds refuge under a linden tree, where "for the first time I found rest in sleep!" We can presume his place of rest, his repose where "all was well again," is in fact the grave. When Mahler quotes "The Two Blue Eyes" in the third movement of his First Symphony, he reorders the song's stanzas. He begins the movement with tonic-dominant strokes on the timpani, in imitation of the accompaniment to the lover's departure in the second stanza: "I went out into the quiet night / well across the dark heath. / To me no one bade farewell." Against this timpani line in his symphony movement, the muted double bass intones "Bruder Jakob"—with the melody purposefully placed on the fingerboard near the neck of the instrument, where the awkward hand position makes the theme difficult to play in tune. Next in the line of pallbearers after the bass are the bassoon, cello, and then most lugubriously of all, the tuba (starting at 0:49). An awkward, faltering idea in the oboe lets a bit of light and air into the music. As more and more members of the orchestra join in, the imitative texture gives way to instruments doubling each other in impassive octaves.

In contrast to this glum Catholicism, sprightly Jewish music makes an entrance at 2:10. This is the most conspicuously "Jewish sounding" of any Mahler passage: a pair of oboes in thirds enters haltingly against a pair of trumpets, suggesting the *yiddisch* music he would have heard in Bohemia. The music is so stereotypically and emotively *jüdisch* that it sounds like a quotation, a tune designed to pull folks out of their chairs and get them dancing the *hora*. The instrumentation is similar to what we would now call a klezmer group, with woodwinds (oboes, clarinets), violins, and trumpets. Underlining the music's expressiveness are the short ritards that lead into the statements and restatements of the melody. Pitted against this *yiddisch* strain is a brief contrasting section (marked "with parody") where minor momentarily turns to major, and a slight speedup is maintained by the boom-chick accompaniment of drum and cymbals (the instruments attached to each other and played by one musician, in village band style). The Jewish melody then reappears in the violins (starting at 2:53, the line now desiring a healthy dose of vibrato), the contrasting boom-chick music comes back, and then the lurching oboe tune takes over in the strings. There is a surprising turn from D minor to G major along with a shift away from march time, in preparation for the third stanza of "The Two Blue Eyes" (starting at 4:54) in muted violins: "On the road there stands a linden tree, / and there for the first time I found rest in sleep!" Mahler marks this "very plain and simple, like a folk tune," but also harmonizes it with a delicate, richly divided texture of three violin parts. At 6:02, the music turns again to minor, and the violins and oboe quote the singer's departure: "Farewell! Farewell! My companions were love and suffering!"

After a last fleeting quote of the song's title phrase, "The two blue eyes of my darling" (at 6:50), the music nudges up a half step (to E-flat minor) and we hear a reprise of the funeral march in that key, with the "Bruder Jakob" tune now in the horns and woodwinds. But the biggest surprise of all arrives when our transposed funeral is suddenly shoved aside by what sounds like a Jewish wedding: at 8:21, the woodwinds burst in with the *yiddisch* music at its most rambunctious, at a faster tempo than the rest of the orchestra, and wrench the music back to D minor. Mahler's morose defamiliarization of "Bruder Jakob" makes me think of the queasy versioning of "Happy Birthday" in Soviet composer Alfred Schnittke's String Trio (1985). In other words, his denaturalization and confrontation of styles is forceful enough to lend the whole third movement a contemporary feel.

THE FINALE: FROM HELL TO HEAVEN

The finale of the First Symphony is less a musical argument than a kind of emotional-temporal trajectory. The composer initially described it as a motion *dall' inferno al paradiso* (from hell to heaven), which as a program is about as purely emotional as they come. The movement begins by imitating "a sudden outcry from a deeply wounded heart," as Mahler originally referred to the opening gesture, in the unexpected dark key of F minor. As part of that cry, we hear intensely accusatory four-note descents—starting at 0:23 and then more insidiously at 0:42, perhaps intoning that indictment of the Creator. The choice of F minor at the start of the finale allows Mahler a dramatic setup: at the violent stroke opening the movement (a chord that caused one matriarch at the Budapest premiere to jump out of her seat, much to Mahler's delight), the tonic D that ended the preceding movement suddenly becomes a dissonance against the C in the bass that starts the new movement; and the note's resolution downward now sets the finale's descending scales in motion. In a nutshell, the bottom drops out of the harmony.

In broad formal terms, the finale is easily summarized. On its way from a tortured start in F minor toward a final blazing culmination in D major, the movement assembles and then pursues a hurtling and episodic theme—first heard as the four-note G–G–Ab–C head motive in trombones and trumpets at 0:09, and then in complete form in brass and winds starting at 1:03. The variants of this theme include a melodic inversion (at 2:26), a tense G minor rendering (starting at 6:53), a C major victory fanfare (first appearing quietly and parenthetically at 7:36), and a fugue-like section (starting at 14:54). Also over the course of the finale's first half, there are various returns to the slow introduction of the first movement—including the "throbbing" falling tenth figure, starting at 1:34, and the slow bass figure starting at 6:25—as well as to the hurtling *dall' inferno* music from the opening of the movement (starting now at 8:31). The pursuit of this hurtling theme slows and is then interrupted by a contrasting idea in D-flat major that serves as the basis for a slow and rhapsodic section (starting at 3:30), one that becomes songful and confessional enough to stand in for the symphony's missing slow movement. Heartfelt and exquisite, this music is full of hesitations, stutters, and pressings-forth that sound less like music than imploring speech. The melodic line sounds like someone overwhelmed and barely able to speak: turning to a comparison in Mahler's beloved *Tristan und Isolde*, the line isn't very different from Isolde's wondering ecstasy in her *Liebestod*, "Shall I breathe, / Shall I listen? / Shall I drink, / immerse? / Sweetly in fragrances / melt away?"

Those critics who heard disunity in Mahler's First Symphony must have passed over the section of the finale that embodies the work's structural crux, its beating heart and emotional nexus. I'm speaking of the section halfway through where the composer brings back material from the first movement most clearly, plumbs his expressive depths to the fullest, and then somehow manages to bring the work's many threads together while forging ahead to a conclusive clamor. I'm speaking of the eight-minute recollection-digression that begins about ten minutes into the finale. Mahler does astonishing things in these eight minutes of music. This passage—stretching from 9:54 to 18:17—is doubly absorbing because it appears as a kind of detour in the movement and would lend itself to a simple, if also unthinkable, cut. Even as late as 1909, when Mahler conducted the First in New York, one critic complained of "the drawing out of the last movement far beyond its natural conclusion . . . Iteration and anti-climax deadened the effect before the end was reached." But this recollection-digression segment is the nub of the whole symphony, the wondrous point of synthesis that allows the composition to work, and not coincidentally the part of the piece that gave Mahler the most trouble. It also happens to be the point of greatest doubt in the First Symphony—doubt that the composition can or will proceed, in a kind of crisis of faith that would become more familiar in his later symphonies.

This recollection-digression passage interrupts victory insofar as the home tonic of D major has just miraculously dropped from the sky (at 9:05), followed by what sounds like a victory-lap coda section and a looping statement of the conclusive, praising, chorale-like "And He shall reign" theme (starting at 9:22, under a nickname I've chosen because of the music's coincidental similarity to part of the "Hallelujah" chorus from Handel's *Messiah*). But victory is quickly called into question here when the music—vamping along on a stable D major, and apparently moving toward a quick close—grows quiet and then (starting at 10:18) reverts to the slow introduction of the first movement, with its octave and unison pedals hanging expectantly in the air, its elemental motive in descending fourths, and its distant brass fanfares. The clear return to where we first were some forty-three minutes earlier could have been a disastrous tactic. While this static music felt hopeful at the start of the first movement, here—coming right after the exultant D major climax and victory-lap affirmation—its minor-key sparseness suggests disillusionment and interruption. More signal events from the first movement return. A drop in the bass brings the music to C minor, and glimmers of both nostalgia and aspiration come with the repetition (starting at 10:58) of clearly earmarked bits of the first movement: the birdcalls and fragments of Mahler's hopeful morning song, "Ging heut' Morgen übers Feld." A "very expressive" tune arises in the muted cellos and violins but is interrupted by a tense pause, a downward turn toward darkness, and then (starting at 11:52) a return to the laborious, chromatic ascent (originally heard on the harp nine minutes into the first-movement introduction). Again, the recollected material sounds somber rather than expectant, and with all the regression and slowing and quieting, our once-promised D-major victory now seems remote indeed. (As Mahler himself described this digression to Richard Strauss, "My intention was to show a struggle in which victory is furthest from the protagonist just when he believes it closest.")

These "redundant" eight minutes are an illogical detour, but in going back to the symphony's opening Mahler makes it plain that the second half of his last movement ties off not only the finale, but the symphony as a whole. Plus, Beethoven had already made a similar interruption of symphonic victory in the finale of his Fifth Symphony, where he pushed aside the magnificent transformation from dark C minor to bright C major for a literal return of the short-short-short-long motive back in a quiet C minor. Mahler likewise earns our trust in the finale of his First Symphony when he acknowledges just how hollow promises of victory can be, but then goes ahead to deliver victory anyway. The last D major coruscation arrives as a reworking of the climax to the first movement. (Compare the music starting at 16:35 in the finale with the climax starting at 13:29 in the first movement.) Here the woodwinds point the bells of their instruments up in the air, and two extra horns are added to the roster of seven—making an imposing array of nine, or sometimes even more if circumstances allow. And then the whole horn section rises (at 17:27) to deliver the "he shall reign" chorale melody in half notes over figuration and tremolos in the rest of the orchestra—that melody being just a transformation of the dropping fourths from the start of the first movement. The coda section that follows (starting at 18:17) is so thunderous that the timpani part, continuously wailing away *fortissimo* on the tonic pitch D until the very end, is divided between the two players for optimal endurance and volume. In performance, this closing music should be deafeningly loud.

And so Mahler ends his First Symphony, which he'd begun as a practically inaudible circadian buzz, by almost literally raising the roof. The emotional intensity of this work is colored by a certain thrilling obliviousness, and not yet tainted by the disaffections and regrets that come with age. Writers commonly call Mahler's First the most audacious symphonic debut since Beethoven's First, which had its premiere back in 1800. But then Mahler wrote several symphonies in his late teens and early twenties, works—now lost—that were last seen in Dresden archives. If we are ever lucky enough to discover and hear those, the published First Symphony might someday be reckoned less an audacious debut than a transition to Mahler's more characteristically ambivalent scores.

2

SYMPHONY NO. 2

Death and Resurrection

After death, there was a return to life. Mahler began the Second Symphony, like the First, as a symphonic poem with an ambitious program involving mortality—but its genesis proved even more difficult, and resurrection became its ultimate message. The seed for the work was planted one day in January 1888, when Mahler's grandiose and morbid imagination beheld a pile of flowers. After premiering his free reconstruction of Carl Maria von Weber's opera *Die drei Pintos* in Leipzig, he found his apartment swamped with congratulatory blooms. These occasioned a vision of himself stretched out on his funeral bier, pale of face and surrounded by just such a sea of aromatic bouquets and wreaths. The question confronting him at that moment: what kind of music would make an appropriate memorial for a visionary young musician undertaking his final journey? The immediate result of Mahler's flowery vision was an austere twenty-minute funerary procession for large orchestra: the symphonic poem that he titled *Todtenfeier* (*Funeral Rites*), after the epic poem by the Polish nationalist author Adam Mickiewicz.

The original question then became a much larger question, one demanding a metaphysical as well as musical answer: what follows death? *Todtenfeier*, though originally written to be self-contained, soon demanded some kind of follow up. In an action that revealed his spiritual makeup, Mahler felt compelled to devise substantial postscripts for his musical funeral. Five years after his initial inspiration, he added two movements of contrasting character. Now that he had a three-movement symphonic torso, he sought inspiration for a finale that would counterbalance the grave and intense *Todtenfeier* movement. His search ended in 1894 when he heard Friedrich Klopstock's "Resurrection Ode" sung at the funeral of his mentor, the great German conductor Hans von Bülow. Mahler quickly set the Klopstock as his long, sprawling finale, using chorus and soprano and mezzo-soprano soloists. He then prefaced that with a brief song he'd recently written to the *Des Knaben Wunderhorn* text "Urlicht," a lyric verse on seeking God that begins, "O little red rose! / Man lies in greatest need! / Man lies in greatest pain!" After making final revisions to *Todtenfeier*, which now stood as the untitled first movement in his extravagant new eighty-five-minute opus, Mahler had his Second Symphony in hand—complete in five contrasting movements.

Mahler committed himself quite early on to the symphony as a genre, and with the Second was already boldly redefining it. The Second Symphony almost seems to reformulate itself as it unfolds, moving from operatic writing to Lisztian orchestral bombast to songlike simplicity, rewriting the rules as it goes along. A demonstrative and dramatic first movement (the death-commemorative music that he had initially called *Todtenfeier*) is followed by a minuet and then, thirdly, by a scherzo that half-conceals a wealth of nuance and intrigue under its glittering surface. And then finally, after the penultimate preface of the brief and disarmingly simple song "Urlicht," we have in fifth place a long finale involving two vocal soloists and chorus. In brief, Mahler modified the classical four-movement symphony format as follows:

1. *Allegro maestoso. Mit durchaus ernstem und feierlichem Ausdruck* (Quickly and majestically. With the most serious and solemn expression throughout) (24 minutes)
2. *Andante moderato. Sehr gemächlich. Nie eilen* (At a moderate, walking pace. Very leisurely, never rushed) (12 minutes)
3. *In ruhig fließender Bewegung* (In quietly flowing motion) (10 minutes)
4. "Urlicht." *Sehr feierlich, aber schlicht* ("Primal Light." Very solemn, yet plain) (5 minutes)

5. *Im Tempo des Scherzos – Mit Aufschwung, aber nicht eilen* (In the tempo of the scherzo—With impetus, but don't rush) (34 minutes)

Mahler's Second is known as the *Resurrection* Symphony, owing to his conclusive choral setting of Klopstock's "Resurrection Ode": "Rise again, yes, you shall rise again / My dust / After a short rest!" Mahler elaborated so widely on the subjects of nature, sorrow, death, and ultimate triumph in this symphony that in the end he felt it necessary to resort to words and the human voice. Words and voice came last in his conception, last both in terms of writing the piece and in laying out the finished composition. His prototype here was, of course, Beethoven's Ninth Symphony with its concluding choral setting of Friedrich Schiller's "Ode to Joy"; Mahler's Second gives evidence that Beethoven's last symphony was still delivering its message on morality and still provoking composers seventy years after its creation. His finale is most obviously modeled on Beethoven's last movement in its division into an instrumental section followed by a transcendent vocal-choral culmination. (Mahler's canny understanding of spectacle must have been at work here. Surely his audacious invitation of comparison with Beethoven helped the spectacular success of the complete Second at its premiere in Berlin in December 1895. Bruno Walter recalled in his memoir of the composer how "the impression of a great and original work and of the power of Mahler's personality was so great that his emergence as a composer dates from this performance.")

But Mahler's finale isn't so simply described, in that it really shows him approaching Beethoven's Ninth through the intermediary of Wagner and that composer's theatricality. Wagner had himself made claim to Beethoven's Ninth—and to the symphony more generally—when he wrote his music dramas starting in the 1850s. Paradoxically, Wagner claimed a revolutionary's entitlement to the symphony after Beethoven. In an appalling act of self-serving ventriloquism, he put the following words in that great symphonist's mouth when he wrote his historical novella *A Pilgrimage to Beethoven* in 1841:

> But why should not vocal music, as much as instrumental, form a grand and serious genre, and its execution meet with as much respect from the feather-brained warblers as I demand from an orchestra for one of my symphonies? The human voice is not to be gainsaid.

> Nay, it is a far more beautiful and nobler organ of tone, than any instrument in the orchestra. Could not one employ it with just the same freedom as these? What entirely new results one would gain from such a procedure! . . . Now, let us bring these two elements together, and unite them! Let us set the wild, unfettered elemental feelings, represented by the instruments, in contact with the clear and definite emotion of the human heart, as represented by the voice of man.

So Wagner considered himself a kind of symphonic dramatist, a man of the theater who nonetheless followed Beethoven. The young Friedrich Nietzsche agreed, idealizing the third act of Wagner's *Tristan und Isolde* as "a tremendous symphonic movement" that would paralyze the listener with ecstasy if it were freed from words and singers and stage action. Mahler followed Wagner as a self-styled dramatic symphonist, and in doing so he reclaimed the symphony for the concert hall—co-opting Beethoven through Wagner, as it were. In his Second Symphony, Mahler the passionate Wagnerian resorted to words and the voice in order to give the fullest expression to his thoughts on the immense and terrifying topics of death and life. But he went further, combining operatic mise-en-scène (including offstage effects) with the multimovement format and motivic working-out of the "abstract" orchestral symphony. He also made use of the palette of precise orchestral effects that composers like Liszt and Smetana had developed in the symphonic poem—what Wagner called "the wild, unfettered elemental feelings" that instrumental music could provide.

In short, the Second Symphony finds Mahler borrowing techniques from whatever musical corners of the concert hall, opera house, church, theater, or village tavern that he found useful. Apart from Beethoven's and Wagner's own genre-bending projects, others had been blurring distinctions between, opera, symphony, and choral-orchestral forms. Among the examples that Mahler knew, we could mention Verdi's later works—especially his Requiem (1874) and the seamlessly integrated opera *Otello* (1887). And then there was Berlioz's love of timbre and spatial effect in his Requiem (1837), not to mention the same composer's combination of tone painting and theatricality in the *Symphonie fantastique* (1830), and above all his choral symphony *Roméo et Juliette* (1835). Also influential was Bruckner's *Te Deum* (1883) for orchestra, choir, vocal soloists, and organ—essentially a five-movement symphony to sacred texts. Mahler had led a performance of Bruckner's piece in Hamburg in 1893, and amended the title page to describe the *Te Deum* as written "for angels' tongues, seekers of God, afflicted hearts, and souls purified in fire!"—words that actually amount to a beautiful précis of his own Second Symphony, which was still gestating at that time.

To indicate the detail that Mahler as a musician felt able to provide on the profound subject of life after death, I pass along here—in slightly abbreviated form—conductor and philanthropist Gilbert Kaplan's conflation of the composer's programs for all five movements of his symphony:

> *Movement I*
> We stand by the coffin of a person well loved. His whole life, his struggles, his passions, his sufferings and his accomplishments on earth once more for the last time pass before us . . . "What is life and what is death? Why did you live? Why did you suffer? Is it all nothing but a huge, frightful joke? Will we live on eternally? Do our life and death have a meaning?" We must answer these questions in some way if we are to go on living—indeed, if we are to go on dying! He into whose life this call has once sounded must give an answer. And this answer I give in the final movement.
>
> *Movement II*
> A memory, a ray of sunlight, pure and cloudless, out of the departed's life.
>
> *Movement III*
> It may easily happen that this surge of life ceaselessly in motion, never resting, never comprehensible, suddenly seems eerie, like the billowing dancing figures in a brightly lit ballroom that you gaze into from outside in the dark.
>
> *Movement IV*
> The moving voice of naive faith sounds in our ears. "I am from God and will return to God. The dear God will give me a light, will light me to eternal blessed life!"
>
> *Movement V*
> The movement starts with the same dreadful scream of anguish that ended the scherzo. The voice of the Caller is heard. The end of every

> living thing has come, the Last Judgment is at hand, and the horror of the Day of Days has come upon us. The earth trembles; the Last Trump sounds; the graves burst open; all the creatures struggle out of the ground, moaning and trembling . . . The trumpets of the Apocalypse ring out. Finally, after all have left their empty graves and the earth lies silent and deserted, there comes only the long-drawn note of the bird of death. Even it finally dies . . . The gentle sound of a chorus of saints and heavenly hosts is then heard. Soft and simple, the words gently swell up: "Rise again, yes, rise again thou wilt!" Then the glory of God comes into sight. A wondrous light strikes us to the heart. All is quiet and blissful. Lo and behold: there is no judgment, no sinners, no just men, no great and no small; there is no punishment and no reward. A feeling of overwhelming love fills us with blissful knowledge and illuminates our existence.

This program is all but necessary for listening to the *Resurrection* Symphony. Parts of this piece count as the most explicitly and undeniably illustrative—that is, the most obviously programmatic—music that he ever wrote. One example is the passage in the big instrumental section of the last movement where "the Last Trump sounds" and then "the graves burst open" and the dead arise (starting at 9:23). This is also the only work where he quotes the ancient *Dies irae* liturgical chant for the dead, a unanimously recognized leitmotif for death, damnation, and *diablerie* (given by Mahler in trombones and tuba at 6:12 in the finale, for instance). Be all that as it may, the danger persists of getting too bogged down in the details to enjoy the self-sufficient beauties of the Second Symphony. Mahler helped us avoid this when he offered elsewhere a much shorter and more general description of how his work leaves the listener "battered to the ground with clubs and then lifted to the heights on angels' wings." Is Mahler's symphonic conception of resurrection (and angels' wings) a Christian one, or at least based in Christian scripture? His chosen passage from Klopstock doesn't mention Jesus, though it does of course look to God. More astonishingly, there is the anti-biblical twist in Mahler's conception that the dead are raised from their graves to face their creator, only to discover that there is no judgment; instead, death leads us to a state where "overwhelming love fills us with blissful knowledge and illuminates our existence," which can sound like a Christian vision of heaven but which would be better described as a humanist philosophy. The Second Symphony shows Mahler as an eclectic alternative to Bruckner's pious Austrian Catholicism and Brahms's jaded north German atheism—growing up as a Jew in an age of institutionalized anti-Semitism would have made this all but inevitable.

This is resurrection reconciled with the secular Germanic notion of the will, as Mahler would have known it from the writings of Schopenhauer and Nietzsche. He also became intensely involved with philosopher Gustav Fechner's *Little Book on Life after Death* (*Das Büchlein vom Leben nach dem Tode*, 1836), though this was probably more a symptom than a cause of his need to believe "in spite of everything." There's a considerable amount of Fechner in the text that Mahler wrote for the end of the symphony's finale, appending it to Klopstock: "What was created / Must perish, / What perished, rise again!" A redefined state of life must await us as we huddle in the darkness, the same way an unexpectable richness of experience awaits the fetus about to be born. This is a strange, unorthodox Nietzschean—rather than specifically Christian—vision of life after death, centering on the idea of resurrection through individual will. It's possible to hear a necessity for rebirth—"hope" is too weak a word—already in the *Todtenfeier* movement of the symphony, in its chronic need to temper the grim march time and all the downward-moving melodic lines with ascending motions and radiant tone colors. The obsessive funeral march rhythms of the first movement are so obsessive they almost seem to demand hopeful rebuttal. Fixation certainly becomes the mother of invention in this movement: Mahler develops myriad ways here of reiterating, nuancing, and deflecting the one-two-one-two tread of the march rhythm. Among these are his alternations of duple and triplet rhythms. He also strategically shifts emphasis away from the first beat of the measure.

Maybe more directly important for someone listening to Mahler's Second Symphony is its transmutation of *place*: even more than the First Symphony, the Second transplants theatrical musical styles and gestures into the concert hall. The ferocious string tremolos that open the work would be utterly out of place in a symphony in Brahms style, but also in the symphonic works of Beethoven and Bruckner. Bruckner symphonies begin with tremolos, as does Beethoven's Ninth, but only as slow, gradual, steady-state initiations into the symphonic drama. Mahler's tremolos are in fact a shameless crib from the storm music that opens Wagner's *Die Walküre*, an opera that Mahler conducted in

Budapest right around the time he was writing *Todtenfeier*. In broader terms of character, Mahler's formidable opening looks to even more distant music: beyond Wagner, and to the theatrical works of Verdi or perhaps back to the last movement of Berlioz's *Symphonie fantastique*. Its dark bleakness smacks of the theater: we might compare its explosive, gestural sound to some of Verdi's opera preludes, like the pitch-black "curse" motive that opens *Rigoletto* or the somber opener for *La Forza del Destino*.

FUNERALS, RIVERS, AND ANGELS

Mahler was intimately acquainted with Wagner's *Die Walküre* and knew that its opening storm is what forces Siegmund into Sieglinde's arms as well as into the murderous sword of her husband Hunding—he knew that Wagner's storm is, in short, the instigating factor in a miserable death (as well as a passionate and forbidden love). It might be a manifestation of his first movement's programmatic and Wagnerian basis that its musical structure proves difficult to grasp, even while its dramatic effect is so cogent and direct. Analysts have parsed it as a sonata form, of course—but like Berlioz and Wagner and Verdi, Mahler seems to think less in terms of themes than in specific events, timbral groupings, and tones of voice. In a revealing statement to his friend Josef Bohuslav Foerster, he differentiated between symphonic "developers" who "mixed" themes in allocated sections of their forms, and someone like Beethoven who didn't allow development of material to obscure his authorial presence as someone who "always had something specific to say." There's a great deal that Mahler has "specific to say" in the first movement of the Second. Already at 2:15, the first assertion of a stern, descending tutti passage shows a prioritization of outward drama over thematic work. I hear this scalewise descent as Mahler's rendering of another critical element in Wagner's *Die Walküre*, namely the leitmotif representing Wotan's spear. Wotan is the ruler of the gods in Wagner's *Ring of the Nibelung* tetralogy, and his spear symbolizes law and justice. It is something like Moses's tablets, except that it also functions as a weapon for administering said law. As if to emphasize its importance, Mahler uses a version of this "Wotan's spear" idea, longer in range but also sped-up, to close his first movement off at its very end.

None of these musical aspects mentioned so far counts as a theme, and themes are the basis for sonata-form structures. Indeed, the first minutes of this symphony must have given ammunition to those critics who lamented Mahler's habit of writing lines not as melodies but as intermittent, stop-and-go bunches of notes. At times the argument of the movement seems supplanted by unending streams of two-note figures. Then, as if in compensation, the second theme (first heard starting at 2:57) proves beautifully lyrical and upward reaching, seemingly endless, and riddled with sighing figures. But if Mahler's volcanic opening gestures don't sound like themes, he brings them back decisively as if they were. The opening tremolo and bass lunges return at 4:06, now setting off in triplets that lead in fresh directions. Wotan's spear-motive descent continues to hover over the movement, hijacking the processional rhythm and anchoring an unusually stable closing section in G minor (starting at 5:32). Here and elsewhere, it functions as a symphonic equivalent to Wotan's *deus ex machina* role in Wagner's opera—administering, anchoring, and resolving.

The lyrical second theme returns at 6:44, as long-breathed and gracefully ascending as Wotan's spear descent is insistent and encumbering. A pastoral section follows in E major (starting at 7:38). The music is allowed to continue moving unimpeded toward life and air and light, even as it tangles with a return of the processional bass figure in two-note phrases (starting at 8:40), which then moves (in a written-out accelerando) to triplets, then to quicker duple eighth notes. This brighter music survives an apocalyptic onslaught at 10:53, and even manages to co-opt the dark processional impetus in producing a march in a major key (starting at 11:44, in B major). But the result is disastrous, the B major pleasantries running headlong into mortal reality and E-flat minor: the opening bass lunges return as a recap at 12:14, now with added fatal thwacks (one of the few major additions that Mahler made when he revised *Todtenfeier* for the symphony), and these bring about a dismayingly quick collapse. The two-note bass figure arises again (starting at 12:38), quietly leading a ghostly procession out of affirmation's ashes. The *Dies irae* chant for the dead appears (at 13:48, and again at 14:32). The music arrives at a climax in E-flat minor (at 15:04) that hijacks the down-up fourth interval figure from the earlier pastoral section (heard now *fortissimo* in the trumpets). A decisive, three-octave Wotan-derived descent leads us to a penetratingly dissonant chord that is not only unprepared according to any sort of voice-leading rules—like Berlioz, Mahler was accused of writing incompetent counterpoint—but is repeated in *fortississimo* triplet rhythms through a strident and sideways cadence back to the tonic, before a roll on the bass drum ushers in a quite literal recapitulation (starting at 16:01). But Wotan's spear descent again intervenes (at 17:16), followed by another drawn-out cadence and a separate sort-of recap (starting at 17:31) of the lyrical ascending second theme.

There follows (starting at 18:35) an exquisite restatement of the E major pastoral material, its quiet two-note figures now marked by ecstatic slides. This drawn-out music in E major is so rapturously beautiful that it sounds like a final annulment of the movement's obsessive, minor-key marching motion. But then a new tremolo links us to a long coda that's back in the tonic C minor and anchored by the repetitious bass descents and processional tam-tam strokes. Hints of an ending in C major are tentatively floated, but the issue is decided with a major-minor "seal" at 23:13, and then to close we have Wotan's spear descent forcefully closing the argument—closing it shut.

Mahler's second movement is a minuet in A-flat major, starting in a *grazioso* (gracious) fashion, complete with elegant courtly upbeats (often marked staccato) followed by sustained downbeats. (The archaic quality is significant: recall that in his program Mahler described this movement as representing a memory, a figment of the past.) This brief triple-time dance arrives as a quiet, implicitly shocking contrast with the titanic first movement, much as we'll find with the second movement of the Third Symphony—the composer later recognized this "excessively sharp (hence inartistic)" contrast as a "mistake" that should have been avoided. At the same time, this movement's nervous and insistent beat strikes a kinship with the funeral procession of the preceding movement: dancing becomes not all that different from walking to the grave.

The story has been passed down that Claude Debussy got up and left in the middle of this movement when Mahler conducted the Second Symphony in Paris in 1910. Debussy might have just been venting his distaste for musical recapitulations, and exercising his penchant for using them as excuses to sneak out and have a smoke. Or he might have been protesting the self-conscious archaisms in the music, or the structural transparency. Mahler does begin by suggesting a conventional movement with discrete, symmetrical themes and well-defined formal sections. Its form is a very simple, even neoclassical A-B-A-B-A, with none of the unexpected explosions and structural deconstructions we heard in the first movement. When the courtly A material in A-flat major cedes to the following B material in G-sharp minor (starting at 1:46), the almost self-conscious shift of character introduces a certain musical preciousness. When the A music returns back in A-flat (starting at 3:28), the isolated preludial notes suggest an added degree of affectation.

But Mahler soon starts undercutting these historical and stylistic precepts, and I like to think that Debussy left his seat before things started to get interesting. He most likely exited before the long-spanning, *molto espressivo* cello line (starting at 3:43) begins to complicate all the regular phrase structures. He certainly must have been out the door by the time the G-sharp minor B material comes back again (starting at 5:34), this time manic in its rhythm and sounding irate at the movement's continuing strict segregations of mood and style. This minor-key material acquires more of a voice when it arrives at a descending, songful violin line in A-flat major (starting at 6:42). But the section still dissolves in a strangely obsessive way, and then gives way to the last statement of A material (starting at 7:43), the strings now all in pizzicato and the flutes and harps paired in staccato glitterings. This music has a balletic effect of stage-worthy charm. The *molto espressivo* line returns (starting at 8:56), now moved to the violins, adding songlike allure to the capering style. Pizzicato chords end the movement on a coquettish note, the final resolution teasingly delayed.

Rivers and ballrooms are two metaphors that have been used to describe Mahler's third movement. Both suggest life in motion, flowing toward no particular goal in an unceasing flux of unindividualized quantities. (His own score designation "in quietly flowing motion" anchors these various impressions of streaming along, always moving.) In the program supplied above, Mahler himself compared his scherzo movement to "this surge of life ceaselessly in motion, never resting, never comprehensible," while in a remark to Natalie Bauer-Lechner he referred to the "surging surf" of this music. This is revealing, even if his program was a conceptual prop invented after the fact for expectant audiences.

Mahler grounded this movement in his own song setting of the *Des Knaben Wunderhorn* text "Saint Anthony Preaching to the Fishes"

("Des Antonius von Padua Fischpredigt"). This tells the tale of how St. Anthony, going to preach but finding the church empty, takes his sermon to the fish in the river. The aquatic creatures make for a devoted audience, but the lesson isn't learned and their strange behavior continues unchanged: "The crabs go backwards; / the codfish stay fat; / the carp gorge a lot, / the sermon's forgotten!" The fish in the stream are of course a metaphor for senseless humanity, for the absurd and unknowing congregation that allows itself to be carried along unthinkingly in the watercourse of life. Living becomes a futile confluence of relentlessness and oblivion: the creatures find themselves caught up in "this surge of life ceaselessly in motion," as Mahler's own metaphor has it.

Turning to the musical details of the scherzo, we find the flowing motion starts up as if St. Anthony's river were a rickety and reluctant mechanism. Figuration moves on unceasingly between strings and winds. But Mahler manages to express a variety of mercurial emotions and attitudes within such a "surge of life ceaselessly in motion"—silliness, self-importance, cheekiness, lyricism, and maliciousness being a few of them. The motion is given its most vivid single voice by the strident E-flat clarinet, which keeps curling its insolent way to the top of the textural flow (starting "with humor" at 0:54, and again at 1:33). A bit of folkish lyricism also bobs up to the top of the currents (in the oboe and bassoon, starting at 2:06). The harmonic motion stalls on C minor/major with a new emphasis on staccato articulation (starting at 2:31), and then a high pedal on piccolo and flute sets up a *fortissimo* bullish outburst in D major (sounding almost like a sea shanty, starting at 3:32). A repetition of this music up a step is curtailed for a slowdown and a nostalgic idea on the solo trumpet (starting at 4:26), the only point in the scherzo where the "surge of life" ceases to be quite so "ceaselessly in motion," and interestingly a melody that the movement offers just this once.

The bullish outburst music, not to be sidelined, surges back into view at 7:34, now in C major. Its optimism quickly takes on a dark hue, and it shatters at the peak of its emotional repetitiveness. Mahler referred to this eruption at various times as "a terrible outcry," "a cry of disgust," or an "outcry of despair" that spills out in response to the world's suffocating doubt, madness, or senselessness. A conclusive cadence to C major transpires amidst the rubble—as strongly verified by the timpani (at 8:08)—the "ceaselessly in motion" music from the opening of the movement returns in its various forms, and we end on a uniquely hued low C that combines contrabassoon, horns, tam-tam, harps, and double basses.

There follows, without pause, the song constituting the symphony's brief fourth movement. Here, shortly before the finale arrives with its terrifying vision of the Last Judgment and final exultant call to resurrection, we hear a miniature setting of the *Wunderhorn* text "Urlicht" ("Primal Light") for mezzo and orchestra in the distant key of D-flat major. Mahler remarked at one point that the "hero" he saw buried in his First Symphony is redeemed and raised from the dead in his Second. In this fourth movement, we see the hero setting out on a pilgrimage in search of God. This is an operatic scene in miniature, tender and disarming and complete with its own form, individual vocal style, and instrumentation. Shortly after the start, Mahler marks the passage for bassoons, horns, and trumpets "in the style of plainsong" (*choralmässig*), showing the gentler, more churchly side of the brass battery that has created heavyweight onslaughts elsewhere. The pilgrim starts (at 2:48) to relate the tale of encountering an angel on her way, an angel who wished to turn her away from her search for God. The instrumentation and intervals here give the music an orientalist quality: perhaps the search has led this pilgrim to the Holy Lands. The searcher emphasizes with great earnestness (starting at 3:34) how she would brook no obstacle in meeting her creator: "But I would not be turned away; I come from God and I will return to God. Dear God will give me a light, will light my way to eternal blessed life!" This testament of absolute faith closes with a prayerful cadence in the strings, quiet and protracted to the verge of inaudibility.

JUDGMENT DAY

We are delivered immediately from this angelic encounter to the full terror of God's judgment. The gentle D-flat major cadence of "Urlicht" is cut off by the finale's ferocious and noisy entrance on a dissonant B-flat minor ninth chord, clearing the air of all homilies and opening a wide vista of sounds and gestures—as if a curtain is ripped aside. In Mahler's description, the finale begins with "the same dreadful scream of anguish that ended the scherzo." (This musical gesture and term are also borrowed from Beethoven's Ninth, the finale of which started off with the crashingly dissonant chord that Wagner admiringly called a *Schreckensfanfare*, or a "fright fanfare.") After that opening salvo, starting at 1:36, we hear unison horns off in the distance, sounding as—again to use Mahler's words—"the Caller in the wasteland." While the first movement of the Second Symphony was theater music co-opted and wedged into a kind of symphonic form, the finale of the Second Symphony is outright theatrical. The influences and the dramatic media have come full circle here. Mahler returns to the post-Wagner symphony what is Wagner's and, taking up Wagner's precinematic project of correlating music to dramatic events, gets even closer to the modern idea of tightly integrating music with the action of sound films.

Mahler would have recognized such a seamless integration of the aural and the visual, the musical and the dramatic, as a Wagnerian idea, so this finale makes for a suitably Wagnerian ending to what had started as a Wagnerian symphony. Actually, Mahler goes further than his predecessor. If he had created this half-hour, multisectional finale in our own audiovisual age, it would surely have acquired a visual track along the way, and his role would be discussed in terms of movies and sound design. (For what it's worth, Mahler was working on his Second at the same time Thomas Edison, the Skladanowsky brothers, and the Lumière siblings were independently developing the first movie projection devices.) A sound designer is, in parallel with the far-reaching 1960s *auteur* theory of script and film composition, an all-embracing and all-controlling author in sound. Like a sound designer, Mahler shows deep concern for details of acoustic space, different scales of distance, and logistics of sound production alongside details of sound perception. To give an example of this last, Mahler shows unusual sensitivity to the acoustic differences between an instrument played far off and the same instrument played more quietly from a less remote position. When the "bird of death" sings in the "great summons" passage (starting at 16:46), it's startling to hear how very different a familiar symphonic gesture—a loud timpani roll—sounds when heard "from a far distance" offstage (at 17:41 and 18:15). Similarly, the quiet backdrop of a *sempre pianissimo* roll on the onstage bass drum wreaks an indefinable psychoacoustic transformation of this same passage. Here Mahler can only be compared with American filmmaker David Lynch (*Blue Velvet*, 1986; *Lost Highway*, 1997; *Mulholland Drive*, 2001), an auteur who doesn't differentiate between film music and sound effects, and who emphasizes bass frequencies with the theater's subwoofer in order to heighten audience awareness and anxiety.

Mahler shows himself to be a cinematic sound designer *par excellence* in the finale of his Second Symphony. His forces here include the orchestra and chorus and two female vocal soloists that are situated onstage, but there is also an array of offstage players—most of them rejoining the onstage orchestra afterward—who suggest contrasting layers of music-making, musical processes, or even conflicted hearing and consciousness. The "Caller in the wasteland" (starting at 1:36), God's summoning the dead to judgment, is voiced by at least four offstage horns: "the largest number possible, blown very strongly, positioned at a far distance." After the dead rise from their graves, they "all have the same fear" and entreat themselves, in a text written by Mahler himself, "Oh believe, my heart, believe: nothing will be lost to you!" Before these entreaties are sung by the mezzo-soprano (starting at 26:13) and then by the soprano (starting at 27:16, "Oh believe, you were not born in vain!"), they are prefigured twice by the orchestra—first at 5:04, and then starting at 13:12. As the second plea becomes more impassioned and imperative, leading to an insistent line doubled in cellos and bassoons, the offstage band of four players enters in a clashing style (starting at 13:43). Mahler must have modeled the percussion part of this offstage group on the Turkish musical "intrusion" in the finale of Beethoven's Ninth Symphony. (In rehearsing the Beethoven for one performance, Mahler positioned the Turkish-style musicians offstage and had them gradually approach the stage while playing, thus creating an effect similar to that in his own Second Symphony. This suggests, in any event, that he heard such musical-stylistic clashes in terms of spatial difference.) But the music Mahler wrote for his offstage group in his Second conflicts with the simultaneous "Oh believe" music; its banality can even sound like scorn for the sad entreaties of the dead.

As befits the apocalyptic subject of his finale, Mahler's vocabulary encompasses sounds that even mid-twentieth-century listeners must have heard as noise—or, more charitably, as sound effects. At his first rehearsal of the graves opening (the passage starting at 9:23), he insisted that the bass drum be louder than the player thought possible, and then even louder yet, to the point of breaking the instrument. (What ended up cracking, soon enough in the preparations, were the player's sticks.) When the marching, fearful dead collide head-on with the ancient *Dies irae* plainchant and its fearful indication of Judgment Day (at 12:41), the music collapses utterly with chromatic descents in the winds, furious crashes in the drums and cymbals, and futile gestures thrown about everywhere else. (From the rubble of this collapse, the second instrumental prognostication of "Oh believe" will arise in the trombone at 13:12.) As we'll discover at other points in Mahler's output, most notably in the hammerblows of the Sixth Symphony, the need for extraordinarily intense expression later led him to abandon conventionally "musical" sounds for more expedient gestures of "noise."

Our discussion of the finale has to return to the texts. In addition to all the connotation, we also have to hear the denotation: which is to say that Mahler owes as much to music theater with its singing as he does—in some kind of creative historical anticipation process—the cinema and its theorized separation into visual and aural "tracks." In addition to Mahler's raucous dramaturgy, there are words and dramatic scenarios to consider. This is not only a filmic soundtrack created before such things existed, but also an oratorio of sorts with a spiritual message. As a way of getting into these details, it would be best to lay out the movement according to sections, texts, events, and keys:

1. "The dreadful scream of anguish"—B-flat minor, C major (0:00)
2. "The Caller in the wasteland"; "THE VOICE OF THE CALLER IS HEARD, the end of every living thing has come, the Last Judgment is at hand"; first summons—C major (1:36)

   2.1 SECOND SUMMONS—F major (3:52)
   2.2 Instrumental version of the plea "O glaube, mein Herz, O glaube" ("Oh believe, my heart, believe")—B-flat minor (5:04)
   2.3 THIRD SUMMONS—C major (7:29)
   2.4 "The graves burst open, all the creatures struggle out of the ground"—F minor (9:23)
   2.5 "Now they march in a mighty procession"—F major (10:20)
   2.6 Instrumental version of "O glaube"—E-flat minor (13:12)
   2.7 "All consciousness dies as the Eternal Judge approaches"—D-flat major (15:20)

3. "THE GREAT SUMMONS"—F-sharp minor (16:46)

3.1 "The long-drawn note of the bird of death"—F-sharp minor (17:30)
3.2 "Arise" ("Aufersteh'n"), first stanza—G-flat major (19:08)
3.3 "Aufersteh'n," second stanza—G-flat major (22:42)
3.4 "O glaube"—B-flat minor (26:14)
3.5 "OH SORROW" ("O Schmerz!")—A-flat major (29:16)
3.6 "I shall die" ("Sterben werd' ich")—E-flat major (30:48)
3.7 "ARISE"—E-flat major (31:17)

There are several developments going on at the same time here. As with the finale of Beethoven's Ninth, we can listen for strategic contrasts of music in instrumental and idiomatically vocal styles. Or said another way: Mahler follows Beethoven in interspersing his long instrumental section with strategic foretellings of the vocal material—in Mahler's case, the need to "believe, my heart, believe." This expression begins each time with a telltale falling second interval, a traditionally mournful gesture that here leads into an invocation of hope. We could also listen for broader harmonic strategies and conclude that Mahler stabilizes the first instrumental half in the interrelated keys of C major and F major, which the personal vocal reflections (Mahler's words "Oh believe, my heart" and the Klopstock ode "Arise, yes, you will arise") oppose with their imposition of flat keys (starting with the first "Oh believe, my heart, believe" at 5:04, and its surprising shift from F minor to B-flat minor). The first movement began the symphony in C minor, and here the vocal sections contrive to pull the work back concludingly to the relative major of that key (E-flat major).

These are processes. It should be said that Mahler also structures his long finale with important nexus points: in other words, with clear psychological and dramatic points of arrival. (In the listing above, I've marked these in SMALL CAPS.) At each of these points, the listener has the feeling of having arrived at something duly prepared for, but also something new—as if a portal has been opened to a fresh and unexpected vista. Here God's multiple summonses are key junctures of orientation and expectation, much as one would expect. While the first summons (starting at 1:36) is played by the unison offstage horns, the second (starting at 3:52) has the calling figure in onstage horns, though still *pianissimo*. This is the movement's first decisive cadence, meaning its first real point of arrival (at F major, after long preparatory bass pedal C continuations that had started back in measure three). This summons closes with descending bass triplets, like the previous call. Confronted with these calls to judgment, the music retreats to fear: there follows the shift to B-flat minor, and the first frightened suggestion of “Oh believe” in the woodwinds (starting at 5:04). The ensuing passage, focusing on the brass, concludes with a triumphant prefiguring of a line we will hear later in the men’s chorus: “What was created must perish, what has perished must rise again!” (“Was entstanden ist, das muß vergehen! Was vergangen, auferstehen!”) (Compare the ascent starting at 6:46 in the brass to the men’s chorus starting at 27:46.) This brass passage leads us into the third summons (starting at 7:29), now in C major and now *fortissimo*, with pungent timpani thwacks, escalating harps, and madly trilling piccolos, flutes, and clarinets. This is an even greater point of arrival. As before, the summons ends with quiet, slithering descents in the bass instruments. But now the aftermath of the three-fold divine summons: the drums and tam-tam (starting at 9:24) invoke the graves opening and the unleashing of the dead. Here the *Dies irae* comes to the fore, giving rise to the march in F major (at 10:20), appearing in the trombones (11:59), then (in a passage quoted from the first movement) emerging in the trumpets and trombones (at 12:10), and then again in trumpets and trombones (at 12:41) in a statement that starts as a climax but incurs another sudden collapse.

The next major point of arrival marks the start of the third and last section of the finale, “The Great Summons” (“Der grosse Appell,” starting at 16:46). In this section the chorus will come to the forefront to deliver the message—not of judgment, as feared to this point, but of necessary and unconditional resurrection. This is the fourth, last, and decisive summons. The first two minutes are a prelude played by off-stage instruments (four trumpets, the four horns, and timpani) along with the piccolo and flute sounding from within the onstage orchestra. This passage is rooted in F-sharp minor, and is therefore harmonically distant from the movement’s opening C major, if even more distant from the closing in E-flat major. This free and unmeasured passage is the recitative-like preparation for the regular, strophic singing of the “Resurrection Ode” that is about to follow. According to Mahler’s program, at this point “the earth lies silent and deserted,” except for the flute and piccolo who break the silence with the stratospheric song of “the bird of death.” At its conclusion, the men’s chorus steals in (at 19:08), quietly and almost unnoticed, with its first iteration of “Arise, yes, you will arise, my dust, after a short rest" ("Aufersteh'n, jah aufersteh'n wirst du, mein Staub, nach kurzer Ruh").

The bearers of the message are quiet to enter, and they muster their strength as they dispatch two stanzas of Klopstock's ode. Enough disbelief remains that the fearful "Oh believe, my heart, believe" surfaces one last time (starting at 26:14). The harmonies progress methodically from G-flat major (the music that arrives at 24:35, after the solo soprano's "And gathers the sheaves, Us who have died"; "Und sammelt Garben, Uns ein, die starben") to D-flat major (the men almost shouting at 28:54, "Prepare yourself to live!"; "Bereite dich zu leben!"), to A-flat major (at the violins' excited leap up of a seventh at 29:16, prefacing the soprano and mezzo duet on "Oh sorrow, all-penetrating"; "O Schmerz! Du Alldurchdringer!"). Mahler has been carefully marshalling and meting out his resources, not yet allowing them full rein. But he finally unleashes them for the first-person cry of "I shall die, so as to live!" ("Sterben werd' ich, um zu leben!" at 30:48), which is also our decisive arrival in the closing key of E-flat major. But the harmonies quickly start preparing another cadence, and that second arrival on E-flat (at 31:17) turns out to be the climactic, life-defining, final iteration of "Arise, yes, you will arise!" ("Aufersteh'n, jah aufersteh'n wirst du!"). It hardly lessens its effectiveness after one looks at the score and sees how this moment has been manufactured for maximum gooseflesh impact, just as one would expect from an expert sound designer. Here the chorus sings the opening line in bare unisons and octaves, without harmony, electrifying us with their sudden simplicity, and the organ enters here for the first time, with a tonic chord underpinned by a wall-shaking low E-flat pedal. The chorus rises to a *fortississimo* and spreads to its registral extremes to deliver the last words (written by Mahler, starting at 31:52): "What you have conquered, will bear you to God!" ("Was du geschlagen, Zu Gott wird es dich tragen!") A concluding orchestral passage brings, in addition to pealing bells, a critical motive heard at the start of the movement—the falling fifth interval, now lastly expanded out to a triumphant octave in trumpets and trombones.

I've mentioned the necessity of the texts for understanding the Second Symphony. But one also wonders if the work's gestures and sounds actually leave enough room for such words, ideas, and actions. It's hard to escape the conclusion that the sense of redemption that Mahler creates at the end of the Second is more a triumph of musical skill, structural planning, and sonic extravagance than a triumph of belief itself. It's relevant at this point to mention the frequency with which commentators refer to Mahler's genius at exciting the air molecules that surround us as listeners. This applies just as well to the last pages of the First Symphony as it does to the Second. Leonard Davis, a veteran violist in the New York Philharmonic, was moved by a passage in Mahler's Second to exclaim, "I never heard anything like it in my life. You could just hear air moving, with sort of a pitch." The British lyric mezzo-soprano Alice Coote, a fine exponent of Mahler's songs, remarked, "He seems to know, like no one else, how to utilize the 'air space,' the space around the instruments, so that it almost seems to resonate as another instrument." And so we return to the sound design notion, and the conclusion that Mahler triumphs in his First and Second Symphonies not just "musically," but also as a master of acoustic exploitation, as a marshaller of pure and unbridled—and yes, often inspirational—sound.

3

THREE SONG SETS

Lieder eines fahrenden Gesellen, Rückert Lieder, Kindertotenlieder

Mahler is known for his all-embracing symphonies, but songwriting came more naturally to him. Three song sets in particular are prized by singers and listeners alike for their uncontrived vocal writing and their jewel-like encapsulations of emotion: the *Lieder eines fahrenden Gesellen* (*Songs of a Wayfarer*, 1883–1885), the *Rückert Lieder* (songs to texts by Friedrich Rückert, written 1901–1902), and the *Kindertotenlieder* (*Songs on Deaths of Children*, 1901–1904). These *Lieder* groups show Mahler limiting himself to a single singing voice and to traditionalist poetry at pivotal points in his compositional career. Compared with many of his contemporaries, he wasn't adventurous in his text choices. For the *Wayfarer* group, Mahler compiled twelve of his earliest adult compositions, all of them settings of his own idealized, Romantic-folkloric verses. The *Rückert* and *Kindertotenlieder* show him finding renewed inspiration in lyric poetry at a later juncture: he had married Alma Schindler and started a family, and his symphonies were becoming more modern, with a turn away from nineteenth-century manners of program music and tone painting. In some kind of creative balancing act, Mahler the songwriter found himself attracted to the simplicity of lyric verse just when his symphonies were becoming more complex and abstract.

In cultivating this pluralism of symphonies and songs, Mahler demonstrated his unlikely knack for both long and short musical spans, and his grasp of both blatancy and subtlety. He was able to develop the sense of anticipation for getting somewhere, but could also captivate in the moment, spontaneously charming the ear at any given instant. There was little precedent for this kind of versatility. It was beyond Beethoven, the all-authoritative symphonist whose works for solo voice are at best a footnote to histories of song and to his own historical importance (though music history texts commonly mention his *An die ferne Geliebte* of 1816 as the first unified song cycle). Containing such paradoxes within a single original style was also not something allowed to Schubert, a composer whose songs are foundational for nineteenth-century vocal music while his orchestral compositions are a beautiful postscript—and in any event had to wait more than half a century to be published. Such capacity was even beyond Schumann, another great song composer whose four weighty and often daring symphonies are—or so says traditional music hearsay—blemished by textural problems.

Perhaps such a song-or-symphony duality doesn't hold up when we consider later nineteenth-century opera, which often conflated symphonic and lyric writing. Great opera composers like Berlioz, Verdi, Wagner, Mussorgsky, Puccini, and Debussy were just as virtuoso with orchestration and large-scale structural planning as they were with telling tales through voices and words and characterizing individual characters through singing. Simplistic as the song-or-symphony generalization may be, however, it does help us get at some basic genre truths about Beethoven and Mahler, composers at the beginning and the end of the Viennese symphonic tradition. As an inveterate developer of musical material, Beethoven usually seems to be going somewhere in a directional and symphonic manner, and he became known—misleadingly, as it happens—as incapable of writing singable melodies. Mahler, by contrast, was a virtuoso both of the long haul and the individual musical moment.

He would demonstrate the synergistic possibilities between lyric and symphonic most clearly in *Das Lied von der Erde* of 1908—an unprecedented "song-symphony" in six movements where he shows himself just as oriented to large-scale structural proportions as to intricacies of text-setting. At the other end of Mahler's compositional career, there are the first four symphonies and their basis in his own early songs. Musicologist Knud Martner contends in his book *Mahler's Concerts* that Mahler's compositional career really began in 1887, specifically with his free "completion" of Carl Maria von Weber's unfinished opera *Die drei Pintos*. This transformative act of using an archive of preexisting material as the basis for an extended new work—Martner speaks of Mahler's symbiotic and coactive process of "recycling" older music while devising "new and strikingly original ideas"—alerted him to the possibility of doing something similar with his own youthful songs. "In a flash he realized the potential of this same method to create a work of his own," Martner writes. "Hence he selected and refashioned some of his older scores, using their themes and motifs, welding them all into a new composition." Symphonic composition thereby became a kind of archaeological dig for Mahler: while Weber had been dead for sixty years when Mahler began work on *Drei Pintos*, one can only wonder if he somehow needed to declare his own youthful songwriter-self defunct before he could reprocess his own *Lieder* in his first four symphonies—if he had to kill himself off before he could refashion the songs in such dramatic, often invasive ways. In those earlier symphonies, then, songwriting becomes inseparable from symphonic writing, the lyrical from the developmental, and the beauties of the moment from the necessities of the wide expanse.

At first glance, Mahler's song and symphony combinings can seem unlikely. The German art song—the *Lied*—is a short and usually quite simple work with words, an accompanied setting of lyric poetry for one singer. It's a musical version of poetic introspection: the composer helps us, on his or her own terms, to eavesdrop on the poet's thoughts. Often a simple melody serves both as the invitation to listen and as musical translation of the poem's broader meaning. A quintessential example would be Schumann's two-minute setting of Heinrich Heine's simple two-stanza verse "Du bist wie eine Blume," published as part of his song cycle *Myrthen*, op. 25 (1840). This text begins: "You are like a flower, / So sweet and fair and pure; / I look at you, and sadness / Steals into my heart." The symphony, on the other hand, is an extended orchestral piece that speaks to the august history of so-called absolute music, meaning "abstract" instrumental composition without reference to stories, words, or pictures. The symphony is also very much a public forum, designed as a civic vehicle for grand statements. Here a prime example would be Beethoven's *Eroica* Symphony, timing in at fifty epic minutes, or perhaps the same composer's motivically driven Symphony no. 5. While the song genre epitomizes a kind of lyrical simplicity of vocal style—think of the simpler *Lieder* of Schubert or Schumann, where simplicity can be complicated by intense storytelling or the most desolate emotions—the most quintessentially symphonic aspects of symphonies have been found in the developmental passages where themes are fragmented into motives and subjected to complex polyphony. The ethos of the song was lyric poetry and beauty of line, while the symphony—at least in its Austro-German lineage—was about continuity and long-range structural thinking.

But Mahler had an intrinsic lyric-vocal bent, audible even in his densest symphonic passages of developmental counterpoint. And this was one thing that enabled him to perform such fusions of symphony and song, such recyclings of earlier songs for lengthy instrumental composition. The almost omnipresent sense of line in his music means that he, like Schubert before him, really didn't differentiate in style terms between writing songs and writing symphonies. And this in turn suggests not only that his symphony movements could sound like songs without words, but also more generally that he practiced a certain confusion between the genres of song and symphony—genres that had hitherto occupied different performance venues, ensembles, and historical roles. Mahler was a prolific fashioner of relations and intercessions between the realms of song and symphony, of which the close emotional kinship between the *Rückert* Lied "Ich bin der Welt abhanden gekommen" ("I Have Become Lost to the World") and the *Adagietto* movement from the Fifth Symphony is just one example.

When he took a songwriter's approach to the symphony, Mahler's main task was structural rather than stylistic: he had to reconcile the brevity of the art song with the protractedness of the symphony; he had to integrate short and long. This was similar to the project undertaken by Schubert, who some forty years before Mahler's birth had worked—whether successfully or not, the question has been debated—to imbue large-scale symphonic thinking with the lyrical ingenuousness of the *Lied*. In the words of French author and cultural historian Marcel Schneider, Schubert took it as his life's ambition to "magnify the lied to a conception of symphonic dimensions." For Schneider, Schubert achieved this kind of expansion in his last piano sonata, the forty-minute Sonata in B-flat, which he heard as "a sort of prolonged, unending lied, so long and varied and luxuriant, so personal and at the same time so universal, that it seems to belong to eternity." Schubert made a similar attempt in his last and longest symphonic work, the fifty-minute "Great" C Major Symphony. In both the sonata and the symphony, Schubert's daring approach was to practice an expansion and slowing-down of the symphony, adapting the symphony to the more leisurely pace of the song rather than the other way around. Both these pieces begin songfully and as if they have all the time in the world, picking up the pace only when the opening themes start to be extended and developed.

SHIFTING FROM EPIC TO LYRIC POETRY

As a fledgling composer in his twenties, Mahler set poems by Heinrich Heine and Richard Leander, but was especially drawn to the collection of texts that Achim von Arnim and Clemens Brentano had published in 1805 and 1808 under the title *Des Knaben Wunderhorn* (*The Youth's Magic Horn*). The charm and the morbid grotesquerie of these old-style folkloric poems proved deeply influential on all of Mahler's music up until about 1901. The *Knaben Wunderhorn* texts are as much character studies—sketches of doomed soldiers, starving children, yearning lovers, wandering pilgrims—as they are about actions and emotions. The picturesque characters speak for themselves within the song, sometimes in rustic dialect: the soldier tells the story of being wounded ("Revelge"), the boy begs his mother for food ("Das irdische Leben"), the cuckoo and nightingale compete for best songster of the forest ("Lob des hohen Verstandes"), and the drummer boy describes being led to his own execution ("Der Tambourgesell"). These are mini-dramas, usually grotesque or eerie or tensely satirical, and often harrowing in their portrayals of death. But as readers, we are made just as aware of specific protagonists telling tales as we are of the actions taking place.

Mahler conjoined his main influences when he produced his first song collection, the *Lieder eines fahrenden Gesellen*, by writing his own texts in *Knaben Wunderhorn* style and then arranging them in something like the overall narratives that Schubert and Schumann had popularized in their great song cycles *Die schöne Müllerin*, *Winterreise*, and *Dichterliebe*: namely, the heartbroken lover setting out for places unknown, and ultimately meeting a dark fate. So the *Fahrende Gesell* songs are first-person lovesick narratives modeled on the great early-century song cycles, but with an added dose of self-pity and some of the quirks and rustic "local color" of the *Wunderhorn* texts thrown in:

1. "Wenn mein Schatz Hochzeit macht" ("When My Darling Has Her Wedding Day") (5 minutes)
2. "Ging heut' morgen übers Feld" ("I Walked Out This Morning onto the Meadow") (4 minutes)
3. "Ich hab' ein glühend Messer" ("I Have a Glowing Knife") (3 minutes)
4. "Die zwei blauen Augen" ("The Two Blue Eyes") (6 minutes)

The set begins with the song "Wenn mein Schatz Hochzeit macht," the jilted lover telling us how he dreads the day his beloved will marry someone else. The song begins with, and repeats obsessively, a lilting but minor-key rhythmic figure that suggests interrupted celebration with its back-and-forth swing from "quicker" to "slower." Here the narrator ponders a wedding dance but then always catches himself mid-phrase, when he realizes someone else will be the celebrating groom. A major-key, folklike strain arises when the would-be lover ponders his own sad retreat from the festivities (starting at 0:56, "Geh' ich in mein Kammerlein"—"I'll go to my little room"). Empathetic nature arises as a solace (1:59, "Blümlein blau"—"little blue flower"), but only adds to the melancholy when it becomes clear nature has left spring and its attendant hopes behind (2:51, "Singet nicht, blühet nicht"—"Do not sing, do not bloom"). In the second song of the set, "Ging heut' morgen übers Feld," the narrator is distracted by the morning loveliness of nature as a metaphor for spiritual renewal. The pace in this song is brisk and regular, as befits a spirited morning jaunt. The good cheer is such that the narrator lets out a spontaneous "Heia!" (at 1:16) and bids the world good morning, but then (at 2:42) he gets his cruel comeuppance for such optimism: "Nun fängt auch mein Glück wohl an? / Nein, nein, das ich mein', / Mir nimmer blühen kann!" ("Will my good fortune also now begin? / No, no, / It can never bloom for me!")

The *Fahrende Gesell* set takes a darker turn with the despairing third song, where all the pent-up pains are unleashed. The metaphors are likewise transformed: no longer an agent of nature, emotion instead becomes "a knife in my breast," a sharp and red-hot blade that "cuts so deeply." A vision of the beloved gives momentary distraction from these incisions in the soul (starting at 1:18, "Wenn ich in dem Himmel seh'"—"When I look up at the sky"), but the song ends with a despairing, grandiloquent collapse into blackest E-flat minor (starting at 2:25, "Ich wollt', ich läg auf der schwarzen Bahr'"—"If only I were on my black bier"). Mahler is setting epic and dramatic texts here. In his *Fahrende Gesell* songs, he presents us with utterances by caricatures or stock characters: people and even animals who are drawn in such a way that we can marvel at and maybe empathize with the sentiments they articulate, but not share in them. There is a pastness and a foreignness to the goings-on, an array of chivalric emotions and often a retributional cruelty administered by nature, that suggest the long-long-ago and far-far-away of the folk ballad.

A case in point is the fourth and last song, presented as a funeral march. "Die zwei blauen Augen" blurs any distinctions between striding out into the world and trudging toward the grave—as in Schubert's *Winterreise*, the walking journey becomes terminal, and the promised escape from love becomes an outing unto death. Like Schubert's protagonist, this heartsick journeyer has arrived in a town in springtime, fallen in love, and hoped for marriage, but now—in the dead of night and haunted by painful memories—he leaves the town for an indefinite destination, a destination that we come to realize is actually the grave. In the third stanza, set mostly in a higher vocal register, the heartbroken lover lies beneath a linden tree and "finds rest for the first time in sleep" ("Da hab' ich zum ersten Mal im Schlaf geruht!," starting at 2:48). The song—and the *Fahrende Gesell* song set as a whole—then ends with a return to the halting funeral march, now with no response of words or the human voice. Clearly, or maybe not so clearly, our heartbroken lover has found an eternal state of rest.

Scholars divide Mahler's symphonic output into an early "*Wunderhorn* period" encompassing the first four symphonies, and by implication a "post-*Wunderhorn*" phase that comprises the later, remaining works. As we would expect given Mahler's symbiosis of songs and instrumental music, this paradigm shift between the Fourth and Fifth Symphonies follows a basic change in his approach to poetry: namely, his taste in texts shifting from the exterior narratives of the earlier folkloric ballads to the more subjective, interior, psychological dramas of the Friedrich Rückert poems that he set between 1901 and 1904. In talking with the younger composer Anton Webern, Mahler called Rückert's work a quintessential example of lyric poetry: "After *Des Knaben Wunderhorn*, all I could do was Rückert—it's first-hand lyric poetry, everything else is secondhand lyric poetry."

What does the word "lyric" mean, exactly, as a term that Mahler chose to emphasize so strongly? Aristotle differentiated between epic, dramatic, and lyric forms of poetry: storytellers telling lengthy tales of the past, characters acting out their own involvements in the present, and a first-person self describing their own subjective sphere of experience, respectively. Lyric poems don't involve folkloric storytelling, explicit imagery, or stagey drama; they frame a short expanse of language in a way that showcases the beauty inherent in human feeling. They frame lovely rather than characteristic emotions, and do so in an irrefusable invitation to empathize with universal, unnamed characters. We could demonstrate the difference between epic and lyric by contrasting the character archetypes and dramatic scenarios of the texts in *Knaben Wunderhorn* style with the Rückert poems. The last of the *Knaben Wunderhorn* songs in its 1901 edition, "Der Tambourgesell," tells the drummer boy's sad story of farewell after he is captured by the enemy and condemned:

> I, poor drummer boy—
> they're leading me from my cell.
> If I had remained a drummer
> I would not be imprisoned.
>
> O gallows, you lofty home,
> You look so fearsome,
> I won't look at you any longer
> because I know I am yours.

The narration, delivery, and dark imagery contrast strongly with—to just pick an example—"Ich bin der Welt abhanden gekommen" ("I Am Lost to the World"). This is the most personal of Mahler's later Rückert songs, and it declares that mindset right from the opening lines:

> I am lost to the world
> with which I used to waste so much time,
> It has heard nothing from me for so long
> that it may very well believe I am dead!

The contrasts between "Tambourgesell" and "Ich bin der Welt" couldn't be clearer, whether we consider them as poems or as songs. The earlier "Tambourgesell" text is strong on dramatic portraiture, its story so tautly characterized that it becomes melodrama. The ballad aspect, the protagonist's submission to all-powerful fate, is especially clear in the brutal reckoning of the closing stanza where the boy says his bitter farewells. By contrast, the "Ich bin der Welt abhanden gekommen" text is about nothing other than pure subjectivity. As Mahler suggested, this poetry is solely and essentially lyric: it tells no tales, describes no past chivalries, and offers no lessons. It invokes no sense of time, and it introduces no characters. Just who is this anonymous and sexless first-person descriptor of the retreating self? Knowing the answer would get in the way of the song's message. Or, as is more likely, the narrator's anonymity is part of the message.

The earlier song and the later song are very different in tone. "Tambourgesell" begins with a dark military march on snare drum and low woodwinds, a clear emotional perspective that Mahler marks "measured and muffled" (*Gemessen, dumpf*). The vocal line itself ("I, poor drummer boy, / They're leading from my cell. / If I had remained a drummer / I would not be imprisoned") is basic and quite narrow in range, a clear presentation of character. By contrast, "Ich bin der Welt abhanden gekommen" offers a remarkable mix of simplicity and elusiveness. The voice part here is a model of austerity, and much of the orchestral writing similarly consists of solos, with no doubling between different families of instruments. The song takes only three or four notes, and hesitant notes at that, to captivate the listener. We first hear a single, isolated pitch: a low B-flat on the harp, buzzy yet generous in tone, something between a gentle call to attention and a loving tap on the shoulder. Then a two-note rise in the English horn, followed by a daub of pastel color in the violas—a warm third interval that arrives (at 0:07) like a soft benediction or a kept promise. After that, the bassoons hesitantly appear, then the clarinets, horns, and finally the muted violins (at 1:05), before the voice enters on the same rising interval the English horn had introduced.

In typical Mahler fashion, a musical statement is unfolding before our very ears—a long-limbed melody, first parsed as two notes, then three, then four, slowly gaining expressive momentum, tempting the ear ever forward. And then at the close, while the drummer boy in

"Tambourgesell" trudges off resignedly to his death ("I cry out with a clear voice: / I take leave of you! / Good night!"), the anonymous recluse in "Ich bin der Welt abhanden gekommen" concludes (starting at 4:33) with a determined motion toward spiritual retreat, a paradoxically steadfast move toward withdrawal:

> I have become dead to the world's tumult,
> And I rest in a quiet realm!
> I live alone in my heaven,
> In my love and in my song.

These kinds of contrasts continue between Mahler's *Knaben Wunderhorn* songs and his *Rückert Lieder*: the earlier and later song sets couldn't be more different in terms of their messages, their musical signifiers, and their descriptive sound worlds. The later songs shy away from the illustrative character of the earlier ones, suggesting the later symphonies and their journeys inward and interior psychologies—in short, the abstractions and ambiguities of his later instrumental music. Mahler's later lyric Rückert songs are not at all obvious in their meanings. Even when he turns to a poem that is explicit in what it is saying, his musical setting tends to blur the specifics. Though it qualifies as a lyric poem, Rückert's "In diesem Wetter" ("In This Weather," from the writer's 1834 *Kindertotenlieder*) is a prime candidate for the most straightforward of all Mahler's song texts. The narrator tells us of his children becoming lost outside in a storm. They have become endangered by the powers of nature, or are perhaps already dead: "In this weather, this raging storm, / I'd never have let the children out; / But they were carried from the house, / I had no say in the matter." Yet Mahler sets the turbulent weather and the parent's heartache in such ambiguous musical terms that the song could be heard as narrating a dozen different narratives.

THE RÜCKERT SETTINGS

Mahler's five Rückert songs don't constitute an actual song cycle, in large part because the composer didn't have an overall narrative or dramatic arc in mind, and therefore didn't specify any one particular ordering. And then there's the fact that he didn't orchestrate one of the five songs usually performed as part of the set. ("Liebst du um Schonheit" was arranged by one Max Puttmann, a staff member with the Leipzig publisher C. F. Kahnt, making this song the only Mahler piece that is heard regularly in someone else's instrumental colorings.) The five Rückert songs are performed in various sequences, most often following the order of the original Universal Edition publication:

1. "Blicke mir nicht in die Lieder!" ("Do Not Look at My Songs!") (2 minutes)
2. "Ich atmet' einen linden Duft" ("I Breathed a Gentle Fragrance") (3 minutes)
3. "Ich bin der Welt abhanden gekommen" ("I Have Become Lost to the World") (8 minutes)
4. "Um Mitternacht" ("At Midnight") (7 minutes)
5. "Liebst du um Schönheit" ("If You Love for Beauty") (3 minutes)

No one order of the *Rückert Lieder* can be definitive or even really satisfying, as Mahler himself probably recognized. "Blicke mir" makes a good starting point, since it shows the songwriter in the act of creation. The act of absconding described in "Ich bin der Welt" makes that a difficult song to follow up on, so it would work as a good capstone to the set, but then its final cadence is so much more graceful than definitive that an audience might feel disinclined to applaud. The two shorter songs, "Ich atmet' einen linden Duft" and "Liebst du um Schönheit," also deal in slighter emotions than the others—meaning they work best as interior to the sequence. A mystical nocturnal ritual, "Um Mitternacht" hosts the most dramatic progression of all, from A minor in bare textures and low registers to a blazing A major (starting at 5:59). So it makes the best closer for several reasons, though Mahler's scoring for only winds and brass—all the string players sitting this one out—means it can't summarize the set on a timbral basis.

Beneath their lovely lyric surfaces, the *Rückert Lieder* are steeped in irony and unpredictability. "Blicke mir nicht in die Lieder" is a song that thematizes creation—yet it urges attention away from the author's songs, at least until they are finished. The title line translates most directly as "Do Not Look at My Songs"—but is better read as "Do Not Look at Me through My Songs," which more accurately renders the implicit warning not to confuse author and work. (The Universal-Philharmonia edition offers "Look Not, Love, on My Work Unended" as a clumsy but plausible singing translation, suggesting right off that the author is shy about his or her work because it is still being labored over.) The last line of the first stanza (starting at 0:36) suggests the author is serious in wanting to avoid scrutiny: "Your curiosity," it scolds the listener, "is treachery" ("Deine Neugier ist Verrath"). It would be easy to imagine a dark, mistrustful setting of this verse, but Mahler's rendition shows his gift for lighthearted humor: his song is whimsical and funny, even adding a layer of self-ridicule to Rückert's nervous self-effacement. Beginning with a busy orchestral passage that suggests both coyness and needless toil, Mahler's near-rigidity of rhythm hints at obsessiveness. The pauses in the vocal line tend to be awkward and abrupt: is the person out of breath from labor and worry, or is the rhythm incompetently composed?

If "Blicke mir" demonstrates Mahler subverting songfulness, he sets the much more conventional verse "Ich atmet' einen linden Duft" to a swaying, hovering vocal line largely in 6/4 time that manages to be both a memorable lyrical idea and an evocative representation of the poem's "gentle fragrance" wafting through the air. The violin line in constant eighth notes is the thread that weaves its way through the entire song—representing perhaps the poet's sensory vigilance. "Um Mitternacht" is a more obscure text, evoking some manner of pagan, nocturnal, mystic ritual. Mahler manages to pull a lyrical vocal line from it, and—eschewing strings entirely for winds, brass, harp, and piano—traces a progression in coloration from darkness to bright, glorious splendor. Finally, as a song on love-persuasion, "Liebst du um Schönheit" counts as the most demure and restrictive ever written. It is a methodical ticking-off of reasons not to love the author. Don't love me if you love for beauty, youth, or wealth, none of which I have; but yes, please love me if you love for the sake of love alone, because I'm rich in love. (This Rückert poem is strophic, in a way that highlights its conventional nature as a love song. Clara Wieck Schumann set the text to music in 1841, in a song that follows earlier, more generalized and formulaic notions of strophic text-setting. Mahler aims much more intently for the punchline in the last stanza, namely the changeover—at 1:37—from the threefold "O nicht mich liebe" to the final "O ja, mich liebe!")

The *Kindertotenlieder* are Mahler's only true song cycle, and his last work for solo voice until *Das Lied von der Erde*—the summational yet groundbreaking song-symphony that followed four years later. The *Kin-*

dertotenlieder heading was Friedrich Rückert's own; Mahler simply carried it over to his own cycle when he selected five of the 428 poems that Rückert had penned while grieving the loss of his own two children. These "dirges for children" are dedicated more to the subject of adult bereavement than infant death. Mahler again presents us with an array of five songs:

1. "Nun will die Sonn' so hell aufgehn" ("Now the Sun Will Rise So Brightly") (6 minutes)
2. "Nun seh' ich wohl, warum so dunkle Flammen" ("Now I Will See Why with Such Dark Flames") (5 minutes)
3. "Wenn dein Mutterlein tritt zur Tur herein" ("When Your Mother Comes through the Door") (6 minutes)
4. "Oft denk' ich, sie sind nur ausgegangen!" ("I Often Think They've Just Gone Out!") (4 minutes)
5. "In diesem Wetter, in diesem Braus" ("In This Weather, in This Storm") (7 minutes)

In choosing among Rückert's many *Kindertotenlieder* texts, Mahler homed in on five poems that are especially oblique, or even self-delusional, in their discussion of death: these verses are neither sentimental nor sensationalist in the way they broach the unthinkable through metaphor or even outright self-denial. The five songs are narrated from the parent's point of view and have widely different styles, ranging from the foursquare "Wenn dein Mutterlein" to the more rhapsodic "Oft denk' ich"; from the operatic melodrama of the long-breathed "Nun will die Sonn'" to the avant-garde storm setting of "In diesem Wetter, in diesem Braus." Tying the cycle together at the end is a long orchestral postlude with solo horn that counts—along with the end of the Fourth Symphony—as Mahler's most luminous and unclouded image of serenity. He instructs that this postlude be played "like a lullaby," making it his first presentation of death as serene transcendence.

To begin with the first song, "Nun will die Sonn'" inverts several Romantic literary clichés on mortality. It was common practice for poets through the early nineteenth century to find consolation and empathy in nature, attributing human sentiment to natural objects in a practice that Victorian critic John Ruskin impugned as "the pathetic fallacy." But in this particular Rückert text, the sun illumines the earth even more brightly than before the poet was bereaved: "The misfortune fell on me alone! / The sun, it shines on everything!" ("Das Unglück geschah nur mir allein! / Die Sonne, sie scheinet allgemein!"). Mahler's song is tempted into brief major-key optimism in the second line, when the poet speaks of how the sun shines "as if no misfortune had befallen in the night!" ("als sei kein Unglück die Nacht gescheh'n!"), but as soon as the line finishes, the horn (at 1:18) drops the major third back to the minor. In a fascinating display of subterranean emotion, Mahler finds several outlets for grief in this repressed and largely strophic poem. In the second stanza (beginning "Das Unglück geschah nur mir allein!"), the horn is even more emphatic in its stressing the optimistic major third (at 2:38) before it returns again to the minor third (at 2:44). Thus begins an orchestral interlude that starts really bringing out the mournful anger that lies buried in the text. After the B section of the poem pleads for light over dark, Mahler inserts an eight-bar orchestral interlude (starting at 4:00) that fully vents the pain of bereavement, twisting itself into chromatic, torturous knots before the last couplet and its forced "Hail to the joyous light of the world!" ("Heil sei dem Freudenlicht der Welt!"). Indeed, these eight measures are analogous to a panic attack, tracing the bereaved parent's thoughts as they grow ever more distant from reason.

The second song, "Nun seh' ich wohl," is more stream of consciousness than the first, as befits the preoccupied and opaque text—the parent haunted by the inscrutable glance he remembers from the departed child's face. Mahler gives the poem a fluid setting, closer to text-based recitative than melodious aria, and with deceptive cadences that promise to anchor the chromatic wandering but end up taking the music only further away from stability. The opening five-note rising gesture in the cellos apparently originated with the exclamation "O Augen!" ("Oh, those eyes!"), and this returns as a kind of *idée fixe* amidst the song's plethora of sighs. Heavily Wagnerian in its chromatic, yearning instability, this is Mahler's most obviously Tristanesque music. At times, the song wanders absentmindedly so far afield that the singer has to be vigilant in keeping his or her pitch. And then at its close—the end can hardly be called a cadence—the music drifts (at 4:57) sideways into the tonic E-flat minor, thus hesitatingly asserting the home chord at the conclusion of a song that spent most of its time avoiding it.

The third song, "Wenn dein Mutterlein tritt zur Tur herein," returns us to harmonic stability and a clear narrative-poetic posture. This is one of Mahler's most folklike and clear-cut songs, with a metric text and short line lengths, and its sense of melodic containment jars poignantly with the unflinching realism of the words: this is the one nondelusional song that acknowledges the fact of death. The narrator finds the child's absence most painful when the mother enters the room alone, without the usual presence at her side. The song begins with the dark and mournful tone of the English horn, a sound that haunts the music as persistently as the voice itself. A pair of horns relieves some of the gloom with a splash of metallic brightness (starting at 1:29), but then the returning English horn and the strophic recall of the original melody (at 2:40) prove almost suffocating in their implicit melancholy: they are like a burdensome thought that comes back to a mindset of quiet dread. The narrator rises for just a moment out of this strophic depression when he forcefully laments (starting at 4:23) the "too quickly extinguished gleam of joy" that was his child, after which the third and still-quiet returns of the English horn and the opening strophic melody become too crushing to incite any further verbal or musical comment.

The fourth song, "Oft denk' ich, sie sind nur ausgegangen!," is the brightest and most melodic of the cycle—but that is because it inhabits a state of denial. Looking out the window, the poet thinks his children "have merely gone out" and that "we go to meet them on yonder height in the sunshine!" ("Wir holen sie ein auf jenen Höh'n im Sonnenschein!"). Each of the text stanzas begins in the minor, but each soon shifts to major-key optimism when the false promises appear: "Oh, don't be anxious! / They are only taking a long walk" ("O, sei nicht bang! / Sie machen nur einen weiten Gang"). The horn often becomes a sound of assurance and hopefulness in Mahler's scores, and it certainly adds to this song's air of wishful thinking. When the narrator ends with a vision of how "the day is beautiful on yonder height" ("Der Tag is schön auf jenen Höh'n!," starting at 2:59), a self-deceptive reference to Elysian fields, the vocalist "protests too much" with an extended, crescendoing turn up to the last word.

The final song, "In diesem Wetter," plunges us from fair weather into a tempest. The fact that the storm is a past event, now recalled, hardly lessens its intensity and danger. Though Rückert's use of past tense must have complicated matters, Mahler should have found these lines easy to set. Storm depictions are an old subgenre of orchestral representation, going back at least as far as seventeenth-century French opera. Liszt started reinventing them in concert orchestral terms in his *Les Préludes* and *Dante Symphony* and Tchaikovsky followed suit in his own symphonic poem *Francesca da Rimini* (1876): roaring timpani, sudden *fortissimo* outbursts, dissonant chords, furiously descending scales, and so on. But Mahler's setting of Rückert's "In diesem Wetter," though certainly ominous, is considerably more ambiguous as a musical illustration. He somehow preserves a storm's sense of dread and danger while utterly transforming its musical rendering. I want to call this a cubist take on a musical storm—in the sense that "cubist" was an early synonym for "modern," but also because "In diesem Wetter" shows a new syntactical rearrangement of various "storm" signifiers like the cubist painters were soon to do in fragmenting and rejuggling natural forms. Mahler gives us an abstract, even kaleidoscopic view of a storm: the descending scales are still there, as they were back in Jean-Baptiste Lully and Rossini, but the insistent, indeed rather square beat makes the invocation repetitious or even methodical.

The strange trills in the lower strings, muted and dropping stepwise through hazily voiced close thirds, hint at an interior torment that wails more powerfully than "the howling gale" outdoors. Mahler marks these lower string parts to be played *fortissimo*, more loudly than any other line of the texture, but this is because they have to shout to be heard in this register and with their mutes on. It's difficult to hear nothing symbolic in the fact that the composer has both suppressed and coerced a section of his orchestra. Which is to say "In diesem Wetter" is a psychological tangle, even from a purely textural standpoint. One soon notices the prevalence of the past tense in the text, and wonders how much of the song is really about the weather and how much is about the narrator's personal emotional tempests: "In this weather, this howling gale, / I'd never have let the children out, / I feared that they would fall ill; / These are now idle thoughts." While the narrating parent was powerless to protect his progeny, it becomes clear nevertheless that this is a song about guilt.

It's really in two longer orchestral passages of the *Kindertotenlieder* that Mahler mediates most fully between us and the poet, imparting us with his fullest musicality, empathy, and sense of conscience. In "Nun will die Sonn,'" his sparing use of the glockenspiel calls for comment in that it illustrates his most cogent response to Rückert's "first-hand lyric poetry." His earlier songs in *Knaben Wunderhorn* vein might be accused of obviousness in their text illustrations, meaning there's nothing in the music that can't be traced back to the specific words being set—or at least connected with them. That is testimony to the clarity and "exteriority" of Mahler's settings of texts that don't hide what they wish to say. But in "Nun will die Sonn,'" it's difficult to locate the textual or illustrative importance of the glockenspiel strokes—a repeated aspect of the song, one that becomes so prominent it's almost inappropriate. And Mahler calls for only one pitch from the instrument, the tonic D. What do these conspicuous, high, metallic strokes mean with their intensely focused, single pitch? The simultaneous clarity and arbitrariness of the glockenspiel strokes, and of the song more broadly, imply a whole layer of interpretive subjectivity between the composer and the outside world. They should warn us away from taking a simplistic approach to interpreting any of Mahler's passages—whether in the songs or the symphonies.

And yet Mahler tempts us to do just that in the postlude to the whole cycle, where the last stanza of "In diesem Wetter" begins (at 3:29) as a transfigured version of the song's previous four: "In this weather, in this storm, in this tumult, / they are sleeping as though in their mother's house, / frightened by no storm." The all-threatening tempest has transformed into a lullaby, though again the reference to the children's "sleeping" makes it very possible that the bereaved parent has returned ultimately to a state of peaceful delusion. If that is a deception on Rückert's part, it's one that Mahler—marshalling his most luminous orchestral textures, especially with the horn solo that begins at 5:29—encourages us to believe.

4

SYMPHONY NO. 3

Limning the Cosmos

Mahler once said, "The symphony must be like the world; it must contain everything." But it was only in the Third Symphony that he really dared to limn the cosmos. Painting on a large sound canvas and eschewing the operatic stage as well as (for the most part) sung texts, Mahler attempted an orchestral totality with sweeping aural landscapes and confrontational juxtapositions of varied styles and emotions.

The Third and Fourth Symphonies are siblings with an intertwined history. They ended up sounding very different but share an objectivity of outlook. Mahler's First and Second deal in personal narratives, while the Third and Fourth Symphonies look outward—toward universes, children, and chains of being rather than individual, subjective tales of life and death. As he described the Third to Natalie Bauer-Lechner while working on it, "It soars *above* that world of struggle and sorrow in the First and Second, and could have been produced only as a result of these." In 1902, he clarified to a friend that the piece "has nothing to do with the struggles of an individual . . . it is Nature's path of development (from stiff materiality to the greatest articulation! But above all the *life of nature*!)." Bruno Walter, who led a performance of the Third in Vienna in 1909, put this in slightly different terms, saying this music "doesn't have the character of the expression of a personality, but of a force of nature, a cosmic power."

The Third and Fourth Symphonies are beautiful but objective. Outer landscapes have replaced inner landscapes. In the Third, Mahler accounts for the world with one hundred minutes of music divided into six movements, and he places these in a calculated, almost symmetrical order. Coming first is a half-hour movement that by itself lasts longer and says more than any symphony before Beethoven's *Eroica*, and coming last is a slow and hymnlike half-hour movement that serves as a counterweight to the first. The substantial third movement scherzo, almost irrational in its sharp confrontation of ebullience with deep serenity, forms the centerpiece; and the three remaining, shorter movements separate the scherzo from the much longer first movement and finale.

1. *Kräftig. Entschieden* (Strong and decisive) (33 minutes)
2. *Tempo di Menuetto* (In the tempo of a minuet) (10 minutes)
3. *Comodo (Scherzando)* (Relaxed [Scherzo]) (18 minutes)
4. *Sehr langsam – Misterioso* (Very slowly—mysteriously) (9 minutes)
5. *Lustig im Tempo und keck im Ausdruck* (Cheerful in tempo and cheeky in expression) (4 minutes)
6. *Langsam – Ruhevoll – Empfunden* (Slow—tranquil—deeply felt) (25 minutes)

In an elaborate program that he frequently changed and finally just threw out, Mahler envisioned the Third Symphony as a stepwise ascent through the Great Chain of Being. By this account, through its succession of movements the symphony gives voice to flowers, animals, humans, angels, love (God), and lastly the child:

I. Pan Awakes, Summer Marches In
II. What the Flowers in the Meadow Tell Me
III. What the Animals in the Forest Tell Me
IV. What Mankind Tells Me
V. What the Angels Tell Me
VI. What Love Tells Me
(VII. What the Child Tells Me)

The seventh and last movement, a soprano setting of the *Des Knaben Wunderhorn* text "Das himmlische Leben" ("The Heavenly Life"), was eventually deleted from the Third Symphony and became a jumping-off point for the Fourth. It found its final home as the brief and understated finale for that shorter composition.

The German philosopher Friedrich Nietzsche (1844–1900) was hugely influential on Mahler's early worldview. The philosopher's naturalism and atheist views are particularly audible in the Third Symphony, which Mahler at one point considered titling *Die fröhliche Wissenschaft* (*The Gay Science*) after Nietzsche's book of that name. The Third has no time for ideas of an omniscient creator or for the systematic, narrow, and judgmental—the non-gay, as it were—morals of entrenched Christian philosophy. This is entirely in keeping with its Nietzschean perspective, not to mention its roots in Schopenhauer's philosophy. What kind of ascent through the Great Chain of Being does Mahler trace in his Third, exactly? His six movements don't sketch out a hierarchy of Christian virtue, but—as Mahler himself described them—instead represent "the ever-increasing articulation of sentiment, from the dull, rigid, elementary state (of the powers in nature) all the way to the gentleness of the human heart." Or maybe the fancy word for Mahler's jumping-off point in the Third and Fourth Symphonies would be panpsychism, an ancient philosophy going back at least as far as Plato wherein all the world's beings are connected through a common soul and consciousness. The idea is not that earthworms and trees and hummingbirds have individual souls, but that they all share in a single *anima mundi*. (With respect to the Third, it's against such an animistic background that we can best understand the original movement titles beginning with "What the Flowers in the Meadow Tell Me." The underlying belief is that all creatures, including humans, belong to the spirit of Nature and are in communication with it.)

Someone who comes to nature as a set of externals might just see dirt, danger, and anarchy in the forest's wild conflation of sovereign beings. ("Lions and tigers and bears, oh my!," as *The Wizard of Oz* has it.) In his 1960 book *Mahler: Eine musikalische Physiognomik* (*Mahler: A Musical Physiognomy*), the German philosopher and social critic Theodor Adorno found Mahler's Third "complicit with chaos." A kind of musicalized commotion is indeed audible: even on a first listen, the huge first movement seems more a heard event than something written, more improvisatory than designed. While Beethoven and Brahms symphonies orient us to earlier reference points, in short cueing the listener to hear present occurrences in terms of past events, Mahler's first movement becomes an exercise in coherent surprise, urging us to listen ever forward. At about two-thirds through, at the close of the development section (23:20), the orchestra is reduced to an offstage snare drum and the cellos and basses. At this point, the score indicates that these two parts of the texture, physically distanced, are to disregard one another and proceed at different tempos—the drum going back to the tempo of the march's beginning (19:59). The effect is of a single drummer who's wandered off, out of "the music," only to disrupt things by suddenly starting up at a tempo that everyone else has forgotten. Furthermore, the snare drum does this interjecting (this barging in from a distance) at full volume and at a strategically strange place in the form: a point where the rest of the orchestra is effecting a structural transition along with a diminuendo.

Looking at the broader picture, there is something provocatively chaotic to the central theme in the first movement of the Third, a musical idea that proves highly changeable across the course of the movement—indeed, so inconsistent and moody that you might hesitate to call it a theme at all. Its rhythm, riddled with triplets and lurching between quick values and long held notes, seems designed to resist consistent phrase structures and the polite "small talk" of style conventions. This music almost seems to speak: it sounds like recitative, as if it were setting conversational prose. The theme moves along like a living, breathing thing that freely follows trains of thought, becoming an uncontainable threat to rational musical structure. While laboring over the Third Symphony, Mahler wrote to Natalie Bauer-Lechner, "It is fearful the way [the first] movement has caused me to grow beyond everything that I have ever composed. I am literally gripped with terror when I see where the path ordained for music leads and that it has become my terrifying office to become the bearer of this work."

This theme is vocal in several ways: it's shifty and uncontainable, it's mostly played by wind instruments (and therefore indicative of human breathing), and it's punctuated by monosyllabic emphases and rhetorical flourishes. The line starts to sound like the vocalizations of a sentient but wordless being, gruff at one moment and wistful the next; if we followed Mahler's original program for the Third Symphony, we might allow ourselves to think of this musically "speaking" creature as Pan himself. As the composer told Bauer-Lechner, "Nature hides within itself everything that is frightful, great, and also lovely (which is exactly what I wanted to express in the entire work, in a sort of evolutionary development) . . . It always strikes me as odd that most people, when they speak of 'nature,' think only of flowers, little birds and woodsy smells, no one knows the god Dionysus, the great Pan." Since phrase structure and rhythm are better explained through verbal analogies than through analytic musical terms, I've taken it upon myself—with apologies to the composer and to competent poets everywhere—to throw together a few foresty words that would fit with the trombone solo at the point where the theme/idea comes to the fore (starting at 6:42):

> Here,
> Fear!
> Hear the woodrushes growing,
> Fall,
> Here flaming red as leaves on the oak tree grown tall,
> Ever so tall,
> Taller still
> Than hills and valleys tell.

My point here is the prose-like, ever-shifting quality of Mahler's line, and how in imitating the rhythms of an odd kind of everyday speech, it differs from the equal line lengths and regular rhyme and meter that are suggested by more traditional music—including most Brahms, Tchaikovsky, and Bruckner symphony movements.

Mahler referred to a "Pan awakes" scenario for this movement in the early program mentioned above, and Pan became more and more important to his conception of the first movement, and indeed to the Third Symphony as a whole. As he told Bauer-Lechner in July 1896, he even considered titling the entire symphony *Pan, Symphonic Poems*. To give an overview of the wind material's "awakening" in the first movement, a formal table might be called for; the titles in quotes are Mahler's own. What I call the "Pan's voice" material here—extrapolating from Mahler's description—enters and exits the argument of the first movement, sounding different at each point but at the same time similar enough to be a continuation:

"Pan Awakes"
[(a) "Reveille" (*Der Weckruf!*): the horns give the annunciatory wakeup call (0:00)]

(1) Pan's voice: eight horns playing in *fortissimo* octaves (2:40)
(2) "Pan is sleeping" (*Pan schläft*) (5:16)
(3) Pan's voice: solo trombone (6:42)
(4) Pan's voice reemerges "with the greatest power," as climax in eight horns (sounding like a recapitulation, but starting the development section) (14:16)
(5) Pan's voice: trumpets (15:18)
(6) Pan's voice: solo trombone (16:00)
(7) Pan's voice: English horn (16:49)
[(b) "Reveille": the horns recapitulate, returning us to the very start (23:38)]
(8) Pan's voice: trombone, heard overtop funeral march (25:32)
(9) Pan falls asleep? end of the voice, cellos giving the cadence (27:48)
(10) Last, fleeting memory of Pan's voice (rising interval now expanded to an octave) (32:45)

Much of the "Pan's voice" material is given over to the solo trombone, an exceptional sound presence that Hector Berlioz described in his 1844 instrumentation treatise as the most epic of wind instruments, able to "chant like a chorus of priests, or utter threats, then muffled groans, then a subdued funeral knell, then a resounding hymn of glory, then a piercing shriek, then a mighty fanfare for the waking of the dead or the death of the living." As a start along the journey of Mahler's shifts in the everchanging "Pan's voice" music, I'll suggest that entrances (2) and (3) pull the material into more distant keys; appearance (7) grounds it in a more stable key while also leaving it open-ended and couching it in a new tone color, a double reed instrument rather than brass; statement (8), arising within the recapitulation, rounds off Pan's soliloquy by sounding like a return to the lengthy trombone statement we heard at (3); and finally (9) presents "Pan's voice" as it wistfully and unhurriedly diminishes into a decisive but restful cadence in the tonic D major, with the cellos having the last word by, in effect, quietly singing "Pan" to sleep.

According to Mahler's early program, in addition to hearing how "Pan Awakes" we also hear how "Summer Marches In (Bacchic Procession)." Not for the last time, he structures a musical span as a confrontation between, and elaboration on, two contrasting kinds of material. The flexible, ametrical "Pan's voice" recitative on the trombone makes up only half of Mahler's thirty-minute first movement. So what kind of music would contrast with this? Why, a march, of course: as Pan awakes and then presumably returns to sleep, the movement is stealthily taken over by the insistent and banal one-two, one-two (left-right, left-right) rhythm of the parade and the military advance. The suggestion is that once summer has started its incursion, it becomes unstoppable. And while Pan "speaks" as an individual presence in a continuing soliloquy, the march is a communal occasion. A "Bacchic procession" would be a drunken orgy on the march, a group celebrating the ancient Greek god of the grape harvest, wine, fertility, and organized debauchery; and Mahler's march is truly a rambunctious affair, a riotous mob on the move.

It's a ragtag crowd—riffraff crashing the party. Mahler wrote "The Rabble!" (*Das Gesindel!*) in his manuscript at the point where the march enters decisively (19:59). As musicologist Peter Franklin reminds us, Mahler is referring here specifically to Nietzsche: in *Also sprach Zarathustra* "the rabble" are the ignoramuses, the great unwashed, the hoi polloi who spoil everything they touch. The prophet Zarathustra works to sequester himself from their common taint, from "the grinning mouths and the thirst of the unclean." Mahler, on the other hand, welcomes the rabble to his gleeful marching horde, and then does nothing to discourage them from taking his "Bacchic procession" to new levels of rowdiness. His orchestration almost becomes an anti-textbook exercise in crowdedness and rivalry rather than summoning traditional, luminous tonal blends; in the larger climaxes, each orchestral participant almost outshouts the next. At one point in the second segment of "Pan's voice" (at 15:40), he indicates in the score that the strings must play "with the greatest power, so that the individual strings, as a result of the violent vibration, almost come into contact with the fingerboard . . . A similar effect applies to the horns."

Though wild and Bacchanalian, Mahler's march is also a wily thing—stealing in with deceptive quiet. It peeks through at 5:58, surfaces more decisively at 9:43, and then—after the "rabble" reinforcements arrive—emerges in full orchestral guise at 12:21. Once it's gotten ahold of the whole ensemble, the marching becomes so manic it leads to an all-out skirmish, complete with piccolo and snare drum in the manner of a fife and drum corps. (Mahler wrote "the battle begins" in his manuscript at 21:45.) Shortly afterward (starting at 22:34), the marching multitude finds itself swept up in a southern gale, a passage where human ferocity is dwarfed by nature's fury (or by nature's fecundity: "Such a wind, I'm sure," Mahler told Bauer-Lechner in describing this passage, "is the source of all fertility, blowing as it does from the far-off warm and abundant lands"). But then the tempest subsides almost as quickly as it started. The following list summarizes the musical course of summer's march, and it should be considered alongside the "Pan's voice" plan given above:

"Summer Marches In"
"The Herald" (*Der Herold!*) (5:56)
First, brief appearance of the march (5:58)
Reappearance and continuation (9:43)
Main march (exposition?), led by three horns (10:53)
The gang's all here! *fortissississimo* march in full orchestra (12:21)
Main march starts taking over the whole movement; sounds like a development section (17:42)
"The Rabble!" (*Das Gesindel!*) (20:01)
"The battle begins" (*Die Schlacht beginnt*) (21:54)
"The southern storm" (*Der Südsturm*) (22:35)
March approaches from the farthest distance (28:23) and takes over
March leads to a riotous coda that begins as a repeat of the end of the exposition (31:45). Compare with the music starting at 12:55; the effect is like finally returning home after a false detour

The duality between "Pan's voice" and "summer's march" shouldn't prevent us from hearing the musical subtypes that Mahler concocts in his first movement, not to mention his marvelous transitions. And then there are the provocative ways he starts and ends the movement. To begin at the beginning: eight unison horns, playing accented and *fortissimo*, cleave the silence to rouse all creation with a "wakeup call" (a "Weckruf," as Mahler described the opening; "reveille" would be the equivalent for non-German speakers). The line is elemental and implacable with its multiple cadences—especially stern starting at 0:13, where the drums sound like gunshots as they drive the chord progressions home. In its simplicity, this theme predicts the "Summer Marches In" music. After the long chain of cadences (starting at 1:01), the bass drum has a mysterious four-bar solo that suggests the "Pan Awakes" music with its strange, swaggering triplets. Mahler described this section in abstract terms, as representing "the gloomy rigidity of merely elemental being." A stuttering figure (starting at 1:17, marked "heavy and muffled"), sounding vaguely funereal, enters in representation of "chaos." Some mighty organism seems to be gradually stirring to life against this backdrop, the bass drum reporting its capricious and fearsome pulse. Fragmentary trumpet ascents and detonations in the strings and timpani keep the music driving forward, as the horns reenter—now paired in octaves in a vehement forecasting of the "Pan's voice" music (starting at 2:40). The mysterious bass drum music reappears, and then a delicately orchestrated passage (starting at 5:16, marked "Pan is sleeping" by Mahler) with string tremolos and oboe and violin solos, followed by the first hint of the march (at 5:58), and then the grand appearance of the solo trombone (at 6:42), where Pan's soliloquy gets underway.

As mentioned, Pan's rousing intersects with summer's progress in the first movement of the Third Symphony: summer is able to get its own march underway only after Pan is fully "awake" around 9:00; as Pan's parting word before the full "rabble" joins the Bacchanalian procession and the march becomes irrefusable, a lyrical and long-limned melody relieves us for a moment from the one-two, one-two of the pageant (the lyrical melody entering at 18:41, first in solo horn, then solo violin, solo cello, and lastly and most beautifully the full cello section). Jumping ahead to the final relaxed inhalation before the march's last onset at 28:23, we have the passage where the cellos cadence for the trombone and put Pan to sleep, as it were (27:46 to 28:15). The movement could have ended at this point of closure in the home key, but irrefusable summer has other plans. The march, hesitantly testing the waters of C minor right after Pan's restful conclusion in D major, steals back in in a delightfully sly way once the coast is clear. And summer arrives noisily and in full orchestral regalia, the ensemble gradually getting larger and larger. There is a brief diversion to D-flat major (at 32:32), in direct reference to the end of the exposition some twenty minutes earlier, but now the harmony is resolved sideways through G-flat major to the F major with which the movement ends. Having sidestepped this harmonic question mark, the final arrival is all the more triumphant—as the timpani are "struck hard," the trumpets raise their bells, the string players use the wood part of their bows, and the final cadence is rendered "with the greatest power" (*mit höchster Kraft*).

MOVEMENTS TWO THROUGH FOUR: THE CIRCLES OF CREATION

The first movement was the last part of the Third Symphony to be composed, and became a prequel, an add-on, to Mahler's early circles of creation scenario. It's only with the fairly brief second movement that we start the itemized ascent through forms of life: starting here with "What the Flowers in the Meadow Tell Me," and then going on in movements three through six to "the Animals in the Forest," "Mankind," "the Angels," and lastly "Love." Following the unclassifiable and unprecedented first movement, the second is a study in combined genres: an essay in the classical symphony dance movement of the minuet, and an exercise in the Romantic character piece salon tradition of the *Blumenstück*, or "flower piece."

But any initial suspicions of triviality in the second movement minuet don't last for long. The charm of this music proves deceptive: right off, Mahler breaks the classical minuet mold by adding a redundant measure to create an opening phrase that is an off-centered nine rather than an even-keeled eight bars long. When the harp and second violins come in in the relative minor key (at 0:53), with the violins largely in triplets, the music takes on a darker hue even though it moves higher in register. Contradicting that is a swooning interjection (at 1:15) where the full quartet of horns comes in and the violins play a two-bar figure in octaves, *molto espressivo*. The pace ratchets up a notch (starting at 2:14), and the rhythmic language becomes even more quick and nervous by emphasizing sixteenth notes and pentuplet rhythmic groupings. The shifts start coming faster and furiouser. Mahler brings in a third, new theme (at 2:30) now in insistent 2/4 time; then a chattering fourth theme in the dominant minor (announced with a cymbal crash at 2:42) with impulsive subdivisions of the 9/8 meter.

The original opening material then comes back (at 3:07) with new countermelodies and various tweaks, its relaxed tempo and streamlined string scoring now shocking us all the more with their comfortableness. The recap makes us ask: how did we journey so far from this cozy schmaltz, almost imperceptibly and in less than a minute? The second theme also returns (at 5:25), now varied and abridged. The third theme comes back (at 5:37) but now in the distant key of G-sharp minor and moving into a vein of manic tragedy. Themes three and four return in combination (announced again by a cymbal crash, at 6:18), bringing with them their metric decenteredness. The original A theme returns (at 6:52), at an "again leisurely" (*wieder gemächlich*) tempo. This material is varied, most conspicuously with rhythmic complications and embellishments in the violins as a reminiscence of the fourth theme. A substantial coda (starting at 8:54) ties off the movement's variety but along the way adds a few intrigues of its own, including a threatened detour to D-flat major. But charm becomes the parting shot: by the close, we've traded Schumannian estrangement for delicacy in the manner of Felix Mendelssohn.

Once we pass the first movement of the Third Symphony with its "Pan Awakes / Summer Marches In" plot and get farther into "part 2" of the Third Symphony, the "Great Chain of Being" program becomes less and less specifically useful to the listener. The third movement is a radically reconfigured scherzo: all of eighteen minutes long, and following a second movement that is weighty in its own way. Perhaps even more than the big first movement, the third holds a variety of moods and materials. An up-tempo scherzo character certainly marks half of the movement, but then the lengthy post horn sections (marked "very relaxed," and then "almost slowly") are essays in such deep and motionless interiority that—though often interrupted by faster music—they start to sound like the whole symphony's "slow movement," or at least as its folkloric heart. This movement is an ambitious expansion of Mahler's "Ablösung im Sommer" ("Changeover in Summer"), a brief song written in 1892 that explains how the nightingale assumes forest singing duties upon the premature death of the cuckoo. Mahler didn't simply take the earlier song as is, as he did with the *Knaben Wunderhorn* song "Urlicht" in the Second Symphony. Nor did he make just a passing reference, as when he alluded to the song "Lob des hohen Verstandes" at the start of the finale of the Fifth Symphony. Rather, he did nothing less than elaborate on and refashion the earlier piece after first presenting it quite literally, much as he did the song "Des Antonius von Padua Fischpredigt" for the third movement of the Second Symphony.

The third movement of the Third Symphony becomes confrontational in its means of "containing the world." This movement shifts between two extremes: (1) a perpetual-motion-skitterish style, comprising forest animal scurryings and polka-style raucousness, and encompassing score markings like "crude" (*grob*) and "merry" (*lustig*); and (2) a quiet-static-nostalgic manner where the folkloric post horn instrument is heard from an evocative distance, spinning out endless melodic lines from almost out of earshot. The first of these two styles is objective, illustrative of the outside world in a way that could be called programmatic ("like a sound of nature" is a marking that occurs more than once), while the second is a more subjective view of inner feelings ("as if eavesdropping" is one strange score indication in this section). The first sounds direct and in the moment, and the second suggests a world dreamed or recalled from memory. The disparities between these two musical qualities are also a matter of harmonic rhythm: the first material is constantly cadencing with square oom-pah bass figures, while each appearance of the second becomes a single, fluid, blissfully drawn-out cadence that suggests slowly falling asleep on a warm summer day. Or, to hear this duality in terms of actual musical sound, the movement switches between (1) music-making that emphasizes physical effort (the strings using the wood of the bow or playing on the bridge at several spots, the winds raising their bells into the air); and (2) sustained playing with the edges smoothed away, gradually increasing in sound or slowly dying away ("drawing somewhat nearer," *sich etwas nähernd*; "becoming fainter," *verhallend*; "completely disappearing," *gänzlich verschwindend*), with instruments placed at a distance or asked to sound that way.

"Ablösung im Sommer" must have functioned as Mahler's jumping-off point for the movement. His symphonic presentation of the song at the start inspires a parade of delectable instrumental colorings, each of the wind instruments impersonating a different creature of the forest. The clarinet is the cuckoo, the piccolo is probably the nightingale (entering more eloquently than the cuckoo, and assuming the vocalist's entry from the original song), the oboe the titmouse, and the clarinet closes with an unmistakable cuckoo figure (taken from the singer's ironic line "Cuckoo is dead! Cuckoo is dead!"). Then closing this first stanza of "Ablösung im Sommer" are pairs of bassoons (creaking and gamboling in tandem under the clarinets) and trumpets (moving downward with a choreographed, arm-in-arm formality that Constantin Floros hears as polka-like). The harp enters at the start of the song's second stanza, where "Mrs. Nightingale" is praised as lovely, sweet, and "always joyous," and the music accordingly changes from minor to major. Other instruments enter—the strings, a trio of horns—as the novelistic cast of characters grows and the orchestral landscape widens. A sudden loud cadence brought the original song to an abrupt end; at the corresponding point in the symphony (1:30), the move to *forte* both closes the song and propels the movement off on its extra quarter hour of orchestral adventures.

The movement develops the various forest-creature rustlings and twitterings of the original song, while the largely introverted sections dominated by the post horn solo are newly composed for the symphony. Mahler spoke of these two kinds of music (perpetual-motion-skitterish, as opposed to quiet-static-nostalgic) as a confrontation between "the quiet, undisturbed life of the forest" and "the appearance of man." It would be limiting to hear the movement as a detailed representation of this duality. At the same time, that scenario can help us register various features: for one, the movement's division between (1) a concerted agglomeration of contrasting timbres and kinds of movement, and (2) a more thoughtful series of enunciations dominated by a central voice—much as (1) the forest is a combination of details that survive with no single overriding intelligence, and as such is confronted by (2) an eloquent if forceful humanity that is, one hopes, guided by singularity of thought and able to ponder, dream, and remember. Mahler brought a film director's sensibility to his juxtapositions, intercessions, and transitions between these two worlds. At the start of a kind of slow dissolve (at 3:00), we can sense the perpetual-motion-skitterish music slowing down, the instruments sounding less soloistic, and the texture consolidating around a specific tone of voice: humanity seems to be approaching, or its presence at least sensed. The movement reaches a self-consciously symphonic climax (the animals in panic, maybe?), complete with a furious downward scale in brass unisons and octaves, only to have any sense of cadence undermined by a reduction of texture and a shift back to the transitional style in C major (at 4:20). The movement seems to keep looping back to the same points, as if in expectation. After the climax, we go back to the music that immediately followed "Ablösung im Sommer," before a trumpet fanfare on C (at 5:27), promising a new key area and a new kind of music, ushers in a slight slowdown in tempo.

Long awaited, the quiet-static-nostalgic music finally arrives in F major—at 6:16, carrying with it the various thoughtful-humanistic (second) connotations indicated above. This music marks a radical texture change, as mentioned: the post horn (sounding remote, the player instructed to sound "as if from a far distance") floats above a seamless, slowly shifting veil of first violins. Both the timbre and the sense of space are evocative: Mahler substituted a modern flugelhorn for the earlier, obsolete post horn when he went back and revised the symphony, but the sound is still suggestive of messengers and mail carriers announcing their arrival by horse carriage after traveling great distances. (The logos for the modern-day postal services in various central and Eastern European countries, including those regions where Mahler lived, still contain the emblematic image of the post horn.) We can imagine the post horn as humankind's distant incursion into the forests the composer remembered from childhood. Even at the end of the nineteenth century, the instrument suggested nostalgia for a simpler and less hurried way of living. Mahler instructs the soloist to play freely and in leisurely fashion, before a pair of regular French horns (entering "songfully" at 8:26) start ushering humanity's quiet-static-nostalgic style of music toward repose. After a brief return of the forest rustlings in F minor, the post horn returns along with its pair of cadencing horns. When the horn-led specter of humanity finally achieves its blissful cadence in F major (starting at 10:37), the arrival is punctuated by four soft strokes on the bass drum, an instrument not heard since the first movement.

But this lulling of humanity doesn't calm the movement's tense duality. Quite the opposite: the perpetual-motion-skitterish music returns with a vengeance, arriving again at the stern scalar descent, before a noisy ("Grob!," "crude!") dance party breaks in (at 12:46). The revelry turns manic, the high, strident woodwinds harking back to the Bacchic procession in the first movement of the symphony. After the pair of trumpets announces humanity's return and we hear a few lingering calls from nature, the orchestra quiets down again. The post horn reenters (at 13:55) and this time finds restful embrace in a pair of violins before the cadential horns enter, as twice before, with sleep's arrival marked by the tolling sound of harps doubling bass drum. The perpetual-motion-skitterish music erupts for the last time in its most violent protest so far (at 16:52), now wrenching the music down to the surprising harmony of E-flat minor. Horns and trombones issue a stern edict above string tremolos in a passage heard by scholar Peter Franklin as "a call to order," at the same time pressuring the music down yet again to the key of D-flat. The music drops down once more (at 17:17), to the C major already established as the home key of the movement back at the second, nightingale stanza of the "Ablösung im Sommer" song. Now, with nature trumping humanity at the end of the movement, Mahler's astonishing rush to the last double bar sounds like an end-of-scene climactic action. It was inevitable that a filmmaker would use this passage. Ken Russell adopted it in his biopic *Mahler* (1974) to underscore a scene (starting at 40:45) where the young Mahler, wandering without direction in the forest at night, is approached by a white stallion. Terrified at first, the boy manages to calm the animal, mounts it, and then gallops off—and so we see the pubescent composer triumph over nature, in a symbolic encapsulation of his journey from inept child to adult genius.

Movements four and five, originally titled "What Mankind Tells Me" and "What the Angels Tell Me," are simple vignettes, blocks of uniform color and mood rather than musical arguments. The fourth movement ("O Mensch, gib acht!") is Mahler's only setting of a text by Nietzsche. It's not difficult to see why very few composers have ever set this "midnight song" from *Also sprach Zarathustra*, since the text—though written as a dance song, as a roundelay—doesn't lend itself to musical setting. The line lengths change and the meaning is obscure: Zoroaster instructs humankind in poetic verse, a strange locutionary manner for a prophet to adopt, offering opaque statements on death and sleep and dreams, and their relation with real-world externality. Since any kind of literal musical realization of these words would have been impossible, Mahler sublimates the text, creating a dark and nonmelodic character and countering the nocturnal air with string harmonics in a glassy stratospheric shimmer. The vocalist is instructed to sing "with mysterious-obscure expression" (*mit geheimnisvollem Ausdruck*), and Mahler obscures the orchestral sound by having the strings play with mutes. He writes for the mezzo-soprano as if she were an instrument, perhaps a French horn, rather than a human character. And he sets the words in a kind of lyrically monumental style, neither annunciatory in the manner of one of Wagner's female prophets, nor locally expressive in an art song manner. (Regarding this last: his strange, fawning style for the line starting at 6:34, "Weh spricht: vergeh!"—"heartache says: perish!"—would be out of place in German *Lied* traditions.)

The melodic and harmonic inertia of this Nietzsche setting makes a strong contrast with the preceding movements; attention is focused here not on broad thematic processes and dramatic scenarios, but on individual tone colors and local major-minor shifts. The movement goes nowhere harmonically or melodically—it just shimmers and oscillates like some force of nature before it ends exactly as it began, with "mysterious" murmurings in the cellos and basses. The mezzo's vocal line begins as a single pitch ("O Mensch!"—"Oh, humanity!") before she moves on to two ("Gib acht!"—"Pay heed!") and then four ("Was spricht die tiefe Mitternacht?"—"What does deep midnight say?"). Harmonically speaking, the movement has a subterranean feel by the way it sits mostly on an unchanging D major chord. At a more expressive section—starting at 3:12, after "tiefer als der Tag gedacht," "deeper than the day imagined"—the D triad is finally left behind and the strings remove their mutes. Here the instruments reach up more rhapsodically and then emphasize D *minor*, support a forlorn rising third interval in the oboe, and then usher the music toward the dominant key of A major. The singer picks up on the oboe's plaintive rising major thirds for her lines "Tief ist ihr Weh!" ("Deep is its woe!"); "Lust, Lust" ("Joy, joy"); and "Weh spricht . . ." ("Woe says . . ."). The opening murmurings return, and then the singer doubles the strings when they return to their emotive line ("doch alle Lust will Ewigkeit," "but all joy desires eternity," at 6:51). Twisting D major to D minor, an accented F-natural in the orchestra darkens the key and incites a shutdown of the movement by pushing the music back yet again to its opening murmur—suggesting matters half-spoken but profound, and in any event left unresolved.

The fifth movement uses bright, clear, incisive sounds to suggest notions of "What the Angels Tell Me." This is a *Knaben Wunderhorn* text about a pilgrim seeking redemption, as we already saw in the fourth movement of the Second Symphony: bells peal away as a tearful sinner is told to "Only love God forever, Thus will you attain heavenly joy" ("Liebe nur Gott in all Zeit! So wirst du erlangen die himmlische Freud"). The register in this fifth movement is as high and the timbres as bright as the coloration of the fourth movement was low and dark: Mahler uses a choir of women, as well as a boys' choir stationed "in a high gallery," probably in imitation of the boys who sing "from the apex of the dome" in the Grail scene of Richard Wagner's *Parsifal*. The text mentions Jesus and the apostles at the Last Supper, a Christian reference that clashes ideologically with the mystical Nietzschean aphorisms of the preceding movement. Mahler illustrates the bell ringing by doubling the boys' chorus ("Bimm, bamm") with an orchestral bell. A women's chorus then delivers the text ("Es sungen drei Engel einen süßen Gesang"—"Three angels sang a sweet song"), after which the solo mezzo tells the tale of the weeping sinner. The movement sounds more and more like a Protestant chorale setting as it goes along, at one point offering four bars of unaccompanied chorus (at 2:54, "Liebe nur Gott in alle Zeit!"—"Love Only God forever") and then (at 3:51) bringing in a solo trombone as an equal partner, as if intoning a chorale tune in a Bach cantata movement. Typically for the ever-paradoxical Mahler, this brightest and most concise movement of the Third Symphony is the one with its darkest episode. Starting at 2:12, in a passage marked "The whole orchestra steadily and slowly crescendoing," the steady "Bimm, bamm" becomes more and more insistent, turning into a funereal tread that's underscored by menacing strokes on tam-tam and cymbals. But the darkness quickly dissipates, and the movement ends with the bell strokes fading gently into silence.

And then the last movement arrives—or, better said, quietly suggests itself. The Third Symphony presents such an array of emotions, textures, styles, sounds, and thematic events that Mahler half-jokingly said he would be crucified at the premiere. And the more variety a piece contains, as most composers discover, the more difficult it is to conclude—which means Mahler could have concluded the Third in so many ways, or indeed might have found no plausible way at all. Certainly quietly insinuative music is the biggest surprise Mahler could have sprung at this point in the composition, at the beginning of the end of his longest and most capacious work. His unique performance instruction is "slow, tranquil, deeply felt" (*Langsam – Ruhevoll – Empfunden*). According to the score, this "tranquil and deeply felt" finale is to follow the bell-ringing fifth movement without interruption. Having the finale steal in quietly adds to its quiet provocation: the rhythm is mostly in simple groups of quarter notes and half notes, and Mahler instructs the violins to render the melody "very legato, sung very expressively." The composer has been long preparing, in some ways subtly and in some ways obviously, for this opening fourth rise in the violins to the tonic D major—and with that simple motion, the most elemental movement in tonal music, the listener can almost hear Mahler's finale click into place as an event both satisfying and inevitable.

What to call the finale of the Third Symphony? Resolution, confession, benediction, summation—the movement performs all these functions. Beethoven had done something similar when he began the last movement of his Sixth Symphony, the *Pastoral*, with a slow and sustained "song of thanksgiving." But Mahler's melodic material is less folkish than Beethoven's, his ambition and scope greater. A specific Beethoven string quartet is more immediately relevant: Mahler begins his finale as an almost note-for-note copy of the start of the earlier composer's slow movement to his String Quartet in F Major, op. 135, transposing up a half step from D-flat to D major. Since Mahler references the Beethoven so explicitly, we can borrow a description from Beethoven himself, who labeled his own quartet movement in a sketch as a "sweet song of rest" or "sweet song of peace" ("Süßer Ruhegesang oder Friedensgesang"). As indicated by Mahler's opening instruction to the violins, he wants his own song of rest or peace to be "sung very expressively."

Mahler alludes almost right away to the *Lento assai* of Beethoven's quartet and to its ineffable quality of what German speakers call *Innigkeit*—inwardness, intimacy, and sincerity. Continuing in elaboration of Beethoven's "sweet song of rest," he scores the first five minutes of his finale for strings alone. (Mahler made string orchestra arrangements of quartets by Beethoven and Schubert for his own concert use, so was well practiced with such adaptations.) Restricted in tone color, his opening section is also simple in terms of form: a straightforward three-part structure, the contrasting section starting without the violins and with the melody given this time to high cellos; followed by a return to the opening music at 2:30, now with the melody an octave higher; and then a twelve-bar coda. A second part follows (at 5:30) mostly in F-sharp minor, with the strings now colored by wind instruments—first the oboe, then the horns. We then arrive (at 6:47, a passage marked "passionately") at Mahler's first quotation of material from an earlier movement of the symphony, showing how his resolution-confession finale is also becoming a summary and a tying-off of this wide-ranging hundred-minute work.

The first thing we heard at the start of this finale was a slow, quiet, smoothly dispatched quarter-note upbeat leap, a radiant and comforting affirmation of the tonic chord. I call this the "serene leap" of the movement, and it becomes thematic and formally strategic in itself as the movement proceeds. The serene leap comes back many times as both a comforting point of return and a moving-ahead to new things, something like the sound of a well-worn page being turned in a treasured old storybook, or like each verse of the old hymn "Amazing Grace" being introduced by the same consoling interval—a rising fourth. Mahler's serene leap, returning after a transitional passage, expands to the full octave D to D when it reintroduces the opening material at 9:24—one of the most remarkable moments in all Mahler, the familiar melody now cloaked in the silvery sound of doubled flute, oboe, and clarinet. This time, in addition to being differently colored, the theme grows more restless, more quickly impassioned, and more harmonically fluid.

Mahler makes strategic use of this serene leap in his finale. He foils expectation at 11:00 when he uses it not to pull us into the tonic D major, but rather into a contrasting (and recurring) section in D minor that uses the new color combination of horns and solo violin. The movement then starts moving to more remote harmonies, distancing us from the D major tonic that we've been made to anticipate. Transitional, shifting material introduces the new key of C-sharp minor, then E-flat minor; a bass drum roll introduces E-flat major, then further key changes. We reach a point of arrival in D minor (14:11) where the horns conflate the climactic point of the first movement development (as we had heard it there at 14:16) with the "Tief ist ihr Weh" figure from the fourth movement. Teasing anticipations of the serene leap occur at 14:46 and at 15:45, each time not following through but leading instead somewhere other than the opening theme. The horns seem finally to initiate a proper cadence to D major at 16:33—but this passage also quickly turns in another direction, the return started but then supplanted (starting at 16:50) by another emphatic recollection ("mit höchster Kraft"—"with the greatest power") of the tense climax from the development section of the first movement.

This tense recollection of the first movement seems to derail the argument of the finale, the way the protagonist of a novel might be traumatized by a reminder of some tragic event: the thematic recall marks a disintegration of the orchestral texture, followed by a new focus on upper-register instruments. A wandering line on the flute and piccolo leads to an expectant string tremolo, and then (at 18:32) the serene leap up to D and a return to the opening material, now in the different color combination of solo trumpet supported by trombone, soon to expand to the full trumpet and trombone sections. The style and the tone colors now suggest a Protestant church service. The long-expected full arrival in home harbor has not yet been granted, the movement's thematic and harmonic moorings obscured by the strings' continuing tremolo and the bass line's avoidance of the tonic D. It becomes clear that this ongoing expectation—and, one assumes, eventual reassertion—of the symphony's thematic origins is being strategically used to counteract the immense and wildly varying structure of the Third Symphony as a whole. (All loose ends have to be accounted for here, in conclusion of this—as Donald Francis Tovey describes the Third in his 1939 *Essays in Musical Analysis*—"musical phantasmagoria in which all the elements that have ever been put into a symphony before are conglomerated with all the musical equivalents of a picaresque novel and a Christmas pantomime.") Mahler's manipulation, and eventual rewarding, of the listener's expectations later in the finale are like the huge pinions, anchored deep into bedrock, that support a suspension bridge; the spans of time involved and the grandiosity of gesture are proportional to just how far afield these six movements have wandered, and show how they have to be corrected for so the symphony can come together as a satisfying whole. (We can best appreciate the summational power of the finale by hearing it as a strategic coordination of three climaxes: the recollection of the fourth-movement "tief ist ihr Weh" in G minor at 14:11, the first-movement voice of Pan in G minor at 17:06, and lastly the conclusive arrival on the last movement's D major at 22:42.)

The finale of the Third Symphony ends with yards and yards of D major, strenuously and repeatedly affirming this key as the work's safe harbor. We enter this home key domain at 21:20, the point where the full orchestra finally arrives at a stable root-position D major harmony and the opening theme is finally allowed to unfold completely, as it was originally heard. The arrival becomes more emphatic a minute further in, where the serene leap to D is heralded by a timpani roll and then underscored (at 22:42) by a decisive cymbal crash and bass drum stroke. All eight horns enter imposingly in *fortissimo* unisons, joined together much as they were at the "wakeup call" starting the first movement. The timpanist reiterates the final tonic arrival no fewer than fifteen times, but Mahler shuns blatancy at the close by requesting an ensemble sound that is "saturated and noble" rather than one marked by "crude power." Thinking back to his original "Great Chain of Being" program, this is the composer's most specific indication of just where his hundred-minute-long phantasmic tapestry has taken us: to a position of majesty that stops short of force or authoritativeness. (In an interview with Michael McManus, conductor Mariss Jansons interpreted this last peroration and "saturated and noble" score marking as saying that we remain firmly on earth even when we are absorbed in praise for the Almighty: "This is like a hymn to God and to the heavens, but it's not a triumph, not a victory . . . I think he wanted to say 'I'm happy that I'm here [on earth].'") Mahler indicates that the last chord is to be held "long" and with no diminishing of the sound—quite a feat for an orchestra that's been playing for an hour and a half with no intermission. With this full-stop closure to an extreme, even ridiculous, stretch of musical ambition, Mahler—at this point still a young idealist and still writing long instrumental stretches under the influence of song—aims to translate both "the highest articulation of sentiment" and the necessity of symphonic closure directly into sound.

5

SYMPHONY NO. 4

Mahler's Symphony of the Child

I've said that Mahler gained a new objectivity with his Third and Fourth Symphonies—works that look outward, away from the earlier self-occupied narratives. The Third Symphony was an expression of love and sympathy for various aspects of creation. The philosopher Arthur Schopenhauer, one of Mahler's decisive influences, spoke of compassion (*das Mitleid*, literally "shared suffering") as our only escape from the destructive individual human will and our only source of moral value. The definitive example of compassion in musical terms was Wagner's *Parsifal*—an opera that echoes Schopenhauer at several points, and a piece that Mahler recalls in the luminous last movement of his Third Symphony. The Parsifal character, the valiant young fool, practically quotes Schopenhauer's *Über die Grundlage der Moral* (*On the Basis of Morality*) at the climactic moment in Wagner's third act, when he miraculously heals Amfortas's incurable wound. He tells the king, "O blessed be your suffering, that gave compassion's highest power and purest wisdom's might to the timid fool!" When Mahler at 14:11 in the finale of his Third Symphony returns to the "tief ist ihr Weh!" ("Deep is its woe!") phrase—an Amfortas moment if there ever was one—he is thematicizing compassion à la Parsifal, building out of that ineffable and inherently undramatic sentiment a conclusion that is at the same time climactic and anticlimactic.

If Mahler's Third Symphony is about compassion, then the Fourth—which was written as an offshoot of the Third, though in terms of initial conceptions it actually preceded it—could be called his "symphony of childish empathy," or maybe just his "child symphony." The Fourth is like the Third in that it doesn't illustrate any specific thing; rather, it invites us to empathize with the child. Mahler's starting point for the whole Fourth Symphony was the *Lied* "Das himmlische Leben" ("The Heavenly Life"), a *Wunderhorn* song that he originally intended to use as the finale for the Third Symphony. Here the child sees heaven as a place of serenity, wonder, and quirky overabundance, a place to frolic with saints and share in their delectable foods and mellifluous music. This cheerful tale of plenty has a dark twin in his song "Das irdische Leben" ("The Earthly Life"), which tells the tale of a child who dies tragically of hunger and want. Mahler himself saw his diametrical pair of "Leben" songs as the alpha and omega for his whole compositional output. They represent the duality of heaven and earth, blessedness and mortality, the two opposing themes he gravitated to his entire life: in this instance, bliss after deliverance and suffering unto death, as told through a child's own words.

The hypothesized and empathized-with child in the Fourth Symphony could be Mahler himself. There remained something infantile and regressive, in the better senses of those words, to the adult composer's personality. Mahler was a full-grown child who had a special bond with his fellow child-children, relating to them as equals. According to Mahler's early biographer Richard Specht, "he was actually a grown child," one who possessed a "pure, untouched childlikeness of being." And yet his childlike nature harbored distrust as well as purity: "He was trusting one minute and suspicious the next, as a child is." The composer's childlike aspect was also noticed by Maurice Baumfeld, a music critic and family friend of the Mahlers in New York. I'm speaking of Mahler's unpredictability of mood and tone, his shapeshifting in terms of emotions, guises, and roles. Baumfeld brought this up in the context of Mahler's interaction with his daughter Anna, in a statement chronicled by Kurt and Herta Blaukopf:

> Anyone who saw him playing with his little daughter fully understood the gentleness, indeed lovableness of this basically taciturn nature. To entertain children so that the child is really the one entertained is rightly considered a special gift. Now whether Mahler was the magi-

> cian or the fairy, the wild beast or the faithful dog, whether he improvised his utterly funny tales from the present or tried to turn them into a parable with a didactic purpose, he always showed that fine understanding of the child's awakening soul which he was able to express in so many of his compositions.

Though Baumfeld wasn't speaking of any one specific Mahler composition when he wrote this, his last sentence serves as the perfect point of approach to the Fourth Symphony: his line about Gustav's "fine understanding of the child's awakening soul" shows how Mahler escaped the Victorian understanding of children as lovely little nothings, as naïve and charming sub-adults. The Fourth Symphony itself, as it progresses from first movement to last in its classical—or just naïve?—four-movement design, demonstrates an awakening to bliss (an awakening to "The Heavenly Life") that is itself blessedly childlike:

1. *Bedächtig, nicht eilen* (Deliberate, not rushed) (17 minutes)
2. *In gemächlicher Bewegung, ohne Hast* (In leisurely motion, without haste) (9 minutes)
3. *Ruhevoll, poco adagio* (Restfully, somewhat slowly) (21 minutes)
4. *Sehr behaglich* (Very comfortably) (9 minutes)

It's of course important that the "awakening to bliss" occurs at the end of the symphony and not elsewhere. The first three movements can't be heard as a series of "ordeals" or other such stages in any childlike "progression" toward bliss: they have episodes of darkness and sorrow, but really present nothing that needs to be overcome. What Mahler's four movements do trace is a general motion from complexity to simplicity—from a certain hustling mischievousness toward greater clarity of sentiment and musical texture. The heavenly bliss that's reached in the finale is a state of restful enlightenment not untouched by irony.

The soprano's last lines in the "Das himmlische Leben" text of the finale recount how "The angelic voices / gladden our senses, / so that all awaken for joy." As the composer said himself, "Das himmlische Leben" is both the starting point and the culmination of the whole Fourth Symphony; and, under the title "What the Child Tells Me," it originally served as the apex of the Third Symphony as well. The very last word of the child's text is "erwacht" ("awakes"), though by that point the music—with its gentle tapering off over a rocking, triplet-based 6/8 meter—suggests restful slumber more than it evokes elation. What kind of joy does the child's soul awake to in the Fourth Symphony? Being childlike means being nonegotistical and changeable, but it also means being celibate and unknowing—and various commentators have pointed out a chaste aspect of Mahler's music that's separate from any joyfulness and innocence. Composer Alfredo Casella heard this quality in tandem with a "pure goodness," a chasteness, that helped define Mahler's style: "It seems that this man can express all human feelings except sexual love, of which you will hunt in vain for a trace in his works."

A CHILDLIKE MUSICALITY

Mahler's Fourth Symphony often seems to make sense only according to a child's way of hearing, feeling, telling. Or is it better to speak here of a child's distractions, non sequiturs, and pretend realities? To start right at the beginning of the piece: how to explain the sly regularity, the bounce and frisk of the repetitive opening of the first movement? Mahler's critics accused him of banality, but a child has no inkling of such things. The steady, relentless, yet playful rhythms of the first movement suggest the repetitive syllables youngsters use to model motion in make-believe scenarios, whether it be walking or rolling along on wheels: for example pitter-patter, waddle-waddle, or the put-put-put-put of a toy car.

Mahler works in similar terms to create a teasing squareness of phrase structure in the Fourth, except in the slow movement. In the first movement, toward the end of the transition section (starting at 1:28), two clarinets deliver a juvenile nyah-nyah-nyah schoolyard taunt. Just as childish is the theme we first hear (at 6:38) played by four unison flutes. This melody reeks of the playground, sounding like "Jingle Bells" overlaid with "Three Blind Mice." Like "Three Blind Mice" or "Row, Row, Row Your Boat," the melody starts with a juvenile one-two-three rhythm and includes periodic pauses that invite an answer from another voice, or seem to ask for canonic treatment. Listen also to the accompanimental figures beneath this four-flute melody: the cellos are along for the ride, just bouncing, lolloping, sauntering, frisking, and capering ahead. In this melody and elsewhere, adult niceties like cadencing seem an afterthought at best. Those involved in the fine art of writing themes expend a lot of effort closing them. Conversely, one way that Richard Wagner revolutionized musical form—making it possible to build his music dramas out of uninterrupted hour-long acts—was by devising ingenious ways of evading cadences. Now consider how Mahler happily throws all these formidable and hard-won masteries out the window and ends his four-flutes melody just by hitting the final tonic pitch three times in the one-two-three rhythm, and that's the end of that. But then both the first movement and the second end in cheekiness, the first with an off-to-the-races sprint toward the final cadence, and the second with a snook-cocking in the high woodwinds.

And then there are the sleigh bells, the very first sound we hear in the Fourth Symphony. Mahler said he intended these as a kind of timbral joke, and they certainly contrast with the thunderous unison horns that opened the Third Symphony and the dead-serious solo trumpet that would open the Fifth. (In his movie *Mahler*, Ken Russell again shows his uncanny musical understanding when he uses these sleigh bells to underscore Alma shaking a baby rattle for daughter Anna. At another point in the film, we see Alma pushing along Anna's stroller to the accompaniment of the Fourth's ambling tuk-tuk-tuk-tuk rhythms.) The second childlike coloration in the first movement, especially remarkable as it arrives in the bright, unexpected new key of A major, is the four-flute melody in the development section (at 6:38) that I've already mentioned. When these four flutes play *forte* and in unison like this in a fairly high register, they sound light and disembodied like an overblown flute, or like a penny whistle. And these four flutes keep their quaintly chummy ensemble going for a while, putting in an especially sassy appearance at 8:02.

This emphasis on the flute is symptomatic of Mahler's top-heavy orchestration throughout much of the Fourth. The orchestral writing glitters and pipes and glistens, sublimating childlike wonder directly into sound. Mahler's Fourth reminds us what it was like to hear with a child's ears: the orchestral toyshop colorations, the myriad timbral hues that shift and shuffle. The themes often shunt impulsively between disparate sets of timbres, inhabiting one for only two bars before jumping off into another. This kind of timbral capering gets most impudent when the development of the first movement begins heating up: starting at 7:40, within just half a minute we hear in succession (1) flutes doing their sleigh bell imitation from the opening (but now without the bells), over a stalking line in the oboe and then the bassoons, punctuated by the rasp of stopped horns; (2) flutes and trumpets doubling cymbal strokes; (3) low strings opposing high flutes and clarinets; (4) a loud tag descending through oboe, clarinets, bassoons, and contrabasses; (5) high woodwinds (including the four flutes, as mentioned above) splayed against triangle, harp, and horn; and (6) a cymbal stroke against *col legno* violins, followed by a quartet of stopped horns and a cadential roll on the bass drum. To hear these kaleidoscopic changes is to have a child's short aural attention span, moving from the chirp of a bird to the aural sparkle of a bell to the sound of raindrops on the roof. Mahler includes bells, glockenspiel, and a retuned violin in the second movement, but omits the counterbalancing sound of tuba and trombones, instruments having a long association not only with death and the Last Judgment but also connoting full-tilt orchestral romanticism: trombones had made their debut in the standard symphonic repertory in the blazing C major finale of Beethoven's Fifth. It's only in Mahler's third movement, the stately *Poco adagio*, that the ensemble sounds deep-seated rather than fragile.

The most childlike aspects of the Fourth are its unpredictability and its short attention span. No single mood or train of thought sticks around for very long, and there are plenty of surprises and dead ends. These stark juxtapositions and quicker-than-sudden changes in tempo and humor are the musical equivalent to the irrationality, the "very easily provoked suspicion" that Specht saw in the "child Mahler." In the second theme area, a one-bar outburst (at 3:30) promises a cadence, but it instead accelerates headlong into a general pause and comes up empty-handed (except for the considerable challenges this measure poses for the conductor). Perhaps most fickle of all is a sequence two-thirds of the way through the slow movement. This passage comes shortly after the darkest moment in the whole symphony, as punctuated (at 12:22) by a succession of four swooping downward laments from top to bottom of the orchestra. But the heartbreak proves short-lived and all pain is forgotten only a minute later, when we return (at 13:24) to the serene music that opened the movement. Indeed, the theme that returns here soon scampers off to new merriments. The hijinks happen in an accelerating crescendo: at 14:38, the key shifts up a half step without warning, the tempo suddenly swings into an allegro, foursquare repetition makes a comeback, and trills hint at all manners of naughtiness. The tempo jerks up yet again, only to break off after only five bars to a slower andante section (at 15:00) that soon flowers into what could well be the most celestial passage in Mahler's entire output (at 15:24, richly chorded in divided strings). Hearing this section is like seeing a child do something daft, only to see them contradict it with some moment of quiet divinity. There's a dizzying juxtaposition of emotions and tones in this span of less than three minutes: we've undergone drastic and sudden shifts in tempo, and traversed feelings of calamity, deliberation, happy agitation, breathlessness, and finally transcendence.

Capriciousness was nothing new in Mahler's music. But it is all the more striking in the Fourth Symphony because it seems at odds with the straightforward and concise structures. The first two movements of the Fourth, in particular, count as Mahler's most easily followed forms. Though some hear the first movement as a rondo form, it really becomes a textbook exercise in sonata structure—not least because the themes confirm their expected keys and are easy to discern from the fluctuating transitional material that separates them. We have a foursquare first theme in the tonic of G major, a quite predictable transition toward A major (the dominant of the dominant), a short pause (a neoclassical formality used here by Mahler to suggest, in Donald Tovey's words, "the abruptness of Mozart's most perfunctory style"), and then a lyrical second theme in D major written in a different kind of texture (starting at 1:42, in the dominant key, and marked "broadly sung"). With this second idea, Mahler even seems to imitate Brahms's own second themes (for instance, the first movement of his Symphony no. 2) in the way he has the cellos sing out above the rest of his orchestra. Mahler's only formal prank is his brief mockup of an exposition repeat (starting at 3:56) before he's even finished with the exposition. But some unexpected harmonic events also contribute to the cheekiness of the first movement. At several points the music's harmonic simplicity is overstepped with an unexpected supertonic chord: one such moment is in the first movement transition (at 1:21, and at 4:46 within the false exposition repeat), where a foursquare pair of measures is just repeated up a half step, as if the composer couldn't think of anything better to do. (Mozart pulled a similar stunt in his *A Musical Joke* to suggest compositional incompetence, or maybe just plain laziness.)

The closing section (starting at 4:54) feels all the more stable for being in the home key of G major rather than in the expected dominant key of D. The development section then starts (at 5:41) with the opening sleigh bell idea moved to the clarinets and trailed by a wheedling line in the solo violin. The shifts in event and color infuse this development with new and increasing urgency. This tension dissipates for a moment when the four-flute theme arrives (at 6:38), but is then heightened again by tense exchanges between contrasting orchestral colors and registers. This capricious and unpredictable part of the first movement chooses not to display compositional rationality so much as it decides, turning to Tovey's apt words, to "develop what it likes, and settle where it likes." Material is sequenced progressively higher, and several times the music seems to have found its harmonic roost, only to fly off again. Our flute quartet suggests F minor as a place of rest, but the development finally arrives at C major, and with this onset the schoolyard nyah-nyah-nyah melody takes over as the emphatic apex of the movement: all that musical effort, Mahler's first listeners probably wondered, just to arrive at a theme that sounds like the work of a five-year-old. (The C major culmination starts at 9:23, with ecstatic tam-tam strokes and the G held in the bass, making the passage sound both stable and expectant.) But then the C major is sabotaged (at 9:45) by an explosive, tantrum-like ninth chord—the child will have no more of it! The opening sleigh bell rhythm is hinted at in the post-climactic flotsam, and the tension quickly dissolves in a coloristic-comic manner. There's a pause, as if the music has to collect its thoughts, and then (at 10:20) we're suddenly in a recap of the opening theme as if the development had never happened.

We're reintroduced to the opening theme at this point, without its telltale first two bars—though in retrospect the sleigh bells at the end of the development might have substituted for it. This deletion (or dislocation) of the first theme's opening is especially sneaky, considering the distances traversed in the development and how strongly we're anticipating the theme's return: as Tovey describes the passage, "[It is] as if the theme, after having traveled round the world, were to walk in to breakfast unannounced, remarking, 'As I was saying . . .'" The recap section works up grand restatements of the four-flute melody and the second theme area, but they are now puffed up to be brassy and insistent instead of lyrical and pastoral in character. With help from the juvenile and emphatic one-two-three rhythm, which was stressed in the development but now threatens to take over the argument completely, the music gets more and more clamorous—with the timpani and cymbals firing off a raucous rum-ti-tum. This climax repeats the earlier passage leading up to the dissonant "tantrum" ninth chord, but now does something very different in directing the music to a dissonance-free arrival on the dominant chord. There is a timpani stroke and an emphatic pause, and (at 11:14) the second theme area comes back—no longer peacefully expressive with long bowed notes on the high cellos, but now in its loud Sunday best, transformed into a kind of grand processional in full orchestral dress. Emphatically orchestrated and belaboring the one-two-three rhythm, this is loud and decisive enough to sound like the "real" recapitulation, superseding the elided return of the first theme shortly before. The other themes then come back in their own turn, along with the sleigh bell figure (at 13:34)—which again returns without the telltale opening of the first theme. The playful, even childish strategy behind this omission from the first theme is finally revealed at the end of the movement, where—after a slowdown and a gently radiant arrival on the dominant key of D major—the first theme finally arrives as a whole (at 16:12), with the first violins slowly belaboring their previously withheld opening notes *pianississimo* and *grazioso*, making sure we appreciate each and every one of them, until the movement sprints through a quick and short *stringendo* to a slam-bang close.

If the first movement of the Fourth gives us the child in all his silliness, the second—the scherzo movement of the symphony—shows his intermittent irony. This movement sharpens the hectic charms of the first while rejuggling some of its elements. The movement can sound like the first, as reheard from another aural perspective. Mahler recombines previously heard figures in a way that would happen again, to different effect, in the first two movements of the Fifth and Sixth Symphonies. The second movement of the Fourth is in triple time and the solo violin, as soon as it enters in the seventh measure, strikes up a dance "like a fiddle" (*wie ein Fiedel*). The concertmaster is told to play like a rough folk fiddler, in short to avoid the sweet tone of the conservatory graduate, and Mahler's instruction that the instrument be tuned up a step from the normal violin (to use the proper musical term, Mahler stipulates *scordatura* tuning) makes it sound all the more strange and anxious. On the occasion of one performance in 1904, Mahler described the movement as a "dance of death" (*Todtentanz*); in such a scenario, the solo fiddler would be the Grim Reaper luring victims off to their demise with catchy, irrefusable tunes. But this movement gives at most a picture-book death, a shadow play, a children's story told with no mortal ramifications.

If there's anything uncanny or hypnotic about this movement, it's the amount of repetition. I lose count of how often one particular rising four-note melodic figure (A–D♭–F–E) reappears in Mahler's vinegary and denatured violin solo—it is the very first thing presented in the solo violin, and it pops up at least twenty times. Even when the movement arrives at two contrasting, idyllic trio sections, such diversion from the opening music only ends up emphasizing its return. The music gets so repetitive that it seems to be counting off: this scherzo is infected with the arithmomania of Anton Bruckner, a composer whose symphonic scherzos wallow in manic repetition and manifold returns. Even Mahler's use of a recurring trio section harks back to Bruckner's rustic, or in dull performances simply exasperating, third-movement diversions.

But the repetition turns out to be a ruse for Mahler: this second movement makes it clear that repetition is actually serving as a vehicle for his almost embarrassingly rich palette of variation. And of tone colors: an orchestration course could spend the whole semester just on Mahler's kaleidoscopic alterations in this one movement. More paradoxically, the repetition also gives free rein to Mahler's impish love of surprise. Shortly into the movement (from 0:45 through 1:00), the music shunts briefly and unexpectedly from E-flat major to C major, though with ill-behaved emphases on F—creating intervals that are unstable in either E-flat or C. When things are repeated in this movement, they are tweaked and retweaked—most often in terms of orchestral color, with a cymbal brush added here, a quasi-improvised timpani stroke there—to the point where one wonders if variation is actually masquerading as repetition, or vice-versa.

It's fascinating to compare the large-scale repetitions—or variations!—of material, for instance with the contrasting trio section (in F major, first heard starting at 1:34). This opens with yodeling alpine trills but quickly moves on to more "sophisticated" things: we come to a bewitchingly lyrical melody (starting at 2:13), complete with courtly grace-note ornaments, music that invites the kind of affectionate rubato one would give to Strauss's more elegant and sumptuous waltzes. When this trio section comes back (at 4:43, again in F major), it does so with fairly subtle changes in the orchestration, but when the lyrical melody comes back (starting at 5:36) it is scored for solo strings—a momentary string quartet, a private soliloquy educed from the full ensemble. But there's an even bigger surprise in store when this material is further extended, spun out at greater length, in the radiant and entirely unexpected key of D major (starting at 6:12). It's as if the composer couldn't bring himself to let go of the melody and needed an unanticipated key to cast new light on it. (Following this, when the movement's opening material comes back starting at 7:05, Mahler's variations in scoring are so tart and inventive they would call for another page of happy explanation. And so it goes.) Likewise, when the earlier C major diversion (originally heard at 0:45) comes back at 3:26 and again at 4:18, the F-natural pranks are reorchestrated and reinterpreted. When the C major diversion comes back for the last time at 7:52, these F-naturals move upstage to the solo violin—at which point the bass drum, tam-tam, and low harp collaborate at the back of the orchestra to put the mischief in a briefly darker context.

RESTFULNESS AND JOY

Mahler left different hints about what was going through his mind when he wrote the slow movement, which he gave the unusual marking *Ruhevoll* (restfully). He remarked to Bruno Walter that the music was a reflection on "one of the church sepulchers showing the recumbent stone image of the deceased with the arms crossed in eternal sleep." So this movement's restfulness could be the restfulness of death. Elsewhere, he said that while writing the movement he had a vision of his long-suffering mother "smiling through her tears," as a poignant reminder of her ability to "solve and forgive all suffering by love." These two scenarios share a sense of the past speaking gently through the present, prefiguring for us listeners the peace—the consecrated, all-correcting *Ruhe*—that can only come when the individual ego surrenders to all-powerful eternity. Mahler once claimed that his Fourth Symphony contains no *forte* markings, a statement that's literally incorrect, but figuratively true of the tranquility at the heart of this movement.

In this slow movement, peaceful surrender is modeled through a (for the most part) calm outpouring of boundless, spontaneous lyricism. Time is now maintained not by higher instruments in the orchestra—the sleigh bells are set aside for the duration of the movement, and even the violins are late entering—but by those faithful shepherds of the bottom of the orchestral texture, the double basses. The double basses set Mahler's slow movement in motion with bell-like pizzicatos on beats one, two, and four, originating and encouraging a sixteen-bar melody in the upper cellos against slow-shifting chords in the rest of the ensemble. This bell-like motive will recur throughout the sections, unifying this lengthy movement. Also, the omission of beat three sometimes suggests a shift in the meter, which helps draw the movement forward with sustained interest. Constantin Floros hears the bell motive as a reference to the bells that summon the Knights of the Grail to Communion in Wagner's *Parsifal*—which would make it yet another Fourth Symphony reference to eternity and redemption. But such dark colors are pervasive throughout this slow movement. In contrast to the bright and reflective colorations of the earlier movements, this one begins with only the lower strings, the violas and cellos and basses divided into a sepia-hued but quite complex texture of six parts. The violins enter only in bar seventeen (at 1:07), the wind instruments in bar twenty-five, and percussion—timpani the first to appear—more than halfway through the movement. In these and other ways, the movement gives the impression of growing slowly into life before it reaches (about two-thirds of the way through) the dual impasses of tragedy and gaiety. The heartbreaks in this movement are quickly forgotten, as already mentioned, suggesting a child's emotional changeability—or perhaps a young and self-renewing mindset of optimism combined with trust. In contrast to the darkness that settles into other movements by Mahler, here hope is never lost.

Mahler said this was the most accomplished of all his slow movements. It comprises a set of double variations: two distinct theme areas, one serene and the other pained in character, evolving seamlessly and continuously in new directions. Here he seems to encompass every possible human emotion within a single improvised and unconstrained musical span. His instrumentation is likewise ever changing but strategically deployed. For instance, the violins, oboe, bassoons, horns, and harp were late arrivals in the slow movement; and now these same instruments guide us into the second thematic material when it first appears. This second theme (the B material entering for the first time at 4:29), marked "plaintive, very expressive," is introduced by the oboe with backup from the horn and bassoon, and the basses momentarily dropping out. The lamentation reaches a "passionate" peak (at 6:45) before a four-fold plunge from the top to the bottom of the orchestra leads to a mournful rejoinder from doubled violas and cellos, the double basses take up the bell motive again, and tension dissipates through a rise to the brighter, sparer colors of horn, flute, harp, and solo violin. The key returns to G major, and the tempo picks up for the unexpected return (at 8:13) of the original A material, the main melody now in the high cellos and harking back to the rudimentary rhythmic vocabulary of the first movement. The music becomes ever more animated and dancelike, before a dark pall again falls over the music—this time not precipitated by any crisis, and so sounding self-willed yet lasting longer than the previous downturn—and the lamenting oboe and horn reintroduce the plaintive secondary material (the B theme returns at 10:08). This section presents inventive variations on the plaintive B material, which is first stated in the tonic parallel minor key (G minor). There's a large change of texture when the melody is stated more emphatically in octave doublings in the strings, leading into a climactic statement in C-sharp minor (at 11:01) and then an even more decisive statement in F-sharp minor (at 12:03). With its expressive and vocal gestures, the music sounds like a confession.

I've already mentioned this passage as an example of the Fourth Symphony's childlike unsettledness. But the key passage in this movement's twisted path from serenity to heartbreak to glee, and possibly the most intriguing stretch in the whole movement, is the major/minor vacillation that precedes the last return of the A material. This starts in F-sharp major at 12:55, with a minimal orchestra gradually diminishing in volume over a timpani roll. The major third (A-sharp) comes to be stressed over the minor (A-natural), but the minor third still lingers as a kind of doubt-compulsion. But the music just sidesteps the question by shifting up a half step to the tonic G major (at 13:24) and then launching into a more audacious passage: an accelerating and multisectioned (Andante, then Allegretto, then Allegro) variation on the serene A material. Mahler asks for a "sudden and surprising" swing (at 14:38) to E major and an Allegro tempo. A quick shift to an even faster speed

(Allegro molto [subito]) is underlined by the jingle of orchestral bells, and ends with a D major cadence punctuated by timpani and cymbals. The movement catches its breath, and then delivers a positively celestial G-major passage in divided strings (at 15:25). This leads back to the *Ruhevoll* music we heard at the very opening of the movement, suggesting this recap in the tonic key will serve as the movement's final destination. And any other composer would have ended things there.

But the biggest surprise is yet to come, and it's presented not in the home key of G major, but in E major. After an impulsive leap upward from the violins followed by a half-second *Luftpause*, the orchestral floodgates open and we find ourselves in the midst of a resounding, full-ensemble exclamation (starting at 17:31). This is capped by a cymbal crash and bass drum roll. (The only passage comparable in sound and suddenness is Haydn's modeling of a godly miracle, the point in his oratorio *Die Schöpfung* [*The Creation*], where God creates light out of chaos to the tune of a huge C major chord.) Youthfulness reasserts itself when Mahler's trumpets contribute a slowed-down version of the schoolyard taunt we heard earlier on four flutes. The slow harmonic progression that follows is somehow both beatific and convoluted, roving through fourth- and third-related harmonies from E major to C major (at 18:46, with the harp reentering), then to F major, D major (at 19:15), and finally the tonic G major (at 19:24). After a short dalliance with E minor, the bass moves down a step to the final chord of D major—and we end the movement on a gentle question mark, with glassy and expectant *flageolet* violins, the inconclusive dominant harmony rather than the tonic, and the bass instruments dropping out of the texture.

The last movement, though the shortest and simplest of the four, is also the lynchpin of the whole symphony. This is the song "Das himmlische Leben" ("The Heavenly Life"), a *Knaben Wunderhorn* text setting that Mahler had written eight years earlier and titled "What the Child Tells Me" when he planned to end the Third Symphony with it. The song presents a child's vision of heaven, detailed and unsentimental, and set to music in an unassuming style. Mahler wrote "Das himmlische Leben" for a lyric soprano, not for a big operatic voice, and he instructs the performer to sing "with serene and childlike expression." The actual text, in line with the folklike, childlike perspective of the *Des Knaben Wunderhorn* poems, opens with an account of the joys and luxuries of paradise. Note the use of "we," suggesting the communal vision is ours to share:

> We enjoy heavenly pleasures
> and therefore avoid earthly ones.
> No worldly tumult
> is to be heard in heaven.
> All live in greatest peace.
> We lead angelic lives,
> yet have a merry time of it besides.
> We dance and we spring,
> We skip and we sing.
> Saint Peter in heaven looks on.

This voice, placed at the end of the symphony as a whole, becomes an oracle of naïveté. If earlier movements of the Fourth have asked us to empathize with the child, this song closes with the child's own voice. It's debatable whether the singer does need to bring "childlike expression" to the table, since the composer has written such expression into the vocal line itself—through skipping and dancelike rhythms, a considerable amount of repetition, and highly expressive pitch intervals.

As shown in an early formal sketch, Mahler had planned to incorporate not only "Das himmlische Leben" into the Fourth Symphony, but also its tragic counterpart, the song "Das irdische Leben" ("The Earthly Life"). While the child in the latter starves to death, the child in the former—the song that became the Fourth's finale—encounters lovely music as well as gustatorial plenty. Though a blissful vision, it still has curious and ironic aspects, typical of the *Knaben Wunderhorn* poems with their old German *Unheimlich* flavor. King Herod has somehow been admitted to heaven but conscripted as the butcher; as for the livestock animals themselves, they happily line up for the slaughter after getting a modicum of pity from the heavenly citizens. Similarly self-sacrificing, the saints are happy to prepare the food, though having Martha labor as the cook seems unkind, since according to the Gospel of Luke she was too busy serving others to listen to the word of Jesus. But the sanctified kitchen staff outdo themselves in a labor of love. The "Himmlische Leben" text includes an over-the-top menu, which makes sense only when one thinks of this song in relation to "Das irdische Leben," which paints a picture of starvation from want of something so basic as bread—a fate inconceivable in "Das himmlische Leben," where angels have been entrusted with the baking. (In any event, in the third stanza, starting at 3:36, Mahler sets the long list of vegetables, fruits, and game in a semi-breathless fashion—"Gut' Äpfel, gut' Birn' und gut' Trauben; / Die Gärtner, die alles erlauben"—suggesting the heavenly harvest might be too much of a good thing after all.)

This unassuming movement is the quiet keystone of the Fourth Symphony as a whole, the first part of the piece that he wrote and the source for musical material in all three preceding movements. As Donald Mitchell put it in the second volume of his *Gustav Mahler* series, "Das himmlische Leben" is "the controlling presence which orders and determines the total conception of the work . . . the symphony in its entirety emerged from, and has its life in, the idea of the song." In using sleigh bells right at the start of his Fourth Symphony, Mahler refers to the song immediately. "Das himmlische Leben" is simple and innocent in tone, but interspersed between its stanzas is the sleigh bell music that Mahler came to use—in a more gentle rewrite—as an introduction to the first movement of his symphony. In the song, the loud sleigh bell repetition—instead of suggesting innocence or playfulness as it does in the symphony—suggests angry protest, a mood that somehow passes quickly and without explanation. Or this music may symbolize the pastoral violence in the *Wunderhorn* text: when Saint Luke slaughters the ox in stanza two, the words prompt bovine protests on the bass clarinet and horn (at 2:37 and 2:41), a figure we first hear in the symphony in the between-stanzas sleigh bell "refrain."

There are clear paradoxes and tensions in this heavenly vision, but Mahler still forges a lasting peace in his final stanza—the one that shifts the focus from heaven's food and dance to its music. The sense of conciliation is palpable: we begin with the noisiest of the sleigh bell refrains (at 4:33), but its shrill remonstrations are pushed aside after only seven bars. We then quickly and quietly settle down into E major, with the performers instructed to sound "very tender and cryptic through to the end." Having started in G major, the symphony now ends in E major—in the major version of the relative minor, an arrival prepped already by the symphony's opening bars in B minor, not to mention the E major exclamation later in the third movement. Introduced by the harp, the finale's E major music is enchanting enough to cause Saint Ursula's eleven thousand virgin martyr followers to dance. Such a sight makes their patroness laugh, and Mahler stretches her reaction ("Sankt Ursula selbst dazu lacht," at 6:21) over an extravagantly wide twelfth interval. The last line repeats the musical phrase and completes the rhyme: the composer sets the words "Die englischen Stimmen / Ermuntern die Sinnen, / Daß alles für Freuden erwacht" ("The angelic voices comfort our senses, such that everyone awakens for joy," starting at 7:13) as a simple descending scale, and then the tolling harp trails off into a state of quiet, immutable blessedness. With their utter simplicity, these last bars almost make us forget that the Fourth Symphony is one of Mahler's more lavish creations. Under its surface of naïve simplicity and within its moderate span of roughly fifty-five minutes, the Fourth manages to pack in twice as many thematic, rhythmic, and coloristic ideas as the Second or Third Symphony. While the piece sings blithely of childhood, its compact intensity looks quietly ahead to the bitter, existential attenuation of the composer's late works.

6

SYMPHONY NO. 5

Journeys for a New Century

With the Fifth Symphony, Mahler looked more intently forward to a modern style. Newly influenced by J. S. Bach's work, he was reconceiving his orchestral textures in more polyphonic terms. He was also turning an ear to emerging modernist composers, and distancing himself from narrative-programmatic ideas and the folkloric tradition of the *Des Knaben Wunderhorn* poems. In short, the Fifth Symphony represents Mahler at his most abstract and forward-looking, but at the same time his most ruthlessly dramatic. This is absolute music written in a severe, realist style; it shows him joining the compositional conversation on the post-Beethoven symphony in a most serious way. Mahler makes this clear when he opens the Fifth with the iconic short-short-short-long rhythm that Beethoven had made famous in his own Fifth Symphony.

The newness of Mahler's Fifth hinges on its formal thinking as well as its tone. Here he replaced late Romantic notions of tone painting and storytelling with the more changeable and open-ended model of what could be called symphonic journeying. The Fourth Symphony had already ended in a different key than it began in. The Fourth doesn't tell stories or paint pictures in tones, but it does have a specific reason for defying traditional rules of harmonic closure. In the Fourth, the journey into a new key supports impressions of the child slipping off to a "heavenly life" ("Das himmlische Leben"). The Fifth Symphony takes up this idea of an unpredictable harmonic journey, this provocative ruse of denying closure, and dramatizes it further. The Fifth starts with no promises whatsoever, and comes to involve an even more dramatic sense of journeying—from the funereal C-sharp minor start of the first movement up a half step to the blazing D major conclusion of the last. We meet so many extremes, detours, and distractions in the Fifth that an ending of any kind is no longer to be taken for granted, and such a sense of doubt must have been shocking at the time in an example of the backward-looking and rationalized genre of the symphony. That Mahler ends on such a message of blazing optimism makes his act of structural and spiritual charity even stranger. (Beethoven had written an overall progression from C minor to C major into his own Symphony no. 5, but keeping the same tonic basis throughout makes that piece more of an inevitable dark-to-light revelation than a journey as such. By comparison, already in his Symphony no. 2 Mahler had started a work in a minor key and ended in its relative major, moving from C minor to E-flat major.)

Mahler completed the Fifth Symphony in 1902. As befits his first symphony of the new century, the Fifth is large in scale, freshly imagined in textural terms, and more objective and plain-spoken in tone than its predecessors. In terms of large-scale form, it is a variation of the classical four-movement symphonic structure, with five movements grouped into larger "parts" that—like the parts of the Third Symphony—make it clear that structures are being played out on several levels. And the central scherzo movement, the longest and most changeable of the five, occupies a part all by itself.

Part I

(1) Trauermarsch (Funeral march). *In gemessenem Schritt. Streng. Wie ein Kondukt* (In a measured tempo. Strictly, like a funeral cortege) (13 minutes)

(2) *Stürmisch bewegt, mit größter Vehemenz* (Stormily agitated, with the greatest vehemence) (14 minutes)

Part II

(3) Scherzo. *Kräftig, nicht zu schnell* (Strong, but not too fast) (18 minutes)

Part III

(4) Adagietto. *Sehr langsam* (Very slowly) (11 minutes)

(5) Rondo-Finale. *Allegro – Allegro giocoso. Frisch* (Quickly—Quick and jocular, Lively) (14 minutes)

Already with the first notes of the Fifth Symphony we hear changes in Mahler's orchestral palette—honed through repeat revisions of the scoring. His ensemble writing was taking on harder and darker hues, especially in the formalized processionals of the first two movements of the Fifth. The symphony starts with a single trumpet stuttering its way up the C-sharp minor triad. The trumpet was known at that time more as a military sound or as a solo instrument than a solo orchestral one, heard up front and undoubled in concertos and operas rather than symphonies. (When he penned the opening of the Fifth, Mahler must have had at the back of his mind solos from two contrasting operas: the distant trumpet that signals the protagonist of Verdi's *Ernani*, a character haunted by his past and bound to a sworn pact, to murder himself at the height of his own happiness; and in Beethoven's *Fidelio*, the offstage fanfare announcing friendly forces as they arrive to liberate prisoners from the tyrannical warden Don Pizarro. Bringing these two examples together, we would arrive at the solo trumpet as a symbol of fate, death, and liberation.)

Even more than earlier works, the Fifth Symphony gives the impression that Mahler is using instrumental color not as a timbral clothing for his thoughts, but as a means of expression in itself. Giuseppe Verdi often spoke of working to find the right coloration, the correct *tinta*, for a particular dramatic situation in an opera, and I believe Mahler's struggles over instrumentation in his Fifth Symphony show him doing much the same thing. He scores his first movement as if he were writing for wind band, meaning the winds and percussion sound together like a complete ensemble unto themselves, while the strings appear as a subsidiary ensemble of wind substitutes. This scoring brings to mind ceremonial music, and the percussion section, especially the cymbals and snare drum, is so substantial as to give the wind band a military tone. The slow, halting, heavily burdened rhythms of the first movement mark it as a processional, similar to the "Marche funèbre" movement of Berlioz's *Symphonie funèbre et triomphale*. That work marked a civic rather than musical occasion: it was commissioned by the French government to commemorate those who died in the 1830 July Revolution, and Berlioz scored the piece for wind ensemble with percussion—recalling music from the earlier French Revolution and from Napoleon's armies. Heard in such a context, Mahler's opening trumpet solo suggests a military funeral or a call to battle—a processional reluctantly pressed onward by vacant tattoos in the trombones, tuba, timpani, and snare drum.

Mahler labels his first movement of the Fifth Symphony a funeral march (*Trauermarsch*) and says it should be played quite slowly and without nuance—"in a measured tempo; strictly, like a funeral cortege." As one would expect of a processional, the large-scale structure is fairly simplistic. What makes a cortege especially inappropriate for the first movement of a symphony, in addition to the slow tempo, is the lack of forward direction: there's no rush in arriving at the grave. A *Trauermarsch* has no pressing forward to summary conclusion, no end-directedness, no reconciliation of opposites, none of these defining aspects of a symphony's opening movement. Rather than speaking of a developing argument, it's better to talk about Mahler's first movement in terms of material being repeated and varied. And then violently interrupted! The movement comprises three basic material types: (1) the repetitious and triplet-laden summons that we hear at the very start on the trumpet; (2) a winding and mutable chant that embodies the funeral march itself; and (3) the more impulsive material that first interrupts as a rapid contrast, "suddenly faster, passionately, wild." There are a few intriguing qualifications to be made with these definitions and distinctions: for instance, material (1) comes to serve different functions (as summoning or annunciatory intro, as outro, and as transition), and materials (2) and (3) are similar enough that when put into the same tempo and dynamic they can be almost indistinguishable. The main rationale of the movement, the thing that maintains tension and keeps it moving, is the stark contrast between the slow processional tempo of materials (1) and (2) and the "suddenly faster" and "wild" tempo of material (3). This stark, even schizoid juxtaposition of opposites implies repressed emotion that then bursts out and never becomes reconciled or mediated: after fighting colossal battles, the movement ends quietly, inconclusively, on a note of hesitation and evasiveness.

It quickly becomes clear that the trumpet has issued a summons to nowhere—it rallies us not into a symphonic melee, but directly into a drawn-out cadence followed by a pause. Here the trumpet intones the note C-sharp, leads the rest of the orchestra up to an optimistic cadence on A major (at 0:24), and then pulls the music back down toward the tonic with a grim, conclusive close on the dominant G-sharp minor harmony (starting at 0:37). In this brief introduction, the summons has served as both annunciation and then—after the A major chord—as an outro from the short climax into the G-sharp minor cadence. As the movement goes on, these two functions of the trumpet figure become separated: the summons will lead us into skirmishes, and it will also escort us out of them. The contrasting chant appears for the first time (starting at 1:08, in the tonic C-sharp minor, marked *pianissimo* and "somewhat slower"). Here, away from the tragic pompousness and stop-start of the preceding summons, we hear the muted songs and the marching footfalls of the bereaved. The chant melody, if it can be called a melody, fixates on particular pitches and intervals—giving it a vocal and distracted, sometimes even tender, quality. Along with the faster tempo, the phrases shorten from two bars to half bars. Little pockets of repetition (for instance, starting at 1:35) invest the chant with further interest over its long, slow stretches of time. Subtle adjustments of instrumentation to the melody also make for continual shifts in the weight and color of the line. For example, the first statement moves steadily downward: it begins (at 1:08) in the feathery sound of the first violins, before being joined by the second violins and then the violas, and then concluding (starting at 1:44) in the cellos.

This sequence (summons-cadence-chant-cadence) becomes the basic pattern for the first movement, starting as a harsh initiation into the symphony but petering out by movement's end. The sequence repetitiously starts and stops its way through the first movement as a shambling, orotund, and barely coherent display of grief. The episodic circularity of the pattern gives the grief a fatalistic quality: we've been here before, it seems to say, and we'll be back in black soon enough. In round two of the sequence, it is extended and more thickly scored. At this second opening summons (at 2:06), the trumpet is joined by winds, horns, and strings. This time around, the cadential chord progression is more convoluted, stretches out from fourteen to twenty-two measures, and goes even lower than before, ending with an emphatic descent in the lower strings and trombone. Continuing in this second sequence statement, the chant is more thickly scored (starting at 2:57), initially for full strings along with clarinet and bassoon. This chant material acts as a kind of refrain but is constantly in flux, mutating and shifting each time we hear it. It is much extended in its second statement—though still mired in G-sharp/C-sharp minor—and goaded on by tattoos in the cymbals, snare drum, and bass drum. There is a color change at 4:24, where the winds drop out and the chant melody reverts to the first and second violins. At its end, the sequence again descends heavily and oppressively toward closure on C-sharp/D-flat.

The fatalist circularity of the sequence (summons-cadence-chant-cadence) has become oppressive by this point. But when the summons returns to begin round three, it occasions a huge disruption: the trumpet enters as before (starting at 5:05) but then brutally yanks us into the new key of B-flat minor, a "suddenly faster" tempo, and a "passionate, wild" style. All the emotion suppressed during the funeral march is released. The meter becomes a steady if also frantic pattern of one-two-one-two, down-up-down-up—more like running than marching. Working against that beat, the surging melodic lines are asymmetrical and unpredictable. Though at first the trumpet continues with the main melodic line, the violins quickly take on a more active role: this is virtuoso and demanding writing for the strings, which thrash about like the hellish winds in Liszt and Tchaikovsky tone poems. The violins get higher and higher, and the movement reaches such intensity that the orchestral texture starts to collapse: the trumpet and timpani, instruments that were coupled in the classical symphonic writing of Haydn and Mozart, become so uncoupled that they trail each other in an uncoordinated call and response (5:39 to 5:48). However, by the time a remnant of the chant returns (starting at 6:08), the strings, winds, and brass come together to articulate the movement's lacerating climax. When the summons returns as an outro (starting at 6:48) to lead us out of the melee, it reaches a smaller climax of its own and then ends with the tuba.

After the interrupted round three of the sequence, round four skips the summons and begins right away (at 7:38) with the chant, now scored for wind band and percussion without the softer, more emotive tone of the strings. The chant is further extended here, and Mahler's typical, piercingly vibrant woodwind writing comes to the fore when doubled flutes, oboes, and clarinets move into higher registers. Round five begins (starting at 9:25) with a transformed summons—sounding forth not on the trumpet, but on quiet timpani. The chant also comes back changed: now in A minor and supported by a dancelike short-short-short-long rhythm. A pair of trombones entwines with the full violin section, leading to a climax (at 10:56, marked "mournfully"), where the expressiveness becomes so intense it melds Mahler's newfound Bachian polyphony into an undifferentiated *fortississimo* chordal mass—snare drums, bass drum, timpani, and cymbals wailing away underneath, and up above all six horns playing stopped and with bells up. The summons returns on the trumpet to escort us away from that debacle. A coda (starting at 11:39) scores the chant for slow-moving winds, brass, and lower strings. The texture quietly dissolves into remote taps on the trumpet, bass drum, and flute, and the movement finally cadences as a mere afterthought, with a belated C-sharp pizzicato on the basses.

CONFLICTED JOURNEYS

The second movement of the Fifth Symphony sounds like a rewrite of the one preceding. Its arrival brings the sense that we're starting over again: the second movement walks the same emotional terrain as the first, and is similar in rhythm and tempo. The first two movements even share material: in a kind of interpenetration, the second clearly reverts to the chant of the first movement when it comes to its own first stable theme area (starting at 1:23). Most importantly, the second movement continues the tense, even exhausting polarities and juxtapositions of the first. What is the relationship between these movements, exactly? Leonard Bernstein heard irony in the oppositional repetitions of the Fifth's first two movements, and understood them in terms of shifting relations between the individual and the communal. In markings in his own conducting score of the Fifth, he describes the first movement as a tragedy confronted by the feelings of empathy that it has also unleashed: "I. Angry bitter sorrow mixed with sad comforting lullabies—rocking a corpse." And then the second movement arrives neither as a contrast nor a palliative, but as an even less restricted expression of the emotions that had been suppressed in the first: "II. Outburst of rage—more 'public' version of private feelings in I. Ends with teeth still clenched."

With the second and third movements of the Fifth Symphony, we return to the question of Mahler's symphonic journeying—as opposed to the storytelling of the earlier symphonies. While the second movement of the Fifth is an intensification of the first, in structural terms it also sounds like the first one turned inside out. Each of the two movements struggles to find musical and emotional stability amidst "angry bitter sorrow," and each movement locates it in a different place. While the grim repression that started the first movement gave way to an almost hysterical outburst in its second section, the second movement begins in a rage that ultimately cedes—with no resolution of any kind—to quiet and reclusiveness. The second movement is marked "stormily agitated, with the greatest vehemence." The wind-band scoring of the first movement has been replaced by a more polyphonic conception with the strings as major participants. The strings start *fortissississimo* right off, and Mahler goes so far as to advise the conductor on the second page, "Violins as vehement as possible!" The melodic lines are full of leaps, and phrasing is asymmetrical and punctuated by brusque gestures that often land off the beat. Countering the unbalanced phrases are stretches of blunt, furious repetition that abut empty silence. The movement reaches its still, stable center at 1:23, a point where the tempo pulls back, the harmony settles into F minor, and then the cellos quote a long-breathed, *molto cantando* passage of chant material from the first movement. (Those who analyze this second movement as a sonata form hear this as the second theme—but all that's come before this has been highly unstable, making this F minor passage sound like the first theme we hear in this movement.) Also taken from that passage in the first movement is the short-short-short-long figure, and this steps more to the forefront as the chant material modulates to C minor.

There is a return to the opening furious music in A minor (starting at 3:31), a newly rigid sense of time ("strictly in tempo," Mahler instructs), and at times a galumphing approach to the march. The argument seems to collapse under its own weight, and then an even more withdrawn, more stable center arrives (starting at 4:17) in the very remote key of E-flat minor. The symphonic argument retreats so sharply here that the music actually stops: there is a three-bar grand pause, with a *pianissimo* timpani roll as the only thread leading into a desolate, slowly expanding gesture in the cellos (marked *pianissimo* and *klagend*, "lamenting") that turns into another varied recollection of the funeral march from the first movement. (Here and elsewhere, Mahler's constant variation of material sounds less like the work of an omniscient Beethovenish genius than the heat-of-the-moment workings of ordinary human memory, in all its emotion and fallibility.) While the Fifth Symphony has a complexity of texture that at times involves twenty or more simultaneous parts, and includes a substantial percussion section, at the E-flat minor retreat the ensemble is reduced to just two lines of music. Where has the orchestra, and indeed the symphonic argument itself, disappeared to in this passage? But that's the trick: just when it seems the Fifth Symphony can't go to any further extremes, it retreats to the most distant key area possible and an unexpected extreme of quiet impassivity. This is the eye of the storm implicit in the opening *stürmisch bewegt* indication.

This cello withdrawal passage brings to our attention something important about the Fifth's new journey aspect. While the first two movements of the work aren't especially violent compared with Mahler's earlier music, the violence now seems an end unto itself, with no clear structural or rational basis—it's become gratuitous. The brutality that Mahler flaunts in the Fifth Symphony could come with the notion of symphonic rhetoric, the idea that a symphony written around the turn of the century was by definition a strategic marshalling of emotional affectation. (Here I think of the nightmare aspect in the " marriage of reason and nightmare" that English novelist J. G. Ballard saw in modernity, while the symphony still counted—even if in name only—as a highly "reasoned" genre of music in Mahler's time.) But then Mahler's contrasting points of withdrawal or near-silence in the Fifth Symphony come to seem more necessary than the violent points, or like obligatory answers to the questions posed by violence. And the issue isn't just violence, but tense extremes between square repetition and long improvisatory spans that start to sound like imploring human speech. The movement's various inclusions of chantlike material count as examples of the latter, while the former sound absurdly crude whenever one listens for them (for example, the mournful four-fold call-and-response between heavily doubled trombones and strings starting at 10:37, and the strings' emphatic but playful ascent starting at 13:03).

Amidst all these histrionics, it's the withdrawn passages that stand out. These episodes—increasing in stillness, poise, and regularity as we go from one movement to the next—form a subterranean journey across this symphony as a whole. In the first movement, the still point was a measured song of mourning (or a chant, as I call it), and then (at 9:25) the summons reduced to quiet solo timpani; in the second, it was the lament in the cello section, edging close to silence and voicelessness; as we will see, in the third it will be a narcotized and sardonic rendering of the dance; and in the fourth, it will be the Adagietto movement as a whole. As we move through the Fifth and its expanding extremes, the question seems to be: if the wheel turns even faster, will the still point grow ever stiller? The symphony sounds like it's searching for a center of gravity, for a place where all the sound and fury makes sense, or—as T. S. Eliot later phrased it for himself in the drama fragment *The Rock*—for "the still point in the turning wheel." For Eliot, the desired still point was a spiritual state. It's more difficult to say what the "still point" could have been for Mahler, other than a point of musical disengagement (but then disengaging for what purpose?); and perhaps for that reason, these very significant and memorable junctures aren't even mentioned in the formal diagrams of the Fifth Symphony that I've seen. But then gaps in the argument, points where the rhetoric retreats, are hardly the stuff of analysis.

On three occasions, the second movement tries to escape these cycles of turning and stillness, each time casting its sights forward to the Fifth Symphony's point of deliverance, namely the ultimate confirmation of D major at the end of the finale. The first of these three attempts starts with the double bass entry at 5:57, not long after the cellos' point of complete withdrawal described above. At this entrance the pace starts to pick up ("From here on, no more dragging!" Mahler instructs), the rate of repetition increases, and at 6:44 a quick melodic reach up a diminished eleventh interval pulls the music into the even brighter key of B major just as it occasions yet another quote from the first movement. In the second of these attempted escapes, starting at 8:00, a reach up a major ninth pulls the music into A major (an arrival commemorated by the timpani) and then (at 8:09) a disguised onset of the recapitulation. (You can recognize the repeated material from the exposition if you listen for the stormy five-note figure in the cellos and basses that we heard at the start of the movement.) This musical return elicits some manic repetition: listen for the five-fold gesture in the strings starting at 8:13, and the stretto passage starting at 8:21 where a rising chordal idea is passed from the horns to the trombones and then to the trumpets. The second theme then returns in forcefully doubled first and second violins (starting at 8:42). The orchestral sound is getting bolder and more forceful: a remarkable *fortissimo* ascent (starting at 9:48) is doubled in octaves and unisons by first violins, second violins, violas, and cellos (playing "with longer bow strokes"), but then in a typical shift the passage ends quickly and quietly.

These incursions into bright keys and melodic unison reachings-up, these efforts all seem for naught when the music descends once again to the dark key of E-flat minor (starting at 10:37, a passage marked "heavily"). A lamenting and repeated figure in the trombones underlines this descent, along with burdened string invocations and a general restriction to lower registers. This is the same key we heard earlier at the *pianissimo* and *klagend* cello withdrawal. The gloom and stasis are interrupted at 11:26 by the third and last escape attempt when an emphatic reaching-up of a ninth interval succeeds in pulling the music up to a victorious, brass-laden appearance of D major. This arrival at D major is celebrated by a new clarity of texture: all the movement's competitive contrapuntal activity is curtailed as the whole orchestra supports a single, chorale-like melody in the trumpets and trombones. The follow-through on this D major eruption occurs with the second, even grander climax at 12:09. Soon afterward the mood darkens with a harmonic shift from D major to D minor, a change punctuated by another recap-like reference (at 12:39) to the bass figures that opened the movement. Strange, disjointed repetitions lead into and out of one last charge, weary but still cathartic. D minor becomes the key for the quiet but remarkable coda that begins at 13:34, with glassy harmonic sextuplets in violins and violas set against a walking bass line on the cellos and basses.

CONFLICTS RESOLVED AND SIDESTEPPED

The third movement is the lynchpin of the Fifth Symphony, and it deserves a chapter all to itself. It brings up questions about the human spirit and about musical organization. Not least because it lies at the center of the work, this is the structural junction where the symphony's lamenting, funeral-march aspect gives way to the major-key optimism that will dominate movements four and five. This is where the tide turns from dark to light, and the sense of tragedy is repealed. The spontaneous, brassy D major eruption toward the end of the second movement, dropped there as a non sequitur (at 12:09), had already hinted at the possibility of such a change. The beginning of the third movement introduces an upbeat waltz, suggesting a traditional, sunlit, major-key symphonic scherzo—there's a whiff of a Haydn minuet in the air. Already with the horns' cheerful opening gesture and the glint of the glockenspiel, we hear a clear declaration of D major and the lift of dance rhythms. There could be no bigger contrast with the openings of the first and second movements: if the start of the Fifth Symphony was dark as night, now everything seems bright as day, the symphony's tragedies and brutal contradictions overcome.

This is one of the most difficult of Mahler's movements to shoehorn into a logical, traditional structure, but then we'd be fools to try. Someone looking at this movement with a musical form textbook in hand might call it a combination of sonata form, simple ternary (ABA) form, and theme and variations. (The composer himself described this movement to Natalie Bauer-Lechner as "kneaded through and through till not a grain of the mixture remains unmixed and unchanged. Every note is charged with life, and the whole thing whirls around in a giddy dance . . . it is simply the expression of incredible energy." Certainly no musical idea is heard the same way twice.) Sonata form is suggested by the clear and consistent points of recapitulation (at 3:31 and 11:11); ternary form by the central retreats to simpler and more leisurely dance rhythms (at 6:46, 10:04, 16:12); and theme and variations by the almost constant parade of varied material (for instance, the variants of the idea first heard at 4:16). But the movement seems to connect these three old-fashioned formal notions in a haphazard way, in a way that shouldn't end up as convincing as it is. Though I haven't considered Mahler's compositional process in this work, I suspect he combined these formal dynamics in a kind of stream of consciousness. He didn't keep any particular external form in mind while writing the third movement of the Fifth Symphony: instead of trying to impose structure on his material from the outside in, he allowed the material itself to dictate the form from the inside out. This movement sounds like an improvisation of the pen, in other words. Mahler must have let himself be led by the style of music that he was writing down at a given moment.

The movement begins as a set of variations on the opening D major waltz theme, including some darker minor-key fugue-like renditions (one fugato in B minor starting at 0:44, another in B-flat minor starting at 1:31). Mahler had been acquiring the Bach collected edition from the Bach Gesellschaft and learning a great deal from the Leipzig master—

as becomes evident in his own ways of manipulating and juxtaposing material. Themes are turned upside down (inverted), slowed down (augmented), and passed from one voice to another before the previous one has a chance to finish (stretto). Formal traditions are still more or less in view when a slower, contrasting trio section comes in in B-flat major (starting at 2:30) with reduced instrumentation. This trio material, which waltzes away in triple time much like the opening music, is marked by upward violin slides that can imply either parody or being drunk, depending on the style of performance and your own mindset. The mixture of tones and styles is becoming rather inscrutable by now—we are witnesses to dancing, drinking, tense and somber fuguing; where in life could all these things happen at the same time? As if to counter this, the movement has a continuity that differentiates it from the stop-start, funereal bombast of the preceding movements. The recap of the opening quick-tempo waltz (starting at 3:31) back in the tonic key indicates we are still in a simple ternary (ABA) form, just as we'd expect in a scherzo movement. But then the minor-key fugato also returns and leads us into new, slower material (starting at 4:41) and a new emphasis on the horns; clearly, the composer is throwing out the ternary form convention as he composes, in real time, in front of our very ears.

Instead of listening to the third movement of the Fifth Symphony by hunting for the usual suspects in the usual musical processes—distinct themes, developmental passages, and strategic key changes—it might be better to listen for specific dramatic moments. Instead of searching for a symphonic argument, we should listen for events and breaches in the argument. I've already talked about trying to hear the Fifth Symphony as a correlation of climaxes, or doing the opposite and hearing each movement as an ongoing search for a "still point"—a moment of withdrawal that involves a unique detachment from the material at hand. In the third movement, these still points are long, beautifully drawn-out cadences—marked *ritardando*, "slowing down." Indeed, this movement shows Mahler devising a new love or even luxuriousness of cadence, one that will mark both his fast and slow movements from here forward. (The Sixth Symphony, especially, can be listened to as a chain of leisurely cadences separated by strategic anticipations of closure. But then there are also the amorous *Nachtmusiken* of the Seventh, the meditative lingerings at the start of the second part of the

Eighth Symphony where the text refers to "the sacred place, / The holy shrine of Love," the idyllic winding-down of the first movement of the Ninth, and many more examples.) Naturally, the beautiful cadences in the third movement of the Fifth wouldn't be so meaningful and satisfying if they weren't acting in opposition to such roaring, catastrophic climaxes.

After we start listening to the cadential "still points" in this movement, we can discern the ways they are approached and the ways they are left behind. And here—finally—a pattern comes into view, really the only one that proves useful once the usual formal-analysis suspects (ternary, sonata form, variations) have gone out the window. And the repeating pattern is as follows, centering each time on a full-scale cadence: (1) an emphatic but far-ranging horn passage, leading into (2) a drawn-out cadential progression, which often expands into the strings; the cadence leads to (3) an expectant pause, which is then followed by (4) a rudimentary, even clumsy triple-time dance rhythm in quiet pizzicato strings or other nonsustained sounds, a dance rhythm that leads to (5) a gradual speeding and/or enlargement into full orchestra.

And so, once the traditional formal interpretations have all failed in this movement—or rather, once the composer has pondered them only to make them fail—we come to the first iteration of the five-stage pattern I mention above. A dramatic eruption in the horns rings the death knell for the traditional formal paradigms, clearing the way for the new, homegrown pattern to take over. In this eruption, the whole horn section comes in *fortissimo* and with bells raised (starting at 5:17), offering an apocalyptic vision centering on a staggered and emphatic unison F-natural. (In his introductory book on Mahler, Deryck Cooke described "an awesome climax with horns echoing and re-echoing as if across mountain distances.") (1) The solo first horn emerges from this welter, sounding above tremolo violins. It continues, in alternation with the orchestra in a gradual slowdown and *diminuendo*. (2) The strings pick up the horn idea, harmonize it, and (at 6:04) start steering it into a drawn-out cadential progression that finally closes on the dominant. A diminuendo and morendo to *pianississimo* arrival on the dominant is then followed by (3) a pause, and then (4) solo pizzicato strings present the same idea as a slow, mordant waltz (starting at 6:46). The oboe then enters, paving the way for clarinet (at 7:35), bassoon, third horn, and then the full strings. Theodor Adorno finds this movement so long, quixotic in emotional changes, and manipulative of the listener's memory that he resorts to gothic horror and memory-related paradoxes from Proust novels. He calls the pizzicato episode at 6:46 "a remembrance of something never heard before," and then alludes to a ghostliness following it when he writes, "the *schüchtern* (timid) oboe entry that follows it has the ineffability of a voice venturing as a living being among shades." (5) Lastly, the orchestra gradually reassembles and speeds up to a *fließende* (flowing) tempo, before the trumpet and first violins (starting at 8:50) offer a short diversion in E minor.

This five-step pattern is a kind of mini-narrative unto itself, a plot outline that's general enough to allow characters and details to change from one reading to the next. It tells a story of renewal and resurgence, transitioning from ruinous textural collapse to a point of rest, then on to a faster tempo that stokes the full ensemble into renewed action. (In a letter to Alma, Mahler himself spoke of this movement as "this chaos that is eternally giving birth to a world that then perishes in the next moment.") The five-step pattern is offered a total of five times over the course of the third movement, in increasingly intense and drawn-out renditions. The second statement follows closely on the first (as described above), and functions as launching pad for the movement's major event of restoration: the large-scale recap of earlier material. As the story unfolds this second time around: (1) The horns reconvene (at 9:25), and (2) lead the cadence through several stages separated by pauses, slowing down to (3) the grand concluding pause (at 10:03), after which (4) the strings start a circling and repeating dance. This almost immediately starts a gradual speedup to the movement's original fast tempo. Here the dance rhythm speeds up more urgently than before: it works up to a madly vibrating B-flat minor chord (at 10:44, the winds trilling at the top), sharp tattoos on the wood slapstick, and a climactic cutoff on an A major chord that leads directly into a recap of the opening theme in the tonic D major (at 11:11), led again by the horns.

This recap is an act of restoration, but not literal return. It's a free recapitulation where the various themes return with reshufflings, modifications, tweaks, and additions (for instance, scales enthusiastically dashing up and down). The minor-key fugato material gets a vibrant restatement on clarinets and oboes (at 11:54). The opening waltz theme returns enthusiastically in the full orchestra (at 12:31), followed by fragmentations of familiar elements. Once again, the composer plays with our expectations of closure. The movement seems to be coming to a close on the tonic D major when a wild flourish on piccolo and violins leads (at 14:12) to yet another variation of the opening waltz material, this time quiet and in a reduced ensemble. But this soon brings us to a changed statement of the "horn apocalypse," now emphasizing D major (at 15:03) before it leads again into the solo horn obbligato line and the climax of the third statement of the five-stage pattern, now interrupted (at 15:16) by a shift to F major and a resumption of the "heroic" horn solo apportioned out in several stages. The expected cadential progression then leads us (at 16:12) back to the pizzicato dance rhythm, this time with clarinet and bassoon altering the tone color.

After coming so close to finishing, we've suffered the indignity of being taken back to where we started: we're apparently caught up yet again in the familiar five-stage pattern, the structural *samsara*, the repetitive furrow of musical death and rebirth. This time the "ghostly dance" section does finish up quickly, but then all the resurging optimism seems truly crushed when the horns, tuba, and basses bring the story to a sad end with a forlorn cadence on D minor (at 16:51). The prospect of a heroic close on D major, promised in the very first bars of the movement, now seems a callous joke. But before giving in, we need to pay heed to the upcoming pizzicato "ghostly dance" music, which has previously been the best forecaster of where the piece will turn next. (While Adorno described this dance material as a "remembrance of something never heard before," in actuality it also functions as a portent of something that will definitely happen.) In this fifth and last statement of the five-stage pattern, the quiet "ghostly dance" now reappears in the bass drum. Are we headed to a happy end or a despondent finish? There is a new vigor that portends well. The second statement of the five-step pattern had worked up enough energy to launch the recapitulation, and now the even more manic fifth iteration promises something yet more decisive. And so it proves. The short coda section moves speedily from "very wild" to "even faster" and finally (at 17:26) "hurrying strongly to the close." The movement plays one last trick with the promised payoff by settling on a fragment of the minor-key fugato material (starting at 17:20), one that now clouds the possibility of a D major homecoming by inserting B-flats. But a last roulade of high optimism from the horns reaffirms the tonic, and a mad swipe of a cadence finally ends the movement.

QUIET RETREAT, COMIC TUMULT

The third movement marks the Fifth Symphony's extremes of violence and retreat, of Mahler's opposition between "turning" and "still centers." But the fourth movement, the so-called Adagietto for strings and harp, trades any sense of competition for gilded beauty. (Confusingly enough, "adagietto" appears as a title for the movement and not as a tempo indication. Mahler's actual tempo directions are *sehr langsam* and *molto adagio* (very slowly), and at one point *wieder äußerst langsam* (again extremely slowly.) The movement eschews extremes for the sake of maintaining a single, unbroken, golden thread of melody. As a profoundly lyrical outpouring written for instruments, the Adagietto harks back to the Romantic genre of the "song without words" (*Lied ohne Worte*), best known by Mendelssohn's fairly brief and unassuming piano pieces of that title. But Mahler's Adagietto movement does have words of a sort, since it is closely related to his song "Ich bin der Welt abhanden gekommen" ("I Have Become Lost to the World"), a setting of Friedrich Rückert that Mahler wrote at about the same time. The symphony movement doesn't quote the song, but more generally echoes its style, turns of phrase, and mood of withdrawal. True to Rückert's text, Mahler's slow movement recoils from the Fifth Symphony the same way "Ich bin der Welt" pronounces itself "dead to the world's tumult, / And I rest in a quiet realm" ("Ich bin gestorben dem Weltgetümmel, / Und ruh' in einem stillen Gebiet"). Such a quiet realm is immediately audible in the Adagietto's reduced instrumentation: while brass, winds, and percussion stirred up cyclonic frenzy in the earlier movements, they sit this one out. In the absence of sounds made by blowing and hitting, this song without words evokes more subdued, slow-burning passions through the uniform tone of bows being drawn across strings. While brass, winds, and percussion require the musical interruptions that are inhalation and hand retraction, strings allow for a sustained, and potentially more blissful, continuity.

But then when we get to the Adagietto, everything has changed from the earlier movements: we've left behind the imitative contrapuntal textures, the obsessive lamentations, and the episodic and interrupted forms. Every preceding movement of the Fifth was brittle, thin-skinned, and multilayered, so even a slight grazing of the surface caused a hidden type of music or a repressed emotion to burst out. Instead of

Bach-inspired counterpoint, the Adagietto configures itself around a primary, lyrical melodic line against which the other voices create the harmonic backdrop—voices that set the melodic line in motion with deep-seated chordal frictions. In musical terms, these chordal frictions are called suspensions—notes that linger over from the previous chord and create dissonance when they become foreign to the new chord. Consider, for example, the third and fourth notes in the opening melody, the E in the first violins. As the third note in the melody, the E is the fifth of the A minor chord that's suggested before the melodic line enters to clarify things. By the time the E is restruck as the fourth note in the melody (at 0:16, on the downbeat articulated by the first pizzicato note in the basses), the other voices have all moved on to the chord of F major. This makes the holdover E a dissonant seventh suspension, creating a sweetly painful tension that impels the E to resolve up to an F, which it then does (at 0:19) as the fifth note of the melody.

As another contrast with the rest of the Fifth, the Adagietto is simplicity itself in terms of form: it follows a ternary (ABA) structure, with the outer (A) sections in F major and the more fragmented inner (B) section (starting at 4:21) moving restlessly through various keys. This inner section has a lengthy stretch in G-flat major—Mahler's usual transcendent half-step area above the home tonic. He makes this simple structure even easier to hear by having the harpist sit out the B section. Typically for Mahler, though, the structure implied by the emotional shifts and swells often fails to align with the form suggested by thematic events—the passions tend to follow their own structural rhythms. A darker turn toward A minor already invades the opening section, and proves strong enough (making a clear cadence on that harmony at 2:06) to threaten the "quiet realm" of the movement. The iridescent sound of the harp goes missing in this somber incursion. But then the minor key is quickly sidestepped, the harp reenters, and (starting at 2:29) we are back in what sounds like a varied return to the opening music. This works its way up to an impassioned arrival on the dominant C major (at 3:21), and this initiates a strong cadence (at 3:41) back to the tonic F major. Thus closes the A section. Disrupting this point of rest, the B section asserts itself (starting at 4:21) and within two bars has established C minor. But the harmonies soon start to move again, and the violins gradually ascend to higher registers, promising—

well, a steady move toward ethereal things and away from depressive gloom.

I described the form of the Adagietto as simple. The compensating moment of complication, the point where Mahler finesses that simplicity with surprise and no small measure of delight, is at the artful return of the first section (the return of A at 7:19). Approaching the later stretches of the B section, his wandering harmonies have gone far—but still plausibly—afield with an arrival at G-flat major (at 4:57) and then a turn to D major (at 6:29) with A held in the bass as if in expectation of a cadence back to D. But then the bass starts to drift unexpectedly down by half steps (at 7:09) before the harmony finally drops obliquely yet entirely inevitably back to the tonic F major at 7:19. After the unsettled central section with its harmonic detours to G-flat major and C-sharp minor, the tonic key is here reapproached by descending steps in the bass concurrent with ascending steps in the top voice. If the central section has spent time in a "transcendent" G-flat major, here at the return to the tonic we've transcended transcendence. The top line (in the first violins and violas) celebrates the return with a quiet glissando, a slow slide down from high D to C. The gesture betrays a taste for rapture. It is a quietly ecstatic sigh, like the last exhalation of one of Viennese painter Gustav Klimt's pale, heavy-lidded, postcoital virgins. Any darker emotions in the Adagietto have been exorcised, and the return of original theme and key are such gratifying events that the melody—the voice of the music—can barely bring itself to carry on. Experiencing an inexpressible and indeed overwhelming pleasure in the moment of return, the Adagietto slides and shudders.

From its opening bars, the finale declares the Fifth Symphony purged of all mournfulness, conflict, and ambiguity. For the first and perhaps last time with this composer, there's barely a minor chord anywhere in earshot. To clear the air for the start of his last movement and set the stage for much upbeat-finale rhetoric, Mahler takes a page from Beethoven: he imitates that composer's Ninth Symphony by having individual instrumental voices intone as if they were singing texts, and does so in shifting tempos. Mahler must have had, at the back of his mind, the introductory plea made by Beethoven's bass: "Oh friends, not these sounds! Instead, let us intone more pleasing and joyful ones." And so Mahler goes on to his own "ode to joy" finale, a fugal-rondo exercise that is both vulgar and virtuosic. As with Beethoven's finale, Mahler goes beyond modeling joy through musical devices like major keys and propulsive rhythms into using out-and-out comedy. With this rondo finale, he is following the beloved genre convention in Haydn's symphonies. In his own rondo finales, Haydn had drawn parallels between major-key symphony send-offs and concluding ensembles in comic opera of the time—madcap points in the comedy where hidden identities are revealed, old debtors suddenly pressed for payment, and all the best-laid plans foiled. If Mahler's marriage of fugal principles with such *opera buffa* convention seems odd at first glance, we only have to think of the conclusion to *Falstaff*—the Verdi opera that Mahler conducted most often, incidentally. Verdi ends his comic opera with an ensemble, structured as a climactic fugue on the text "Everything is a jest, man is born a jester . . . Everyone is duped, Taunt each other, But he who laughs last laughs best" ("Tutto nel mondo è burla . . . Tutti gabbati!"). These words come from Falstaff himself who, after suffering the humiliation of having his amorous delusions publicly revealed, is happy to see his rival Ford duped into blessing his daughter's marriage with her lover Fenton.

After finishing the Beethovenesque introduction to his finale, Mahler presents his first rondo theme on the horn—starting at 0:37 under the indication "Quick and jocular, Lively" (*Allegro giocoso, Frisch*). The opening theme itself is loose and episodic enough to lay the groundwork for later hijinks. Hear at the opening of this theme, for instance, how the half notes are plopped fatuously on downbeats: LONG-short-short-LONG-short-short-short-short-short-LONG, etc. These long notes will become pratfalls—with the first comic splats arriving at 2:15 and 2:19. The opening of this theme, a scalewise descent through a fifth interval, will reappear with cheeky persistence. It will generate the fugue subject proper: compare the horn descent that starts at 0:37 with the eight-note descent starting the fugue subject at 1:43 in the woodwinds, the return of the original horn-descent idea at 2:32, and finally the trumpet's initiation of the fugal climax starting at 12:25. Mahler's fugue is much less strict than Verdi's, being divided into five main sections that are separated by episodic, developmental, and cadential material. He has really written more of a portrait of a fugue—though one that still shows enviable contrapuntal skill—than an earnest compositional exercise. His affectionate portrait borders on caricature, as he shows with the brief quotation of his own song "Lob des hohen Verstandes" ("In Praise of Lofty Intellect") at the start in the bassoon. The song tells the tale of the cuckoo and the nightingale facing off in a singing competition, and the donkey judge giving the prize to the two-note songster rather than the virtuoso because the cuckoo's song is easier on his ears. Mahler intends all this as a sardonic remark on music critics as well as a self-deprecating comment on his own ensuing fugue, which represents his grandest attempt thus far at this most intellectual of musical forms. Just as in the finale of Verdi's *Falstaff*, all sorts of duping and counterduping are going on here; and certainly the Verdi text "Tutto nel mondo è burla" could serve as a motto for Mahler's own finale.

As regards the style of this fugal portrait, it straddles sardonicism and smart-aleck braggadocio. And this is where the rondo-finale aspect comes into play. The fugal sections are just as interested in bustling eighth-note motion as they are in any thematic manipulation, and the individual lines of music seem inhabited by stock comic opera characters: the bumbling old lech, the wily servant, the lovesick young man. The first fugal section (starting 1:10) spins off into busy figuration before it hints (starting 1:27 in the first violins) at the big chorale tune that will cap the finale and the symphony as a whole. The fugue subject per se enters in the woodwinds at 1:43, and in the horns shortly after. This developing enterprise comes to an undignified hiatus with the comic pratfalls at 2:15 and 2:19, followed by a deceptive cadence. To contrast with the hustling figuration in D major, a different fugal section will surface in B-flat major (at 3:06, recurring at 6:29) and later a closing-cadential section in descending chords (starting at 4:16, recurring at 7:21). The rondo's opening music comes back (starting at 2:32) with a charming air of self-importance, and then re-resumes and is interspersed with additional fugal exercises. The first sign that Mahler is setting up some heavyweight summation of the Fifth Symphony as a whole comes at 3:29, where the first violins recall the Adagietto movement ("graciously," *grazioso*). The development section allows some further digressions, including a courtly string line starting at 6:35 (again marked *grazioso*).

A developing climax, with the bustling eighth-note motion now extending into woodwind chords, leads into the start of the recapitulation of the fugue proper (starting in the strings at 8:39). The main project of this section is preparation for and summary restatement of the big D major chorale music that had interrupted the second movement as a non sequitur. The chorale is hinted at in the trumpets starting at 9:02 (where they're instructed to play with bells up), but then quickly gives way to a further fugal section—yet another imitative steeplechase starts up, to the point where the listener starts to lose count of them. The descending D major chorale incipit is reintroduced at 10:12, followed by a contrasting section in G major starting at 11:04 that expands upon the quotation from the Adagietto movement. A startling drop to F major (at 12:04) comes with the score marking "Gradually and constantly faster," followed by—at long last!—a climactic appearance of the long-awaited complete D major chorale tune (starting at 12:25 in the brass), paired now with the "busy" fugal passagework and the ecstatic trills from earlier on. Still in the final and summational key of D major, the movement moves on to an exact statement of the chorale passage from the second movement (starting at 12:46). The manic coda arrives (at 13:12) after a slightly threatening ritardando, with sped-up renderings of the chorale tune in the horns, and then a full statement in the trombones (at 13:20). A threatened last-second diminished-chord derailment pops up (at 13:38) but is swept aside for the last rush to the close—the most exuberant ending that Mahler ever penned, all the more astonishingly happy for its eventual arrival from funereal beginnings.

Or is it? Mahler hadn't shown such a radical change of heart between the first measure of a work to the last, and would never traverse such extremes again. In the Fifth Symphony's overall changeover from darkest dark to brightest light, the joy arrives so blindingly that some commentators have questioned the symphony's integrity—the music's belief in itself. The finale raises as many questions as it answers when it returns to the D major brass chorale heard in the second movement: Is this a conclusive fulfillment of the earlier idea, or a less obtrusive normalization—a taming—of it? Does the second movement chorale look ahead to the finale more intently than the finale chorale refers back? Compared with the other movements, the finale as a whole does seem to obey convention in a way that makes it sound more disciplined and constrained. Theodor Adorno, always more interested in paradox than affirmation, might have been thinking of the end of the Fifth Symphony when he proposed that "[Mahler's] vainly jubilant movements" serve to "unmask jubilation."

Paul Bekker detected another kind of dissimulation in the finale of the Fifth, hearing this movement in different self-contradictory terms, as a "buildup of insatiability." As Bekker heard it, the finale shows an artist allowing himself to become drunk with his own magnificence of resource—a kind of music where the composer becomes "intoxicated by the means of expression and intensification." In another passage in his Mahler book, Bekker described the finale of the Fifth as a musical exercise in strength and resolve: a demonstration of "a path to the free heights of the creative human will, up to which this symphony and this Finale lead in an untiring ascent." From what we know of this composer's visceral need to believe in higher causes, such an ironclad determination toward optimism—toward joy in spite of everything—sounds like a real possibility. As if to demonstrate the fullest power of the human will, Mahler's next symphony would establish a contrary, equally fierce resolve toward darkness and negativity.

7

SYMPHONY NO. 6

The Rigid Embrace of the Narrow House—The Blackness of the Absolute Night

If the Fifth Symphony shows Mahler opening up new possibilities in form and mood and texture, the Sixth signifies a closing up, a circumscription—a limitation of form as well as rhythm, phrasing, and tonal reach. The work's harmonic closure is among the traditional aspects: the Sixth is Mahler's first symphony since the First to end in the same key it begins in. These formal and gestural restrictions become claustrophobic, almost suffocating. Mahler follows a four-movement layout that Mozart might have recognized, with a sonata form in the first movement that is almost textbook, but also includes, at the other end of the symphony, a finale so apocalyptic and so massively conclusive that it bemused even Richard Strauss.

1. *Allegro energico, ma non troppo. Heftig, aber markig* (Quickly and energetically, but not too much. Heavy but vigorous) (21 minutes)
2. *Scherzo: Wuchtig* (Scherzo: Heavily) (12 minutes)
3. *Andante moderato* (At a moderate, walking pace) (15 minutes)
4. *Finale: Sostenuto – Allegro moderato – Allegro energico* (Finale: Sustained—Moderately quickly—Quickly and energetically) (29 minutes)

In the Sixth symphony, Mahler used his most classical scaffolding to structure some of his darkest sentiments. This is at odds with Enlightenment thinking, which maintains that a rationalist worldview is necessarily an optimist worldview—the conclusion that philosopher Gottfried Leibniz had taken to such an extreme in drawing his famous conclusion that God made for us "the best of all possible worlds." In a paradox worthy of Mahler, the conservative Brahmsian (or even Mozartian) layout of his Sixth Symphony becomes part and parcel of the work's pessimism: the closed forms and regular rhythms are like walls that close in on us, especially with the free impulsiveness and progressive tonality of the Fifth Symphony still fresh in our ears. Though there are plenty of lush and beautiful byways in the Sixth Symphony, there are no real surprises apart from its last, terminal howl. Everything in the Sixth is logical and prepared, its grim and mountainous splendors beautifully methodical. (The Sixth therefore counts as the most Brucknerian of Mahler's symphonies, though Bruckner's unshakeable faith would never have allowed him such a nihilistic close.) In Mahler's Sixth Symphony point A leads inevitably to point B, and it's in this sense of surrendering to fate that the overall tonal circularity of the work takes on special meaning: final closure back in the original tonic A minor shows there is to be no escape from the mundane, as we had seen in the Fourth Symphony in G major (which ends in a major version of the relative minor—that is, in E major); nor is there to be the transcendent half step upward that we have in the Fifth (which begins in C-sharp minor but has a finale in D major).

Mahler's rhythmic consistency ticks like a clockwork across the first three movements of the Sixth Symphony, moving the piece inexorably toward its final tragedy. There is marked rhythmic and metric similarity between movements one and two. The first movement is in 4/4 march time. The second, though it's in triple meter, is certainly the least dancelike, the least airy of any Mahler scherzo movement: the marchlike pulsation of the first movement persists here because the triple meter is undercut already in the first measure. This movement has a somber and haunting end. This makes a contrast with the scherzos of the Fourth and Fifth Symphonies, works where Mahler was clear in dispelling any lingering pessimism before the arrival of the slow movement: in those preceding symphonies, the end of the scherzo was the point where a cock was snooked or hats were thrown in the air, putting to bed any doubts of a happy ending. Heard in retrospect, the second movement of the Sixth rehearses the grim certainties of the finale. The third movement, the lovely but confined Andante moderato, is unusual for a slow movement in that it also follows a strict rhythmic pulse. In that way it's different from the Adagietto of the Fifth, music defined by a fluid beat. As for the finale of the Sixth, that becomes a cataclysmic five-act drama unto itself. The final coda (starting at 26:21)—whether heard as a requiem or as a simpler graveside funeral service—refuses to intervene and tell us it was all a bad dream; rather, it acts out a dark finality with uncaring detachment. This is Mahler's only symphonic finale that ends neither in joy nor in a state of transcendence, but in darkness.

I've mentioned the Sixth Symphony's classical four-movement layout. But two elements counteract that rational schema with changeableness and even disorder: I'm speaking of the free, molten flux of the thematic material, and the noise in the percussion section. As regards the first aspect: the Sixth goes even a step further than the Fourth and Fifth Symphonies in establishing progressive changeability of material. Mahler works here with malleable and even commonplace musical ideas. His friend, the pioneering Viennese musicologist Guido Adler, called the second theme of the first movement "melodically weak," but that accusation could be leveled at the whole Sixth Symphony—the third movement aside. This most lyrical of symphonists sharpens the sense of tragedy here by restraining his own melodic gift. And with respect to the second aspect: Mahler introduces various instruments and playing techniques to diffuse and obscure any melodic-thematic information with a wide range of noise. He retains instruments from earlier symphonies, among them the bass drum, snare drum, tam-tam, cymbals, glockenspiel, triangle, and of course timpani. Now added to those are the bundle of twigs called the *Rute* (struck against the rim of the bass drum, and last used in the Second and Third Symphonies), the xylophone and celesta (neither of which Mahler had used before), a new combination of bells deployed mostly offstage (deep, untuned bells as well as cowbells), and lastly a complete innovation: a massive "hammer," emerging three times in the finale to deliver "short, powerful, but dull-sounding strokes of a nonmetallic character (like the fall of an axe)." Alma attributed to her husband a program where the three hammerblows symbolize terrible blows of fate suffered by the hero, "the third of which fells him as a tree is felled."

These new "sound effects" in Mahler's Sixth Symphony suggest a symphonic argument that has overrun normal channels of musical communication. This composer would seem to have such urgent and powerful things to say that he can longer limit himself to traditional instruments. But one person's innovation is another person's gimmick, and Mahler's contemporaries—largely deaf to his expressive profundities—saw these orchestral innovations as stunts. The critic for the *Wiener Abendpost* heard the Sixth's hammerblows as evidence of how "notes fail [the composer], so a blow falls. That is only natural. When words fail speakers at the decisive moment, they slam their fists onto the table." The new noises in the Sixth also indicate a developed sense of tone color—the composer using new instruments not for purposes of rhetoric, but to heighten mood and atmosphere. Some earlier symphony composers had dared to pilfer instrumental colors from theater music. In his *Military* Symphony (his Symphony in G Major, Hob. 1/100, 1794), Haydn had imitated Turkish percussion using triangle, cymbals, and bass drum. In his Seventh Symphony (1883), Bruckner introduced the Wagner tubas of Wagner's *Ring of the Nibelung* operas into the concert orchestra. César Franck scandalized at least one listener when he dared to use the English horn in the slow movement of his Symphony in D Minor (1888), a provocative choice because the instrument was thought appropriate to opera and ballet but not to the concert hall. The cowbells that Mahler introduces in his Sixth present a rather different situation. Composers of concert music had used unfamiliar tone colors mostly to reference a particular theatrical space. But the cowbells had no such history in 1906. Mahler's listeners would have heard these particular "instruments" only as farming sounds, and so it's no surprise they made the orchestra break out into laughter in the first rehearsal.

On the other hand, this lack of orchestral provenance allowed Mahler to use the cowbells to suggest unique, spiritual altitudes. He said the cowbells of the Sixth Symphony evoke "the last terrestrial sounds penetrating into the remote solitude of mountain peaks," while denying they had any specific programmatic meaning in his symphony. A few commentators have heard something utopian in their sound, a conclusion that might or might not relate to Mahler's own reference to leaving the earth, and that might or might not connect with the idyllic or even paradisiacal passages that appear alongside them—especially in the finale. But the musicologist Thomas Peattie reminds us to put any such impressions in the context of the Sixth Symphony's overall tragedy: by his understanding, if the cowbell sound suggests a better world, that suggestion should only sharpen our sense of loss when the Sixth finally denies any such possibility. "And if we accept the premise of its illusory nature," Peattie writes in his book *Gustav Mahler's Symphonic Landscapes*, "it might in turn be thought of as the most powerful reflection of the symphony's ultimately unfulfilled utopian promise."

In the actuality of performance, the cowbells usually sound too random and clanky to suggest a utopia, while Mahler's offstage placement makes them all the more mystical and indistinct. And so I hear the cowbells as a kind of white noise, the buzz of an ebbing consciousness, a "tuning out" of the real world, and the sounding mechanics of pure contemplation. Mahler suggests this with his instruction that they be played in a random manner, and that they appear only in jangling conjunction with the deep bells (*Tiefes Glockengeläute*), celesta, tremolo strings, and/or lower brass. Similarly, in the first movement the bass clarinet models a tuning-out of consciousness while the cowbells are buzzing their buzz and the strings play the chorale in quietly fluttering tremolos. Or perhaps it is a kind of fine-tuning of the consciousness. At the point in question, the clarinet enters at 12:53, quickly reaches and holds a high F, and then decrescendos to a *pianissimo* before crescendoing back again. It's an important, unnecessary, mystical, and utterly arbitrary moment—one that has us listening intently to a nuance in one player's breath in the midst of a piece that's played by ninety musicians.

The celesta has its own connotations. A small keyboard instrument with hammers that strike bell plates instead of strings, it had appeared in orchestras some fifteen years before Mahler utilized it in his Sixth. The instrument was used by Tchaikovsky for the Sugar Plum Fairy in *The Nutcracker*, and before that by Ernest Chausson in his music for Shakespeare's *The Tempest*, specifically for the fairy Ariel. In act 3 of *Tosca*, Puccini used the instrument for the duet where Tosca tells her soon-to-be-executed lover Cavaradossi that they will escape to "new horizons": "As long as we are together the planets will vanish, like the clouds above the ocean." In Stravinsky's 1910 ballet *The Firebird*, the celesta appears as part of the magic carillon (the *Carillon Féerique*) that summons the evil King Kastchei's troop of Monster Guardians. In all these cases, the celesta is a theatrical sound used to evoke magic, dreaming, the imaginary, and otherworldliness. (Its significance was made even clearer late in the century, when it was used in the children's TV show *Mr. Rogers' Neighborhood* to connote passage to the Land of Make Believe. And then of course there is John Williams's use of it in the opening title music for the Harry Potter film series.) And so here is another example of Mahler being the first to import a theater instrument into the concert orchestra: the Sixth marked the celesta's first appearance in a symphony, and in combination with Mahler's other unusual percussion—the cowbells and the "deep bells"—it acts to transport the listener and remake the aural imaginary.

MARCH WITHOUT MELODY

If cowbells are "the last terrestrial sounds" we hear in the Sixth, then we must have begun the journey with our feet on the ground. And the symphony does open with a *musica mundana*—emphatic, sharp, one-two-one-two strokes that sound more like spades penetrating earth than feet tramping on it. Mahler refuses to follow the usual compositional point of a march: namely, using the repetitious one-two trudge as a challenge for writing lyrically. Beethoven wrote a similar funeral march as the slow movement of his Piano Sonata no. 12 in A-flat major, op. 26—a "funeral march on the death of a hero" where the rudimentary melody stays anchored to the meter. As Beethoven did in his sonata movement, Mahler finds creative ways to emphasize the first beat (the downbeat) of each measure without losing the listener's interest. The varied instrumentation also offers plenty of intrigue. Starting at 0:26, there is a two-fold trading off between the oboes (marked "shrill") and the trombones, followed at 0:36 by the trumpets. Starting at 1:12, the strings momentarily distract from the downbeats until a cymbal crash reorients us to beat one. Starting at 1:37, fragmentary grumbles in the lower strings again disrupt the meter, followed by a burst on the snare drum and timpani that leads (at 1:51) to a quiet, chorale-like passage for the winds (derived from the opening march material). This passage proves as liberated from beat and bar line as the march was obeisant to them. A ritard then guides us (at 2:23) to our first obvious thematic (if still "melodically weak") event, the rhapsodic second theme in F major.

Mahler methodically uses the discrete registers of low, middle, and high in a way that, pursuing his reference to things "terrestrial," seems to correspond with the ideas of subterrain, ground, and stratosphere. Critic Otto Neitzel heard such an orchestral stratification and said it showed the Sixth's inability to reconcile its own emotional oppositions. "Cow bells and a celesta!" Neitzel exclaimed after attending the premiere. "Paradise on earth and Elysian fields above! It would all be so simple if Mahler's symphony were content to remain between these two poles. But in the meantime an enormous abyss has opened up, an unappeased longing, a despair, and a struggle on the part of the entire orchestra." (Here, as elsewhere, Henry-Louis de la Grange's Mahler biography is our main resource for learning the reactions of this composer's original critics.) Mahler begins the first movement with stabbing, relentlessly marching As. When our melodic initiation begins at the ascending steps in the violins, it starts out of sync with this pure marking of rhythm in the bass. The melody's frustrated aligning with the march leads to the first real orchestral chord (at 0:10, with all eight horns), and then their final concurrence is marked by an emphatic four-note laceration in the full strings (at 0:13).

There follow many effortful reachings-up and descents, especially in the strings: registers have become shackles, confinements to be resisted. We hear what is becoming a Mahler hallmark: a pair of whole-note chords (first stated at 1:47) dovetailing from a major triad to its parallel minor, and in this instance from brass to woodwinds. Constantin Floros hears this two-chord emblem as Mahler's "seal" (*Siegel*), a telling description in that it can mean both a personal hallmark and a way of fastening a communication shut. At this point in the first movement of the Sixth Symphony, the major-minor seal closes off the relentless, earthbound tread of the march, silencing the lower, terrestrial register of the orchestra and allowing the upper-register woodwinds to float heavenward for their chorale-like passage (which starts at 1:51). With the second theme in F major (starting at 2:23, marked *Schwungvoll*, "with impetus"), we are liberated from the march and have broken through to higher registers. This theme has a spontaneous drive that manifests itself as sporadic and uncentered motion, and it flaunts its hard-won freedom to scale up just as high as it wishes and when it wishes. (Alma reports that her husband wrote this theme as a musical depiction of her; this may or may not be true, but in any event its gushing theatricality doesn't necessarily make for a flattering portrait.)

Having heard the second theme as the incitation and culmination of the first movement's reach upward, now in the closing section (starting at 3:57) we are liberated from the march and finally free to breathe. Mahler has prohibited any changes in the tempo until this point, apart from tucking into the start of the second theme with a short ritard. But now the slackening effect of a pair of slowdowns conspires with lower dynamics and quivering triplet fifths in harp and cellos to give this last repeated cadence (repeating the four-note opening of the second theme) a luxurious or slightly dazed feeling, even as the colors again grow darker. After the exposition repeat (at 4:27), the development begins (starting at 8:49) with a quieter version of the opening march. This quickly progresses to the most emphatic statement of the march in the entire movement (starting at 9:27). But as the development section moves along, we hear Mahler focusing less on the march rhythm and more and more on the quiet fluidity of the second theme, chorale material, and closing section: in a move that could be considered either a collapse or a loosening of earthly bonds, we are slowly shifted from the march and its terrestrial obsessions toward a state of static oblivion.

When the march returns in the midst of this shift (starting at 10:26), it appears as a mere caricature of itself—sardonic and twitching, with trilling woodwinds, xylophone, and affable trombones and tuba. With the march disempowered, the cowbells are able to enter for the first time about half a minute after that. At 11:00 the woodwinds climb down through a remnant of the second theme, and with the cowbell entrance the earthly consciousness is relieved of its duties; a reiteration of the major-minor seal at 11:18 packs it away all the more conclusively. The intoxicating combination of cowbells with celesta, high bass clarinet, and the chorale material in horns and tremolo strings makes us realize we've been escorted far away—or far up, rather, since the orchestra is all in higher registers at this point. A violin solo (marked "caressingly," with the player instructed, "give yourself time") leads to a conclusive point of rest on B-flat major (at 12:53), which is Mahler's usual position of transcendence a half step above the tonic.

We are jolted out of this otherworldliness by a sudden if relatively gentle return to the opening tempo and rhythm (starting at 13:48, in B major rather than the tonic A major). As we will discover, the recapitulation section reverses the themes compared to the exposition, meaning the definitive and climactic portion of each batch of material now comes at their ends rather than at the beginnings. This backloading of emphasis makes the movement more dramatically continuous overall. And so the distinctive portion of the opening march theme doesn't return until 14:54, where it appears as a climax that reinstates the stabbing march rhythm—and thus the "real" recap. The march theme works its way to the dominant key, the major-minor seal is heard again (at 16:21), and then we hear a quickened and reorchestrated version of the chorale material (now brightened by celesta and offbeat pizzicato strings). The second theme (starting at 16:56) is now made to sound like a transition, and introduced without its four-note opening scale ascent or its escapist journeying into higher registers. The closing theme has become more and more important as the movement's capacious reservoir for contemplation and flexibility, and when it returns (starting at 17:38) it leads to the coda section (starting at 18:15) via a pitch-black descent in bass clarinet and bassoon.

This completes the movement's tour of the three registers: if the cowbells and celesta were extraterrestrial, this lead-in to the coda sounds subterranean. With the entrance of the tam-tam and trombones, the passage burrows even more deeply into bedrock. The opening march theme reenters, and after increasingly tense elaboration it becomes the launching pad for the long-delayed second theme. This reappears (at 20:18), finally rejoined with its original opening four-note ascent. A second statement of the theme a step higher (starting at 21:01) overstates the opening four-note figure as a melodramatic pinnacle. Mahler thereby repeats a favorite maneuver: taking the most tender point of a movement, in this case the "caressingly" violin solo from the development, and repeating it as the grandest climax. The throw-away coda that follows is the best example of a trick that Mahler learned from Beethoven: as he described it once to Bruno Walter, the compositional prank consisted of imitating peals of laughter at the point of anticipated conclusion, before racing off to the real close.

This end of the first movement is crucial to anyone hoping to grasp the Sixth Symphony as a whole. The movement has ostentatiously followed certain classical rules, as mentioned earlier, and in doing so set up expectations for the rest of the piece. For instance, Mahler has followed Mozart's practice of abrupt structural articulations: the contrast and reduction in the orchestra coming out of the first theme, the ritard leading into the pause before the second theme, and most of all the predictable, gradual motion toward the dominant of the new key. And coming from such an inveterate modifier of material, Mahler's inclusion of the traditional exposition repeat is almost shocking. These classical observances lead the listener to expect what the following two movements end up supplying in basic outline, but at the same time the expressive content can seem to conflict with such structural clarity and discipline.

This predictability in the first movement, though contradicted by interior thematic changes and workings, makes the joyful, hats-in-the-air coda all the more puzzling as the conclusion to a movement that began on such a dark and militaristic note. There were charms and songs along the way, but the very dark turn at the start of the coda could only have poisoned the musical well. If the second theme is in fact a representation of Alma, then positioning her as a point of triumph at the end of the movement might present her as the composer's own *Mater Gloriosa*, as his redemption from despairing thoughts. But there is something hollow in this concluding glorification of the second theme—not least because of the maniacal timpani part, absurdly doubled by the tuba (at 20:17, 20:39, and then 21:09). Ken Russell uses this first-movement coda as an energetic send-off at the very end of his movie *Mahler*, underscoring a freeze-frame image of the smiling composer (played by Robert Powell). But Russell sets up the exultation—with the composer's face modeling the mood of the coda—to be painfully self-delusive "exultation." Though severely ill, Mahler is smiling here because a doctor showed a lack of concern after giving him an emergency checkup. Alma and Gustav have also renewed their affection for each other after that pronouncement, putting their marriage back on a strong footing. The Mahlers happily take their leave of the doctor and exit their train carriage. At that point, we glimpse another doctor—who is approaching with news from a pathology lab that the bacterial infection is in fact advanced and incurable. But before the second visitor can open his mouth to deliver this death sentence, the pale-faced composer smiles ear to ear and supplies the last line of the movie: "You can go home, doctor! We're going to live forever!"

DESPAIR, THEN CIRCUMVENTION

The strained oppositions of the first movement leave us wondering where we're headed as we head into the second through fourth movements. It's a question that vexed Mahler himself, since he felt compelled to reconsider the order of the inner two movements. He published the work early in 1906 with the scherzo movement second and the Andante moderato third. When he rehearsed and premiered the piece later that year, though, he decided to place the Andante moderato second and had his publisher print an erratum. But the editor of the 1963 critical edition, exerting a strong influence at the start of the critical Mahler boom, set the default when he—citing some undocumented report that the composer had again changed his mind—restored the scherzo to second place. Mahler's own intentions aside, the strongest harmonic and structural arguments are for placing the scherzo second—not least because that echoes the Fifth Symphony's obsessive pairing and interconnection of the first two movements. The fact that they are similar enough to sound like reworkings of each other, even more clearly affiliated than the first two movements of the Fifth, makes the overall structure of the Sixth all the more oppressive. Placing this scherzo second seems retroactively to imbue the first movement with even greater intensity: this order suggests that matters in the first movement are so overwhelming they have spilled over into the second. (Of course, these impressions are dependent on tempo. The speeds chosen by the conductor should be slow enough to make the march rhythms and the phrase structure sound confining, but without allowing the music to drag.)

The scherzo movement is also marked by strategic ambivalence. I've mentioned a strategy that Mahler had developed in the Fifth Symphony: setting up an inner movement as the dramatic or emotional fulcrum within a conflicted work, a movement that suspends elements of light and dark such that the rest of the symphony can end up tipping into either exultation or despair. In the Fifth, this fulcrum movement was the big third-movement scherzo; in the Sixth Symphony, it is the second, scherzo movement. The fulcrum aspect sits with this movement's interplay between two kinds of music that are strongly contrasting, and therefore typical of a scherzo. However, their juxtaposition here is anything but traditional: this is Mahler adulterating Schubert's and Bruckner's naïve scherzo designs. The opening manic material in A minor (marked "powerful," *wuchtig*) is contrasted with an F major minuet-like passage (starting at 2:01) that Mahler specifies as "old-fashioned" (*altväterisch*) and "gracious" (*grazioso*). At first this *grazioso* material seems a conventional and typically heartening trio section—and Mahler has in the past allowed contrasting material to take over a darkly colored movement, rescuing the symphony from adversity. But here the *grazioso* material is interrupted and displaced more and more by the chattering, repetitious minor-key *wuchtig* material and its faster tempo. There are four of these remarkable, threatening incursions on the "gracious" courtly theme: first at 2:30 when the winds barge in, loud and "speeding up"; then speeding up again more briefly at 2:55; and then again at 3:28; and lastly when a major-key version of the staccato contrasting material takes over the *grazioso* at 3:57 and leads the movement into a sardonic, highly nongracious passage in F minor (starting 4:35) that's embellished by muted trumpet strokes, xylophone, and bass drum.

These interruptions happen through quick, manic repetitions of a vacillating interval, usually a fourth or a third. Appearing in lower instruments, a slowed-down version of this depressive single-interval "wobble" works to undermine certainty within the movement in a different way. This more deliberate wobble can either end on the higher note, potentially sending the unstable movement upward, or on the lower note, pulling the argument down. Here the fulcrum aspect of the Sixth Symphony is boiled down to a single interval, and the fate of the work hangs in the balance. The first such wobble (at 0:31) ends on the higher note, a D that sends the music into D minor and the violins sailing up to a high, piercing, drill-like A harmonic. On the next statement (at 1:37), the wobble ends on the low A, somehow sending the strings and winds skyward again, and eventually leading to the *grazioso* trio section (and its own interruptions). More crucial is the wobble that occurs at 5:36, ending on the low A, which then drops farther down (at 5:44) to a lower F that casts a pall over the music, initiates a ghostly series of tam-tam strokes, and gives the general impression that the symphony's battle against darkness has been lost. The entire composition could have been left for dead at this dispiriting point. But the argument somehow dredges itself up from the basses, a wobbling second interval carried upward finally to the flutes and first violins. When the *grazioso* material returns for the last time (starting at 6:50), it is soon undermined by both the repetitious minor-key *wuchtig* material (at 7:26, 8:26, 8:58) and the fourth-interval "wobble" (at 7:57), though by this point these two hostile agents are sounding similar.

This confrontation of themes incites the movement's final showdown and collapse, the pace of events now sped up and the stakes becoming ever higher. This last section begins (at 9:14) with a key change and repetitions of a drooping, almost comically morose figure that sounds like yet another version of the "wobble." This lament leads in turn to a slowed-down, cynical, and noisy rendering of the repetitious *wuchtig* theme in E-flat minor (starting at 9:32), now marked by the dry, clattering rasp of *col legno* strings and sponsoring a dour minuet in the oboes and English horns. The original *wuchtig* material comes back for the last time (starting at 10:04), in the tonic A minor and more furious than ever. It is brought to heel by the ambivalent "wobble" (at 10:32), a vacillation that now even blurs basic distinctions between major and minor. The coda section (starting at 10:41) is in an irredeemable A minor and traces the movement's final collapse—and forecasts, at this crucial point right before the slow movement, the dark fate of the symphony as a whole. The coda begins with a shriek in the flutes and violins, an upward stroke that prefaces a four-octave plunge. The horns carve out their own descent and hand it over to the tuba, the clockwork resumes but with increasing fragility, and then the timpani reach a new level of wretchedness at the very end (at 12:13) when they follow the preceding paired phrases with a single, lonely, and unanswered three-note figure. "Schade, alles ist vorbei!" as German speakers say—"It's all over, sad to say." Or maybe not quite yet, since we still have breath enough to admit defeat.

The slow movement that follows, marked Andante moderato, answers few questions. Its key is the clearest sign of its withdrawal: this movement is in E-flat major, at the farthest possible harmonic remove from the symphony's tonic base of A minor (though Mahler prepared us for this far-off key with the short, noiseful passage in E-flat minor toward the end of the preceding movement). This movement is a lullaby with an epic tone, and its steady tread and methodical progression separate it all the more clearly as a parenthetical statement—an aside—within the Sixth Symphony as a whole. By calling the movement epic in style, I point to its artlessness, stability, and length. Also to the cogent message it seems to carry from days gone by: "epic" is related to the

Greek word *eipein*, meaning "to say." Aristotle and Plato talked about a duality between acting out and telling. So much of what we've heard in the Sixth Symphony so far has been the former, but now the Andante moderato enters with its narrative posture. The melody wends its way between major and minor so intricately that at times it sounds as if it's written in one of the old church modes that held sway before tonal scales. Beneath this simple, quasi-modal melody doing its telling, developing its missive, the lower strings and the harp provide a steady rock-a-bye accompaniment.

The Andante moderato speaks as it sings, but it does so unwillingly. It's in some ways a difficult movement to "read," since it lacks the narrative transitions and interruptions that marked the previous movement. The opening melody's tinge of bittersweet regret suggests a story that is too distant in time and place for us to change its course. This is the first of two basic themes (the A material) that the movement pursues in a standard overall A-B-A-B-A structure (the five sections starting at 0:00, 4:35, 7:25, 8:50, and 12:11). And yet some of the biggest changes of tone and sentiment occur within rather than between these sections. Also serving the movement's continuity are a basic uniformity of tempo and the similarities between A and B material, with B sections sounding like elaborations on motives and ideas given in A. Each section is given all the time it needs, and the big expressive shifts sound inevitable and unhurried, with no sense of intrusion. For instance, the first lines marked *forte* (for horn and clarinets, starting at 4:50) are prepared for four bars earlier with a key change and a shift up to higher registers. When the first *forte* section entrance follows (the violins, cellos, and basses at 5:10), it again feels expected, especially with the beat-early entrance in the violins. The only real transition of the movement (starting at 7:06, as we finish B material and prepare for the first return of A material at 7:25) is a descending chromatic passage for the violins alone that has no bass line and completely disregards the key signature—a sequential free fall that sounds like a sigh that's drawn out, without beginning or end. When the biggest climax begins (starting at 11:09), with some of the thickest textures and heaviest doublings in the whole symphony, the poignant emotion again feels tempered by its surety of placement—its inevitability.

FINALE: DESCENT INTO TRAGEDY

The finale returns us to the Sixth Symphony's malign project, decided through a series of dramatized surges. The early twentieth-century music theorist Ernst Kurth explained Bruckner's intuitive structures as a series of waves. As he wrote in his book on that composer, "Form is neither movement nor its synoptically grasped rigidity, neither flux nor outline, but rather the lively struggle to grasp something flowing by holding onto something firm." In his view, "symphonic waves" are cumulative events by which the music apportions its energies through time into a series of culminating watershed moments.

What Mahler has done in the finale of his Sixth is to dramatize such a wave structure, taking a long, Bruckner-like form and importing it—so to speak—into a theater of symphonic music. Klaus Pringsheim, one of Mahler's vocal coaches at the Vienna *Hofoper*, remembered the Sixth finale as an overwhelming series of emotional peaks when he heard it under the composer's direction: "The chaotic masses of sound fell into place, peaks rose out of the waves, he built them up, piled peak on peak, and so emerged, overwhelming and gigantic, in masses that Mahler never before and truth to tell never again dared to attempt, the last movement." Making them all the more theatrical are the three hammerblows that punctuate the climaxes of the three waves. Mahler apparently did have a specific kind of sound in mind when he specified a "hammer," but one he couldn't realize in instrumental terms. He had a massive chest built for percussionists to beat with wooden clubs but was unhappy with the results in rehearsals. Today's orchestral percussionists disappear into their workshops and assemble wood, metal, and hide in efforts to come up with the be-all and end-all of Mahler hammers. But sadly—or perhaps not—none of them has yet cornered the market in Sixth Symphony *Hammerschläge*.

We can attribute the strictly autobiographical reading of the finale's "three blows of fate" to Alma. Gustav gave his own, more generalized account of his Sixth Symphony well before he suffered any of the three specific "blows of fate" that Alma suggested after the fact: "It is the cruelty which has been inflicted on me," Mahler explained to his friend Alfred Roller, "and the pain I have had to suffer!" He arranged the finale's incursions of fate with an uncanny sense of dramatic timing. Yet their arbitrary one-step decrease in relative loudness—the three blows marked *fortississimo*, *fortissimo*, and *fortissimo*, respectively—sets them apart from Hollywood-style apocalypse and managed to confuse that theatrical pragmatist Richard Strauss.

Mahler begins his finale with two grand, drawn-out gestures that forecast in microcosm the sweeping battles of the whole movement—and demonstrate how those battles will be lost. This opening swoop has a rhythmically loose, recitative-like makeup that distinguishes it from the previous music in the symphony. Like the opening of Mahler's Fifth, the introduction of the Sixth's finale begins rather ambiguously and in the "wrong" key, ascends in a hopeful motion toward air and light, but then plunges back earthward and ends lower and darker than it began. As if to keep reminding the listener of this dark prophecy, the introductory swoop will return three times: at the start of the development section (8:16), at the beginning of the recapitulation (17:08), and to initiate the coda (25:40). The upward flourish itself is an astonishing invention, somewhat Disneyesque in its fictive character and elaborate coloration. With its dramatic spanning of several registers, it demonstrates yet again our three strata of subterranean, terrestrial, and extraterrestrial. We begin with a single, low thunk on basses, cellos, harps, bass drum, horns, and contrabassoons; a sweep upward on the celesta; a quiet chord in the woodwinds; an expectant tremolo in the strings; and then the expansive, two-octave, striving theme on the first violins. This secretive, conflicted orchestral texture suddenly snaps into clarity for the finale's first statement of the major-minor seal in the brass (at 0:18), the stuttering motto rhythm in the timpani (itself symbolizing an imposition of fate), and lastly the strings' four-octave descent into the depths of cellos and basses.

Having heard these introductory prophecies, we enter a shadowy, rarefied, and almost directionless passage with further bass descents and fragmentary motives (the dotted-rhythm figure in the tuba, passed off to bass clarinet and horns; the fluttering tremolo chords in the violas). The shadows deepen at 1:30, when the bells enter to create an ambient "white noise" with the harps and celesta, while the horns pick up the dotted rhythm and take it in a slightly more hopeful direction. At 2:22, three trumpets quickly slide up more than an octave and then down again—a gesture that sounds like a scream from some wounded beast, especially as Leonard Bernstein interpreted it in his 1988 Vienna Philharmonic recording. The symphonic argument manages to collect itself for the first time since the opening and returns to the initial tempo. At 2:34, one piece falls into place in the piecemeal windup that will lead to the first hammerblow: this stepping-stone is the C minor chorale in brass and winds that will henceforth indicate gathering tensions. The motto rhythm returns in the timpani with major-minor seal in the trumpets (at 3:24), but these lead only to more marking of time with sequential motions. At 4:03, the chorale returns, and at 4:30 it leads to C minor and precipitates the first crucial climax of the movement—which is then ominously squelched to make way for development of an anxious transitional figure in C minor.

The tempo picks up slightly for the main section of the movement (*Allegro energico*, starting at 5:00), which begins as a strangely awkward march in A minor set for full orchestra. This leads to a lengthy unsettled, development-like passage with propulsive rhythms. A new climax is dissipated quickly by a cymbal crash, and with disconcerting quickness we come to music of a different character: a stable D major passage of sunny pastoral material (starting at 7:14). Here the solo horn brings back the dotted idea heard earlier above cowbells and celesta. Sextuplets in the winds are perky-cheerful enough to suggest picnicking on red gingham tablecloths at the racetrack. The pastoral takes a rhapsodic turn when the harp enters and the violins pick up the melody (starting at 7:37). The proceedings take on a darker tinge when the anxious transitional figure comes back in the brass (at 7:58), and before we know it we're hearing the opening swoop, now in D minor, as a quick preface to the development section (starting at 8:16). The questing, leaping violin lines return, and then we're back in the otherworldly "white noise" of cowbells, harp, celesta, and string tremolos with the tuba and horns giving the quiet melodic tags. The return of the anxious transitional figure (at 9:27) is briefly offset by remnants of the pastoral music, but it leads inevitably to the rhapsodic material (with its swooping harps) and increasingly tense sequencing. All this functions as a drawn-out prolongation of A major—of the dominant key—which increases in tension the longer it awaits resolution to the D tonic.

That tension is furiously discharged with the first hammerblow at 11:44, dispatched *fortississimo* and with the winds trilling wildly and the horns raising their bells for visual and sonic effect. That stroke is followed by the major-minor seal in the horns, and the strings struggling in its wake. The music once again has no time to recover from disaster, and contradictory styles are thrown together pell-mell, auspicious as well as menacing. The paradisiacal or pastoral topic quickly returns (at 12:27), but is then pushed aside (at 13:10) for a fugue-like passage marked "Everything with brute strength" (*Alles mit roher Kraft*). This, too, is briefly undercut by a different style, this time marked by a reduced ensemble and the frantic time-keeping of the Rute striking the rim of the bass drum. At 14:09, the main section material returns, now in C major and "fiery" and self-confident in character, the melody focused in the oboes and clarinet and then in the violins. A turn to minor at 14:57 leads in the direction of the return of the chorale passage, and at 15:49 this begins the feared sequential windup to the next hammerblow.

This second hammerstroke hits at 16:13 and leaves the strings scrambling furiously and chaotically through scales. The opening swoop and recapitulation follow soon after (starting at 17:08). At this point, now that the various pieces are in place for the musical argument, we can do some summarizing and looking forward to what's in store. What we're hearing here as the finale moves forward is a strategic realignment of the relationship between the movement's two main recurring events: the opening swoop and the hammerblow. At its first statement, the opening swoop was timed to give the impression of leading into the "white noise" percussion music, while its later statements draw closer and closer to the high-tension opposite of those interludes: namely, the hammerblows themselves. In short, the roles of the material types are changing, and we end the finale with a hammerblow stymying the opening swoop, followed by disappearance of the pastoral material and indeed everything else. (To give the actual timings: the first time around, we have the swoop by itself at 0:00, leading into the "white noise" material at 1:30; in the second cycle we have the swoop at 8:16, leading even more directly into the "white noise" passage at 8:33 and remnants of the pastoral music at 9:48; in the third cycle, hammerblow one occurs at 11:44 and leads into the pastoral at 12:27 and the brute-strength fugato at 13:10; in the fourth cycle we have hammerblow two at 16:13, the swoop at 17:08, and "white noise" at 18:37; and, finally, in the fifth cycle the swoop occurs at 25:40 and hammerblow three at 26:00, followed only by the coda.)

If we focus on one decisive shift in the finale of Mahler's Sixth Symphony, it would have to be the ruthless way victory is almost stolen from the jaws of defeat in the recapitulation. This is the main dramatic crux in this long and highly conflicted movement: if there's a point where the tide could turn and benevolence and hope could seize control over the symphony, it would be in the recap. The return of the opening music seems at first to be just as dark as before. But then the "white noise" music (starting for the last time at 18:37) seems to brighten the mood gradually, and when the pastoral music returns in B-flat major with the melody on the oboe (starting at 19:45), it leads into a genteel drawing-room passage of solo strings. All this is promising. Indeed, the pastoral material works up to a climax in B-flat major (starting at 20:32) that's so splendid and conclusive it would seem to dispel all forces of darkness. And when the tempo picks up shortly after, we seem to be in the final sprint to victory. But our hard-won success starts to come off the rails with the fateful motto rhythm (at 21:05), and then at 21:35 the postponed return of the main material in A minor—with bits of the pastoral material now thrown callously into minor in the trumpet. As if this setting-up and dashing of hopes weren't cruel enough, the composer sets up one last possibility of—well, if not victory, then at least reconciliation. This occurs in the outro conclusion of the recap (starting at 24:08), which begins ambiguously but leads (at 24:56) into a hopeful A major rendering of the pastoral music, with the melody now in the trombones.

So things have—yet again—gone from hopeless to less hopeless. A final, decisive showdown is promised when the coda begins with the opening swoop (at 25:39) and the hammer is nowhere to be seen. But then a third blow does arrive as a cruel afterthought, delivering its final mercy stroke and basically ending the symphony's structure at 26:00 (and presumably "felling the hero" at the same time, to use Alma's interpretation). Now is a good time to mention that Mahler himself deleted this third hammerstroke in his later performances, and the 1963 critical edition also drops it. Alma claimed he removed the third iteration out of superstition, but conductor and composer Pierre Boulez says the deletion was a musical improvement. "The third time," Boulez said in an interview with Wolfgang Schaufler, "it's the introduction which comes back, and the hammer has nothing to do with this reprise, this repetition, from the very beginning. And so there is no hammer there." As I argue, however, the last hammerblow having "nothing to do with this reprise" is in fact the point: the coup de grâce arrives when we least expect it, when we seem at last to be out of harm's way. In putting the last stroke where he did, Mahler managed (at least before his revision) to inflect tragedy with arbitrariness, and thereby make his musical representation all the more believable. Given its arbitrary placement, the third hammerstroke looks ahead to philosopher Hannah Arendt's famous line about "the banality of evil."

When the descent from the third hammerblow finishes and the coda arrives (at 26:21), there is a remarkable change in the music's tone and coloration: all the strings and higher woodwinds have disappeared, and any sense of emotional life has been drained from the music. This passage, with its muted colors, seems to be sounding from a distant and unfamiliar place. We begin with the tuba and a quartet of trombones sharing a leaden, even funereal idea over a quiet timpani roll. The dotted rhythm here might remind us of the pastoral theme and its cheerful tone, now a distant memory. Lower winds enter to provide some body to the ensemble sound, then disappear. The remaining horns and trombones all gravitate slowly to a low A. Finally the double basses and cellos, doubled by the lowest woodwinds, deliver the final word. The A is held quietly, *morendo*. And then the denouement: a *fortissimo* crash on the full orchestra, the major-minor seal sounding now without its major chord, the timpani throwing out a last utterance of the motto rhythm, and lastly a single quiet pizzicato chord that sounds like a door being gently closed.

Critics have resorted to the twin ideas of death and interment in discussing Mahler's coda, no doubt because of its sound—all that remains of the orchestra here are the timpanist and trombonists—as well as the radical sense of inevitability in that single, pitiless *fortissimo* chord. Constantin Floros calls the coda "a Requiem" and an "epitaph." Musicologist and critic Richard Osborne offered an unforgettable hearing of the passage as a kind of funeral in sound: "The solemn plucked A which ushers in the coda, and its paler reiteration at the very end of the symphony, is like a clod of earth falling on Mahler's coffin, as four trombones—so many pallbearers—grind out a slow fugato, and the major triad soaring minorward—the Symphony's central musical symbol—is heard for the very last time." As Osborne would have it, the claustrophobia of the Sixth, implied by its suffocating march rhythms and hammerstrokes, has by the coda enclosed us utterly—indeed, to the dark and narrow confines of a coffin. If we can allow ourselves to hear the end of the Sixth as precisely as Osborne suggests—the sonic drama of one's own obsequies heard from inside one's own casket—then we could even hear the last brass notes (at 27:55) as our final contact with humanity and our coming face-to-face with what Edgar Allan Poe called the "unseen but palpable presence of the Conqueror Worm." And then the cataclysmic crash and trailing snare drum as our panicked realization of abandonment and death, our horrific meeting with eternity.

Mahler didn't know Poe's work, but he did share Poe's fear of being buried alive. Mahler specified that his heart be perforated before interment, showing a dread for what Poe called this "appalling and intolerable horror from which the most daring imagination must recoil." Poe detailed that horror in his story "The Premature Burial" (1844), but the narrative of his "Cask of Amontillado" (1846) relates more closely to the finale of Mahler's Sixth. In both the short story and the symphony, it's the naked singularity—the simple and non-negotiable oneness—of death's arrival that proves most horrifying. In "Cask of Amontillado," the peevish Montresor lures his drunk acquaintance Fortunato into the catacombs. He suddenly chains Fortunato to the masonry, and it's only when Montresor starts to wall him in with bricks and mortar that the victim realizes in a sickened panic that he will meet eternity alone, in the fetid blackness. Fortunato will die with no comforts, homilies, or morals. In my comparison, Mahler's final crash is like Fortunato's last, pitiful exclamation: "For the love of God, Montresor!" And his single, quiet closing pizzicato stroke is almost barbaric—compare the three thumps marking the protagonist's death at the end of Strauss's *Don Juan*—in that it utterly excludes assurances or second thoughts.

To interpret Mahler's music in terms of such specific narratives or visual images is to limit it, and the composer himself would have said such wordy explicitness restricts rather than develops the listener's relation with the music. By that line of thinking, it would be better to give the last word to a nonmusician friend of Mahler's who—perhaps feeling like a Fortunato who had been tempted into mortal danger not by sherry, but by the promise of music—had a startling reaction to the Sixth Symphony, again recorded for posterity by Alfred Roller. Stammering through tears after first hearing the piece, the friend asked in disbelief, "How can a man of your goodness express so much harshness and cruelty?"

8

SYMPHONY NO. 7

A Mahler Serenade

The Seventh is the odd man out among Mahler's symphonies, the opus that presents no particular gimmick, rationale, or worldview. At one point, the symphony had the nickname "The Song of the Night" (*Das Lied der Nacht*), a subtitle that didn't originate with Mahler, and one that has fallen out of use. We know from the composer's letters and from secondhand accounts that he did hear the first four movements as vaguely relating to topics of night and darkness—a premise that becomes concrete in the two *Nachtmusik* ("night music") movements, and in his score indication "shadowy" (*schattenhaft*) for the third movement. But then night and dark are mutable or even indefinable things, just as this is an elusive and dark-hued piece of music—hanging together more as a set of shadowy dreams than as cumulative storytelling.

Along these lines, writers—including myself—usually end up framing the Seventh Symphony in negative terms, defining it by what it isn't. And then there's the matter of the Seventh's neglect among conductors and orchestras. Though it had some success at its premiere in 1908, this remains one of Mahler's least played scores. Deryck Cooke called it the "Cinderella" among the symphonies. If the Seventh is the least cohesive of his scores, we should remember that it came right after the tight and highly symphonic Sixth, and could not have walked the same paths. By this reckoning, the Seventh is both an answer to the Sixth and an attempt to leave it behind: where the Sixth is tense and tersely argued, the Seventh is sprawling and digressive; while the Sixth glowers and deliberates, the Seventh diverts. (If there is any consistency in Mahler, it's through such paired contrasts: we've seen it before with the Third and Fourth Symphonies.) Be that as it may, this substantial piece—just as long in timespan as the Second, Sixth, and Eighth Symphonies, if not the Third or Ninth—is certainly about something more far-reaching than nocturnal darkness.

With its circuitous five movements and its guitars and gentle horn summonings, the Seventh is less a symphony than it is a serenade. It shows Mahler connecting with traditions of occasional music—and with the old leisure spaces of nocturnal pleasure gardens, spacious dining rooms, and upper-class entertainment quarters. In terms of structure, a rule of thumb was that the symphony as a generic tradition comprised four movements, while the serenade had five or more. (Mahler's lengthy sonata-form first movement and sizable rondo finale don't rule out serenade comparisons for the Seventh, since Mozart's larger Salzburg serenades had comparably weighty beginnings and endings and could be almost as long.) Mozart's famous *Eine kleine Nachtmusik* originally had five movements, and most of the serenades of the later eighteenth century had five, six, seven, or even eight. It's against this occasional-music backdrop that the nocturnal colorings and five-movement layout of Mahler's Seventh make the most historical sense.

(1) *Langsam – Allegro risoluto, ma non troppo* (Slowly—Quickly and decisively, but not too much) (21 minutes)
(2) *Nachtmusik I. Allegro moderato* (Night Music I. Moderately quickly) (17 minutes)
(3) *Scherzo. Schattenhaft* (Scherzo. Shadowy) (10 minutes)
(4) *Nachtmusik II. Andante amoroso* (Night Music II. Amorously and at a walking tempo) (15 minutes)
(5) *Rondo – finale* (Rondo—finale) (18 minutes)

Heard as a serenade, Mahler's Seventh Symphony reflects a neoclassical approach—but one very different from the formal nostalgia we heard in the Sixth Symphony. The Sixth follows the standard four-movement format of the classical Austro-German symphony in its tried-and-true pattern of forging ahead through the different symphonic facets of sonata first movement, slow movement, scherzo, and then finale. But a five-movement work like Mahler's Seventh is more digressive—

and in that way, more suggestive of night's pleasures and irrationalities than the rational sensibilities of day. Night is a time for leisure, wandering, and lovemaking, and is therefore a time for guitars, serenading under balconies, and a certain impulsiveness, oblivion, and tranquility overall.

Night, cloaking humanity under intimacy and darkness, is also a time for focused listening. As part of its nocturnal theme, the Seventh Symphony sports many ear-catching novelties in instrumentation. These become particularly audible, and beautiful, in the chamber-music scoring of the two *Nachtmusik* movements. Among the instruments here are the mandolin and guitar, used to evocative serenade-like effect in the fourth movement. Carried over from the Sixth Symphony to the second and fifth movements of the Seventh are the cowbells and *Rute*. The two stringed instruments suggest privilege and leisure, and the two percussion carryovers delight the ears with their washes of gentle and perplexing noise. The two *Nachtmusik* movements are colored by the unique combination of mandolin and cowbells, along with prominent passages for the horn and solo violin. The first two tend to create quite a bit of picturesque noise—their pluckings and clankings throw tone colors in all directions. This overall sonic landscape makes for an evocative aural picture of the flotsam and jetsam of nighttime, and the white noise of dreams. Adding to the effect is the unusual amount of repetition in the *Nachtmusik* movements, which gives them a strophic or songlike quality.

A serenade involves less of a musical-structural argument than a symphony does, for the simple reason that serenades weren't written for focused, concert hall listening. So it comes as no surprise that symphonically minded critics have found fault with Mahler's second and fourth movements, the two "night musics." In an interview with Wolfgang Schaufler, conductor and composer Esa-Pekka Salonen complained of "unbelievably banal, painfully banal moments" in "Nachtmusik I." Actually, it would be easier to accuse Mahler of a threadbare musical argument here. But his loosely assembled last movement has come in for heavier criticism for that very reason, particularly given the general supposition that finales become the key movements in symphonies starting with middle-period Beethoven. Beethoven's Ninth, Brahms's First, and Bruckner's Fifth developed a culture where the symphony finale became both culminative and cumulative—a custom that Mahler continued in his own First, Second, Fifth, and Sixth. And yet Deryck Cooke spoke of the last movement of Mahler's Seventh as a "patchwork" finale, while Henry-Louis de la Grange described it as "perhaps the most bizarre and disconcerting piece Mahler ever wrote." Regarding the interpretive and structural difficulties that attend the piece as a whole, veteran conductor Valery Gergiev has confessed—in an interview with Michael McManus—to sleepless nights trying to devise a viable overall interpretative strategy. These various negative verdicts suggest the Seventh isn't so much unusual by choice as it is an example of compositional indecision, awkwardness, or even failure.

The old popular "Song of the Night" subtitle is accurate in one sense, in that Mahler began the Seventh Symphony with the two shorter *Nachtmusik* movements (movements that became the second and fourth of the completed work). Mahler's "Nachtmusik" title is actually a pun, since it can indicate a "night piece" in the sense of rustling nocturnal ephemera, and can also signify a serenade—in the sense of occasional, light music for nightly entertainments, as epitomized by Mozart's *Eine kleine Nachtmusik*. Mahler's two movements embody both these night-music types, encompassing the nocturnal buzzes and rustlings one hears in nature as well as the lighthearted serenading that represents a fair evening's outdoor entertainment. There is a luxurious and unhurried character to these movements, contrasting utterly with anything in the Sixth Symphony—making it all the more remarkable that Mahler wrote them while working on the finale of the Sixth. The *Nachtmusik* movements amble along as if they had all the time in the world. According to Alma, her husband was occupied with "Eichendorff-ish visions" while composing the second *Nachtmusik*, and entertained images of "murmuring springs and German romanticism." She goes on to say that Mahler was specifically occupied with parts of Joseph von Eichendorff's story in verse *Das Marmorbild* (*The Marble Statue*, 1819). To judge from the water reference, Alma could have been thinking of these specific lines from *Marmorbild*, given here in translation:

> Over the glistening peaks,
> It comes from afar like a greeting,
> The treetops are whispering,
> As if they wished to kiss.

> How gentle he is, how fair!
> Voices sound across the night,
> Sing secretly of the image
> Ah, how glad the wake I keep!
>
> Do not murmur so loudly, you springs!
> You know it is not yet morning,
> Into the moonlight's balmy waves,
> I sink my silent joy and sufferings.

It is fitting for us to begin discussing the Seventh Symphony here, where Mahler might have begun writing: with "voices sound[ing] across the night" in the two *Nachtmusik* movements. The Seventh differs from the Fifth and Sixth in having no true Adagio movement, no "still center" since there is no tightly wound existential crisis that would demand it—no consistently forceful Allegro movements to be offset. The *Nachtmusik* movements have aspects of both intermezzo and slow movement, and yet sound like rondos in the way they return insistently to familiar material. They also gain meaning from the way they flank the third-movement scherzo—a peculiar and macabre essay in triple meter that by virtue of its central position tethers the symphony to an irresolvable enigma. The primary intrigue of the Seventh Symphony lies with the strange relationship between the two *Nachtmusik* movements and the scherzo they enclose. The occasional-music pair combine acerbic humor with descriptive music, continual shifts in tone color and major/minor modality, and an overall marchlike character. These shifts in character and timbre range from obtuse to subtle. In "Nachtmusik I," the symmetrical structure matters less than the constant juxtaposition and rejuxtaposition of different kinds of music that the form allows. The shimmering, whimsical instrumental hues become a cloak for what is at its essence a "walking piece" set to a steady, sauntering tempo.

In the *Nachtmusik* movements, we hear nocturnal trickles and jangles within changing soundscapes. These are aural diaries of nocturnal strolls, with the ears open to all manner of novel sounds that daylight would have banished or obscured. Mahler was finishing the Sixth Symphony when he started these two scenic interludes, so there are carryovers from that work—including the cowbells and the major-minor seal (now heard within the descending gestures that start, end, and mark the center of the second movement, with the minor turns appearing at 1:28, 9:06, and 16:13). The writing for solo instruments makes this pair of movements immediately appealing: this is chamber music that demands a beautiful sound and interpretive poise. True to the history of the serenade, Mahler places special emphasis on wind solos. In the serenades and cassations and nocturnes of the eighteenth century, wind instruments were at the forefront in creating sounds that could carry outdoors. And so we begin the second movement with horn players evoking a sense of space, possibly in illustration of Eichendorff's "voices sound[ing] across the night." In this beginning, two horns converse at a distance, the first marked "calling" (*rufend*) and the second instrument—muted and therefore sounding more distant—marked "answering" (*antwortend*). The space the horns open up is then consecrated by trickling water: Eichendorff's murmuring springs are simulated by the oboe, clarinet, English horn, and bassoon. The introduction concludes at 1:30, and then the main section begins. Here we immediately hear another point of contrast with the tragic Sixth Symphony, namely a sense of playfulness. The major-minor seal is used as a simple punctuation, divorced from its earlier fateful symbolism. Offbeat accents and misplaced trills appear as splotches of mordant humor. We hear the clatter of *col legno* strings, and (starting at 2:21) an overlong passage where the basses and contrabassoon have their self-importance punctured by the high-handed timpanist.

All this suggests a composer enjoying himself after oppressive labors on the Fifth and Sixth Symphonies. The leisurely diversions continue in the second movement's two trio sections, which introduce A-flat major and C minor into a movement based in C major. The first (starting at 3:56) is a striding passage that focuses on the strings. It gives way (at 5:37) to a more cadaverous style initiated by the opening horn duet and tinged with the secretive timbres of cowbells, tam-tam, stopped horns, and low woodwinds. An abridged reprise of the main section follows (starting at 6:45), before the mournful second trio begins with quivering oboes (at 7:44). This trio is interrupted by an abbreviated return of the "murmuring springs" introduction (starting at 8:42), after which (at 9:13) the trio music combines two solo cellos in a plaintive duet—introducing a kind of heartsick tango into Eichendorff's landscape. Humor quickly returns as we approach the expected retransition back to the main material. Here Mahler sets up a gradual decrescendo (beginning at 10:14) through disparate registers of lower strings, flute, and harp. What should be a direct springboard back to the tonic key and the original material becomes instead a teasing disengagement: the closer we get to the reprise, the more unlikely it becomes. Indeed, the gradual decrescendo seems to flaunt its own control over our expectations. Finally, the trumpet and the (extremely frustrated) clarinet take matters into their own hands and heave us into the long-expected return of the main section (starting at 10:51).

The second *Nachtmusik* (the symphony's fourth movement, marked "amorously and at a walking tempo") shows the more romantic side of night. The movement begins with a sumptuous yawn on the first violin, a gesture that suggests a languorous form of oblivion. Eichendorff makes no mention of luxury divans fitted out in silk damask, but Mahler's opening phrase puts us in mind of one—with our serenaded paramour lounging on top. The violin line stretches up an octave, F to F, and then descends the scale before horn and oboe dovetail with the melody and the guitar and mandolin enter with their accompanimental twinklings. They twang their way through the movement as part of a reduced orchestra, suggesting a serenade under the lover's balcony. More generally, the remaining melodic gestures are just as luxuriant and solicitous, even tender, as the opening solo. This presents night as an escape into amorous oblivion, perhaps in reference to the lovers' nocturnal tryst in act 2 of Wagner's *Tristan und Isolde*. Wagner, working under the influence of the poet Novalis and the philosopher Arthur Schopenhauer, portrayed evening as a deep escape from the spitefulness, envy, vanity, and deviousness of day. In the most celebrated line from Wagner's act 2, the two lovers entreat the evening: "Descend, / O Night of Love, / Grant oblivion / that I may live" ("O sink hernieder, / Nacht der Liebe, / gib Vergessen, / dass ich lebe"). Here the night becomes a haven not only from daylight, but also from consciousness and from time itself.

Romantic though it may be, this second *Nachtmusik* manages a robust sense of humor. There are moments of buffoonery where Mahler seems to poke fun at his own dark moods. A mock transition section sequences upward with dogged insistence (beginning at 2:11, marked "very graciously") and distances us worryingly from the tonic F major. At 2:53 we arrive at A minor for what promises to be a lengthy stay—and an anguished one, to judge from the stabbing As marking the beat. But before we know it, a quick crescendo and a trill on flutes and violins pull us out of the darkness and back toward some amiable mandolining in F major. By now, misfortune intruding on romance has become an ongoing joke, played repeatedly at our expense, and the movement continues to take time from its nocturnal lovemaking to toy with our anxieties. Nervous upward sequencing keeps leading in various and sundry harmonic directions. An anxious violin solo provides some new melodic interest starting at 3:27. We're back in minor-key note-stabbing mode at 3:53 and again at 5:34, but are soon liberated from it. At 6:03, and again at 6:25, the worries are centered on G-flat minor, but a B-flat major trio section enters to save the day. Anxiety manages to rear its head yet again at 7:40, to the tune of E-flat minor and now with a sobbing idea on the G string of the solo violin paired with mandolin plunks.

The air is cleared of jesting by a luxurious passage that suggests the orchestration of Richard Strauss, and at 9:29 we're safely back in the opening material. But Mahler saves his biggest prank till last. The anxious rising sequence starts up one last time with the guitar entrance at 11:34 and works its way into the mother of all dead-end climaxes—though major chords never disappear from view. All this much-ado-about-nothing is over by 12:10, at which point we're back yet again in the comforts of the ambling first theme. All is forgotten when the end of the movement brings an intoxicating spray of quiet and sublime colors: a clarinet trills over three muted solo violas; the horns, cellos, and double basses calmly locate the tonic F major; the clarinet brightens the picture by calmly raising its trilled note to the major third, at which point low flutes chime in with their silvery, feathery balm for the ears; and the guitar strums two last chords just as the clarinet quietly and slowly unwinds its blissful trill. These last moments must be, whether literally or figuratively, a musical rendering of "the moonlight's balmy waves" described by Eichendorff.

RECONCILING THE SYMPHONY WITH THINGS NOCTURNAL

Having produced these two lovely spin-offs from the gloomy Sixth Symphony, Mahler put pen to paper again the following summer to write the more obviously symphonic first, third, and fifth movements of the

Seventh. The opening movement that resulted, the longest and the most weighty of the five, is an odd amalgam of the serious and the grotesque. At the same time, it has sensuous byways that hint at the earlier *Nachtmusik* movements, and at the Sixth Symphony itself. The first movement is primarily a stern march, centered in B minor with an introduction in E minor, and sounds like a fusion of the march styles that begin the Fifth and Sixth Symphonies. But we don't hear a steady march until three minutes into the movement, when the introduction gives way to the Allegro section. In this Adagio introduction, the shuddering rhythm is in fact hard to parse in the ear and the memory, and it's even difficult to make out the 4/4 meter until the melody enters.

Instrumentation counts among the most original aspects of this music. Most remarkably, Mahler used a rare instrument for the introductory melody: the tenor horn. This is an outlier from wind bands, confusingly called an alto horn in the United States, and is less like a French horn than a smaller euphonium. Its sound is just as tough to place as the accompanimental rhythm Mahler has put beneath it. The ear wants to ask: is it a trombone? a Wagner tuba? The tone could be described as darkly mysterious, if also rather clearer than a trombone in the same register—it is a bellowing sound that harks back to the imposing "voice of Pan" on solo trombone in the first movement of the Third Symphony. (That solo represented the pagan god of the wilderness in the Third, and Mahler similarly heard the tenor horn as a voice of nature in his Seventh: he likened it to the roar of a stag that's gotten itself mired out in the forest.) The sound is fascinatingly diversified when this theme comes back along with the rest of the opening. At that point, it is divided among a trio of low instruments, their dusky timbres typifying the nocturnal tone of the Seventh Symphony: we hear the melody shared between double bass (starting at 13:06), trombones, and lastly the original tenor horn (starting at 13:26). There follows a captivating face-off of not-quite-the-same low brass sounds when the tenor horn and trombone have a duet, punctuated by the tuba as yet another bass voice (offering two notes starting at 14:07). After such a pageant of timbral gloom, the high doubled violins come in as a *fortissimo* corrective (at 14:20)—though any promise of a brightening is negated right away by an iteration of the major-minor seal.

But the most important aspect of the first movement of the Seventh, something that joins with the formal unorthodoxies to make listening a challenge, is its lack of definite themes. Mahler has replaced distinct melodies that arrive and depart with sets of intervals that, when reshuffled and put in a different key, become sort-of new sets of intervals. This intervallic (as opposed to thematic) thinking allows a linear and cumulative, twenty-minute symphonic structure with no verbatim repetition of any material until near the end. It's difficult to think of a Mahler first movement that develops a more powerful sense of unimpeded momentum from first bar to last, despite the prevalence of measured tempos. In the first movement of the Fifth Symphony, he had juxtaposed fast and slow tempos without reconciling them. That provocative approach required the follow-up of additional music in similar style, and so the second movement—also in duple meter, and at about the same tempo—was a necessary supplement. In the first movement of the Sixth Symphony, march time was brought to bear on a sonata structure of Mozartian clarity and simplicity, ending in an exciting coda section. In the first movement of the Seventh, Mahler devises a structure of increasing weight and impact, and manages a linear effect by integrating tempo changes, inventing thematic transformations, and reorganizing listener expectations in a sonata form. So the end becomes both exciting and highly symphonic when, after dominant preparation, we arrive at the coda section (at 20:15) and with it a slowed-down and aggrandized version of the first march theme in the tonic E minor.

Even by Mahler's standards, this first movement challenges symphonic expectations. It starts and ends as a march, but fails to divulge whether it is processional music for the military, for the church, or for some other ritual. The movement begins with an Adagio introduction that sounds both too tentative and too thematic to be introductory. And then we have a clear thematic return even before the introduction can finish and before the main section of the movement can start with its faster tempo. Here the opening melody comes back in three trombones (starting at 2:02), followed by a repeat of the introductory rhythm, and (at 2:21) a return of the tenor horn with its mysterious bellow. Finally, a decisive arrival on B in the bass line (at 3:00) allows a launch into the Allegro con fuoco tempo and the actual main section of the movement, now with an up-tempo march theme given to the horns. In symphonic first movements more generally, it's the slow introduction's job to ask questions and the job of the ensuing faster music to answer them. In this case, however, the questions actually start with the quicker tempo.

Among these questions is the relationship between this new Allegro theme and the introductory theme (as heard at the start in the tenor horn). Does their close intervallic relationship make them the same theme, just played at different tempos and with slightly different rhythm, or is the transformation enough to make them two themes?

The second theme of the Seventh's first movement (the music starting at 7:39), with the main melodic interest in the doubled first and second violins, doesn't contrast by being ideally lyrical, but by being impulsive—in effect, march-resistant—much as "Alma's theme" was in the Sixth. Mahler's marking here in the Seventh is "with great impetus" (*mit großem Schwung*), while the corresponding Sixth Symphony theme was marked "with impetus" (*schwungvoll*). As we already heard in that "Alma" theme of the Sixth Symphony, Mahler's second subjects—harmonically unstable, and reaching and striving across wide intervals—are sounding more and more like transitions rather than themes. (This will become even more marked in Pater Profundus's music in part 2 of the Eighth Symphony and especially in the convoluted, even tortured, second theme in the first movement of the Ninth.) Mahler effects even more continuity by fragmenting these new theme areas with newly intricate textures and other rhythmic instabilities. Expressive impulsiveness is suggested in the Seventh's second theme not through a tempo slowdown, but through a series of fermatas (hold signs, which Mahler says specify in this instance "a trifling extension of the note values").

Mahler's skill in moving this long movement forward becomes even clearer in the development section. Traditionally, the development in a sonata symphony movement would be preceded by a closing theme that is harmonically stable and ends with a firm cadence. And then the development itself, after it starts with some version of the first or second theme, would steadily increase in cumulative tension right up until the recapitulation. Mahler overturns all these expectations, leaving the listener constantly guessing where we are and in what kind of structure. What he does is lead directly and without pause into the development (starting at 6:22), where we have a restatement of the march theme variant. The repetition is literal enough to suggest we might already have started the recap. But then, conversely, Mahler begins to loosen the tension of the argument considerably, and makes new changes in material. Just where the symphonic vehicle should be moving forward with greater intensity, the air is being let out of the tires. The second theme reappears (starting at 6:59) in B minor, but with the texture more varied and complex. With some tension returning, we reach (starting at 8:09) a restatement of the march theme variant.

But then there's a cymbal crash and at 8:30 it sounds like we've segued into a different movement altogether in lieu of a real second theme, much like Russian composer Alexander Scriabin was doing at about this same time in his Second and Third Symphonies. Mahler slows the tempo and the harmony in this new passage, slows down for the first time since the opening bars, with our point of rest now being E-flat major. Dueting trumpets, joined by the solo flute, suggest some of the same nocturnal spaces that will be invoked in the next movement. And the trumpets are supported underneath by "solemn" (*feierlich*) chords in winds and strings, a transformation of transitional material from earlier in the movement. The beat is still regular, but more fluid phrases now carry the music across the bar lines. Staying in line with the nocturnal theme of the symphony, writers have related the passage to something dark or mystical: Constantin Floros likens this music to a "religious vision."

The march tries to reassert itself, but at 10:00 the dueting trumpets and mystical tremolos return—now with added clarinet and other woodwinds. A figure in rising fourth intervals leads into a beautifully voiced chorale-like progression in the brass ("blown very softly," *sehr weich geblasen*), and then (at 11:26) an even greater change, like a curtain being drawn aside. The colors suddenly brighten for a radiant opening to B major ("very broad," *sehr breit*), complete with harp cascades, trilling winds, and rocking string figures. Floros says this "might be considered the center of the movement." Such an impression is underlined by the typically "aspiring" Mahler string line that unfolds in first and second violins, reaching rhapsodically for higher heights while doubling each other in octaves and unisons. Henry-Louis de la Grange points to "the ecstatic melody and sumptuous orchestral texture of its accompaniment" and calls the passage "one of the rare episodes in Mahler's music to radiate the sensuality of Strauss." At the peak of their implorings, the violins repeat a fifth leap up followed by a step down—a high-register figure that Mahler would reuse at a similarly ecstatic moment in part 2 of the Eighth Symphony, at the point where Margarete says her beloved Faust "is still dazzled by the new daylight!" as his remains are borne heavenward.

Structurally speaking, this passage is a big, decked-out dominant preparation—a grand springboard for our return to the original material in the tonic E minor. After such a long and showy windup, when the recap finally materializes (starting at 12:59) it's disturbing in its underhandedness. We hear the introductory theme reorchestrated, as mentioned above—meekly distributed between basses and trombone. The recap of earlier material extends to the march theme (starting at 15:28), and a pause reengages the movement's duality between darkness and light by suddenly plunging us back into E major. This surprise recapitulation, reminding us that we are in fact still in a lengthy E minor march movement, takes off pretty much as expected. The march variant reappears (starting at 16:23) with cymbal replacing the earlier tambourine rolls, but still acting like a second theme. Mahler works up considerable excitement through imaginative variation of the march material. The second theme sounds quite different when it reenters at 17:25, now emphasizing downward motion and now pared back to minimal instrumentation with a focus on the violins and horns, with the trumpet recalling the tag that opened the introductory theme. To give the last segment of the recapitulation a suitably conclusive send-off, over a gradual slowdown the march theme returns in its most recognizable form yet (starting at 18:35), before the trombones and tuba work more and more clearly into the material from the movement's introductory tenor horn solo. The summational coda is introduced by a cadence to the tonic E minor (at 20:15) and a return to the original tempo.

Arnold Schoenberg was thrilled when he heard the new Seventh Symphony—as well he should have been, since the first movement is so similar in its cliff-edged, all-inclusive formal strategy to Schoenberg's own just-completed Chamber Symphony no. 1, op. 9. But Mahler went one better than Schoenberg: not only did he write follow-ups for this ostensibly self-sufficient first movement, he made those follow-ups somehow indispensable. At the same time, the opening movement has a dramatic, heavy-weather style that neither seems necessary to the overall ruse of this symphony nor implicated in the style of the remaining movements. (Unless we allow that the movement's dramatic weight could be involved in the "cry of affronted nature" aspect that Mahler himself heard in the tenor horn solo.) Whatever the first movement of the Seventh might have needed by way of a musical answer, the following four movements don't provide it. The first *Nachtmusik* is just a scenic interlude within the overall plan. The second *Nachtmusik* has the same function, though it does predict some of the rhetoric we'll hear in the finale. Mahler's third movement, the *schattenhaft* scherzo in D minor, poses a more substantial riddle.

WALTZING IN A MADHOUSE AND GREETING THE DAY

Mahler's scherzo calls for a wild simile. The movement holds some of his most inscrutable writing, but also the most consistently danceable dance music that he penned. I would compare this scherzo to waltzing in a madhouse, while clarifying that the comparison comes from a film and not from firsthand experience. The filmmaker in question is, of course, Ken Russell. Yet again, Russell manages to "explain" a quizzical aspect of Mahler's work through a cinematic vision presented as pseudobiography. Russell used the scherzo of the Seventh Symphony to underscore the scene in his film *Mahler* (starting at 1:04:30) where Mahler and his sister Justine visit the composer Hugo Wolf, an old university friend who is now confined to an asylum. Wolf is suffering the delusion that he is Emperor Franz Joseph, and Mahler and Justine play along while the "emperor" determines whether the young conductor is right for the Vienna Court Opera directorship. In the middle of the conversation, as a test of their facility with things Viennese, Wolf suddenly orders his two visitors to waltz. And waltz they do, accompanied by the strains of the Seventh Symphony scherzo as they spin through the asylum's elegant grounds—past Baroque fountains, topiaries, and manicured French gardens.

Mahler's scherzo is nocturnal in its colorings and mad in its syntax. We need to ask just what he could have meant with the score indication "shadowy" (*schattenhaft*). How can an orchestra play a piece of music in a shadowlike or mysterious manner? Perhaps by emphasizing darkness and changeability of expression, two aspects that overlap with constructions of insanity. At the start of the movement, he assembles the waltz in the reverse direction than a Johann Strauss would have taken: from the bottom up, starting deceptively on beat three rather than one, methodically assembling the oom-pah-pah accompaniment before any melody has a chance to appear. And while Strauss usually begins a waltz from the top down, by emphasizing luminous and beautiful tones, Mahler begins at the bottom by sketching in this oom-pah-pah with the darkest, lowest colors: the timpani, cellos, and basses. Falling next into place in Mahler's waltz is the middle of the texture: the violins and lower woodwinds. A semblance of melody finally appears (at 0:42) in the uneasy mixture of flutes and high oboes—the tune, marked "lamenting" (*klagend*), sounding quite unwaltz-like in the event. These dancers are weeping as they move. The violins finally do their duty and make the waltz melody more respectable (at 0:59), but then (at 1:14) they disrupt the ballroom elegance with ill-mannered slides. Texture and sense then collapse, and the waltz is forced to start its reassembly a second time.

We could also say Mahler is engaging in defamiliarization, a process the dictionary defines as "taking something familiar and rendering it unfamiliar by drawing attention to the language or formal devices used." The movement's sheer insistence on 3/4 time makes one think of the children's defamiliarization game of taking an everyday word and reiterating it over and over until it loses all meaning. Some of Mahler's lower winds and brass protest the coercion and loss of sense (for instance, the flatulent tuba at 1:26), while the oboes scream out like pained animals at one spot in the first windup of the waltz (at 0:29). Cadences become forced, even violent, as if the music desperately wants to stop: hear the *fortississimo* timpani hit and tuba slide at 5:32, and the extreme *fffff* snap of the cellos and basses at 7:27. The fluctuation between major and minor keys makes coherence seem more and more improbable: in the fairly innocent trio section (which starts in D major at 3:12), the quick and inexplicable turn to minor (D minor at 3:25) sours the cheer of the dance as if it were milk suddenly gone rancid. In Mahler's grandest statement of the waltz tune (starting at 7:47, marked "wild"), the paired trombones and tuba are along for the ride at the bottom of the texture, giving the music a circuslike sound. But even this big-top rendering can't resist the earthward pull, and the music falls into minor at 7:55. Finally, at the very end, the waltz extinguishes itself through the odd combination of a timpani stroke with a pizzicato chord on violas—the music commits a D major waltz suicide.

The last movement of Mahler's Seventh Symphony practices defamiliarization of a different kind. Having brushed aside all matters nocturnal, this rondo finale bursts in in uninhibited celebration of the day. It's a comic rondo with a vengeance: it makes no pretense of developing anything, and instead states the opening music a total of eight times in a movement that comprises only eighteen minutes (the ritornello clearly occurring, whole or in part, at 0:11, 2:38, 3:45, 5:38, 8:17, 8:51, 11:00, and 15:59). Mahler isn't emphasizing this thematic material because he thinks it original. It is a barely concealed paraphrase of the music representing the Mastersingers' arrival in Wagner's opera *Die Meistersinger von Nürnberg*—and the music Wagner uses to open the prelude to act 1. A number of scholars have pointed out a relation to Mahler's nocturnal scenario for the Seventh, in that Wagner ends his act 2 with expectant evening and starts act 3 with the breaking of St. John's Day. Coincident with Midsummer's Day and Hans Sachs's name day, *Johannistag* is the date of the Mastersingers' arrival for the long-anticipated Nuremberg singing competition, to be followed by the wedding of the heroine, Eva, with the competition winner, Walther. To end a long evening in the theater, the opera's final act arrives as a festive morning, and the final scene arrives full of good-natured punchlines and happy endings. In his score, Wagner specifies a setting "in an open meadow" that exhibits "gay decorations" and hosts "much merry-making."

Mahler was deeply in thrall to *Die Meistersinger*, conducting it a total of forty-six times over his career and extolling it to Natalie Bauer-Lechner in 1899 as the perfect comic piece and even a peak of German art more broadly, a work that "almost makes everything else seem worthless and superfluous." But again, even as Mahler dutifully imitates the Nuremberg singers' arrival, we hear him defamiliarizing a beloved musical institution. His ritornello theme is a near-imitation of the singers' arrival for the contest in the scene described above. Among the separable musical parts of this theme, units that are to be stated, shuffled, and reused, are the fanfare-like cry in horns and trumpets (first heard starting at 0:11), the scalewise ascent in the melody set against the scalewise descent in the bass (starting at 0:28), and then the closing section with its cadential timpani (starting at 0:44). These will all recur again and again in a mélange of high spirits. At the start of his final scene, Wagner has the Mastersingers arrive for the *Johannistag* celebrations in the stage setting described above, amidst great pomp and hoopla. In his repurposing of this music for his ritornello, Mahler makes the

Mastersingers seem more and more off-kilter by having them make their grand entrance no fewer than eight times.

A formal analysis seems beside the point with such a movement, a movement that asks the listener to stop listening and just join the revelries. Simply keeping the party moving betrays a certain compositional prowess: only at one point (starting at 12:05) are Hans Sachs and company encouraged to sound calm and lyrical. It would be more in the spirit of the proceedings to talk about Mahler's orchestrational means for keeping the flood of sound fresh and vibrant: for instance, the pairing of bass drum and cymbal with a minor key at 4:34, or the slightly bizarre appearance of flutter-tonguing in the flutes at 10:18. The importance of the timpani to this movement, even as a solo presence, raises questions of playing and orchestral balances. In her book on the Seventh Symphony, musicologist Anna Stoll Knecht has suggested that Mahler actually merged his love of Wagner's opera with an interest in the circus, which as a touring act was becoming widely popular in Mahler's time in Vienna and in the American east. Mahler's finale certainly coarsens the broad humor of the Wagner comedy, taking it more in the direction of humans doing pratfalls and tumbles and elephants doing hoof-handstands. As Stoll Knecht indicates, the sheer proliferation and collision of sounds in Mahler's music could suggest a three-ring extravaganza—multiple spectacles that compete for our attention. Brass and percussion come to the fore, as do carousel sounds. At one point (11:15), the music actually cadences and stops in its tracks with a circusy "ta-dah!" flourish.

But this finale still must function somehow in performance as the capstone of Mahler's eighty-minute symphony. Veteran conductor Valery Gergiev has found the Seventh Symphony a special interpretive task: how to bring its loose ends together despite a dominating first movement and a last movement that offers more sonic spectacle than symphonic argument? As quoted by Michael McManus, Gergiev outlines the challenges thus:

> [The Seventh] has a strange, unusual shape, which is the key to it. You have to work very hard at shaping it. This is not really about tempi—it's more about working with light and shadow and different levels of power. It is essential not to tire your public too early. You start to feel exhausted yourself and worry about the orchestra too.

> The first movement is so immense you really need to know what to do with the second movement.

Gergiev touches on the Seventh's problems of proportion and formal strategy, much as I discuss them above: namely, the symphony's unusual overall setup of five movements that fail to "speak" to each other, not so much in terms of a lack of shared thematic material but in terms of uncoordinated weights, moods, and messages. By Gergiev's understanding, the Seventh ends up becoming a kind of interpretive black box: the piece either works as a musical entity in performance or it doesn't, and by the time the conductor knows how those efforts are panning out, the hand has been played and it's too late to do anything about the outcome. For Gergiev, that crux—that point of reckoning—occurs early in the finale, and once that movement has begun the performance has already succeeded or failed. The challenge that comes to bear at that place is "to feel [the symphony] is moving, becoming more and more focused on one goal, namely the end of the piece." Mahler constructs such a sense of focus by self-consciously bringing back material from the first movement (starting at 13:31), in a grand attempt to round off the symphony as a whole. When the first movement's march idea returns with a sense of triumph in D-flat major (staring at 14:47, then shifting back to the tonic C major at 15:11), we appreciate just how closely related the various themes of the first movement are. For Gergiev, though, that would seem secondary to the conductor's ability to mold and pace the work as a whole. "For me the terrible thought was that we might play, say, the first five or eight minutes of the final movement and I would find myself thinking, 'it's over, it didn't work again.'"

9

SYMPHONY NO. 8

His Gift to the Nation

Mahler rarely suffered from self-doubt. But when he left Vienna for the Carinthian countryside for his annual composing holiday in June 1906, he must have felt some apprehension. He had just conducted the premiere of his Sixth Symphony to general confusion; and the previous year he had difficulties drafting the Seventh, a work he would have trouble selling to a publisher. As if to defy such misgivings, or just to distance himself from the "cruel" negativity of the Sixth, the Eighth Symphony—the work Mahler produced that summer—became his one categorically positive statement. This is his most public and most affirmative composition. When Mahler conducted the premiere in Munich in September 1910, before an audience including royalty and the crème de la crème of European artists and intellectuals, the ovation lasted twenty minutes. Thomas Mann was moved to call the composer of the Eighth an embodiment of "the most serious and sacred artistic will of our time"; author Stefan Zweig called it a signal event in European cultural history before the two wars; and famed soprano Lilli Lehmann said the music caused her to "give way to emotion which I could not control." The young Viennese composer Alban Berg, known for his mild manner, gave himself over more fully to such emotion, becoming so excited at the Viennese premiere that he almost got himself thrown out of the hall.

When Mahler described the Eighth as "a gift to the whole nation," he must have meant the pan-German nation, of which he counted himself a citizen—born a German-speaking Bohemian, associating with nationalists in his University of Vienna days, and proving himself in the highest musical stations in the Austro-Hungarian Empire. His description makes clear the function of this majestic composition: it was a public address, a musical-spiritual inculcation from someone who had willed his way into the cultural heart of the nation. Still, one wonders just how much of the Eighth's nationalism was real and how much was wishful thinking. Mahler must have been the very picture of an assimilated Jew in Viennese eyes, a success story from the provinces, but now a resurgent anti-Semitism marked the same pan-German sentiment that he aspired to. Despite his outward success, Mahler continued to identify with the Wandering Jew, Ahasver, Christendom's timeless refugee. And here we come to the first paradoxes of the Eighth Symphony: that its proud public face hides deep-rooted uncertainties, and its communal and open nature makes it his least characteristic composition. Perhaps what we choose to hear as its grandness is really the effortful sound of its composer's personal overcoming.

There are provocative contradictions in the composition itself. Mahler initially conceived his symphony as a choral work starting with the ninth-century Pentecost hymn "Veni Creator Spiritus," and going on to a movement in representation of the Christian idea of *caritas*, and finally ending with a hymn relating to "the Birth of Eros" or "Creation through Eros," which itself represents an urge toward human creativity. Thus, the symphony was conceived as a disquisition into the types of love—charity as well as erotic love or, better said, striving and romantic love. His symphony would open with "Veni Creator Spiritus": the Pentecostal hymn addressed to the Holy Spirit, to the energizing drive in and of the faithful. Mahler quickly settled on Goethe's great poetic drama *Faust* as follow-up to the hymn, and at one point considered closing his symphony with the *Walpurgisnacht* scene from *Faust*, the wild orgy-celebration of witches—thus moving outrageously from the sacred to the profane. But he settled on two parts for the Eighth Symphony, equally weighty but different in all other respects:

1. Part 1: Hymn – "Veni Creator Spiritus" ("Come, Holy Ghost—Creator Spirit") (24 minutes)

2. Part 2: Closing scene from Goethe's *Faust* (55 minutes)

The national aspect of the Eighth Symphony is clear in one regard: Mahler's work concerns itself with the spiritual welfare of its hearers, and to that end bestrides the two pillars of Catholic devotion and the most enduring and nurturing figure in German literary history. Mahler had told Natalie Bauer-Lechner that as a principle he avoided setting masterpiece texts, but he went back on that statement with the Eighth—following through on his long-held ambition to put Goethe to music. When we take a broader view, however, Mahler's juxtapositions remain provocative even after he dropped the witches of his initial *Walpurgisnacht* conception: in the Eighth Symphony, Church Latin confronts the vernacular, an ancient liturgical text is juxtaposed with a high-Romantic allegory by a self-declared non-Christian, and a declarative prayer scripture prefaces a non-narrated drama. The thread holding the two parts together is their common message of redemption through external inspiration, and in that sense Mahler's Eighth can be considered a kind of counterpart to Beethoven's Ninth, which in itself represents a musical "gift to the nation." As a sort of answer to Beethoven's "Ode to Joy," here we have Mahler's ode to creativity: creativity as manifest (in part 1) in the divine energy granted to humankind by the Holy Spirit, and as manifest (in part 2) in the "Eternal Feminine" (*Das Ewige-Weibliche*), as both instigator of and haven for all male striving.

I've mentioned the Eighth's clarity, decisiveness, and forthright power. When Mahler described the symphony as his "gift to the whole nation," a remarkable description after the bemusement caused by Symphonies nos. 4 through 6, he was inadvertently pointing to the fact that the Eighth is his least characteristic work. Indeed, the symphony stands quite unique unto itself. (In a letter to the conductor Willem Mengelberg that Donald Mitchell first published, the composer described his symphony as "so peculiar in content and form that it is really impossible to write anything about it.") It is the most accessible of Mahler's compositions, and the most immediately impressive: the least ironic and least questioning of his creations, the least daring in terms of dissonance and chromaticism, suffering no insurmountable crises or "blows of fate" and, most surprisingly of all, encompassing no ambivalence or parody. "In the other works everything still was subjective tragedy," Mahler said to the critic Richard Specht, "but this one is a source of great joy." The sanguine turn was short-lived, since the work following the Eighth—*Das Lied von der Erde*—would return to "subjective tragedy" in its most extreme form, exploring deepest introspection and loneliness.

The national quality of the Eighth is also manifest in its sheer magnitude, and in the composer's newly simplified approach to verbal language. The so-called "Symphony of a Thousand" is Mahler's largest work in terms of ensemble, requiring a large orchestra as well as two full mixed choirs, a children's choir, and eight vocal soloists. (In one caricature, he conducts a very crowded performance and asks the intendant why there's no one in the audience, to which he hears the reply that his personnel demands have left no one behind to buy tickets.) As for the second difference, this is his first symphony to be sung more or less from beginning to end, indicating the new relationship between words and music that Mahler was discovering for himself.

A NEW RELATIONSHIP WITH WORDS

The symphony, as the quintessential absolute music genre in the nineteenth century, exemplified the power that instrumental composition was thought to have in and of itself, without recourse to the banal precision of words. We've seen how Mahler involved himself with that idea of music's possible abstractness in his newly "modern" symphonies—starting with the Fifth, where he left behind both his early tone-painting aspirations and the lyricism of the folk poetry collection *Des Knaben Wunderhorn*. As he himself made clear in his comments to Richard Specht, the Eighth takes a different direction altogether:

> Can you conceive of a symphony that would be sung from beginning to end? Until now I have always used the word and the human voice in explanatory fashion, as a short cut, as a factor of atmosphere, in order to say, with the terse accuracy which words alone make possible, something that, in purely symphonic terms, could be only expressed at enormous length. But here, the singing voice becomes at the same time an instrument; the whole first movement is strictly bound by symphonic form and is at the same time sung throughout . . . The most beautiful instrument of all is guided to its destina-

> tion—and not as mere sound, for the human voice is also the carrier of poetic thought.

So the Eighth marks a big change in Mahler's approach to musical expression, the voice, and the word. He tells us that sung words had served in his earlier symphonies only as a way of nudging the music toward concreteness and directness of expression, while the Eighth Symphony begins and ends with words, making verbal explicitness the meat of the matter. Another way of saying this is that the Eighth, as preoccupied with telling as it is with expressing, is more like an oratorio than a symphony in the classical Austro-German tradition. Or to put this yet another way, because of the continuous presence of words, the Eighth is the only Mahler symphony where the absolute-or-programmatic question becomes irrelevant.

And yet, for the two parts of his vocal Eighth Symphony Mahler settled on two texts where nothing really happens. His decision to yoke two contrasting texts together—a Christian hymn in Latin from the ninth century, and the denouement of an artful German tragedy from the early nineteenth—makes more sense when we see how these texts avoid storytelling, details of the physical world, and everyday human emotions. Or to put it another way, Mahler chose what could be called two post-conflict texts. He enters Goethe's drama only after the fight over Faust's soul; his hymn to the Holy Spirit doesn't invoke despair or enemies, and doesn't lament or give thanks as we find in the Psalms. The themes of Mahler's Eighth are spiritual, perhaps even metaphysical, rather than narrative. He developed a two-part structure to straddle the dualities of *caritas* and *eros*, sacred and profane, classical and vernacular, and churchly praise and theatrical drama. Musically speaking, the Eighth couches those various dualities in an opposition between a mostly chordal or homophonic first part and a considerably more wandering, excursive, and multisectioned second part.

The first movement of the Eighth might be simple and tightly constructed, but at the same time the structure isn't obvious or classically modeled. Counterbalancing the symphony's simple duality aspect are its nearly infinite combinations of human voices into duets, trios, quartets, double choirs, and triple choirs. And then there is the malleable, ever-changing, intricate system of themes. If Mahler's rhythms and phrasing in the Eighth were stipulated by the words he set, his broader conception of themes—as audible things and as components of musical structure—was already becoming more and more dynamic, even incoherent, from the Fifth Symphony onward. Second themes of his first movements start sounding more like agitated transitions than the rational, harmonically anchored, songful themes common to the classical symphonic repertory. They have stopped singing and anchoring the structure, and started bolting at the gate. The second theme of the first movement of the Sixth Symphony, the *schwungvoll* ("with impetus") idea in the string instruments that Alma claimed was penned in representation of her, spans two octaves and veers back and forth between passionate, long-limned arcs and obsessive, small-scale repetitions. When he brings back this theme to close the first movement of the Sixth, he slows it down and focuses on the repetitiveness in order to give it the necessary conclusive coda character.

In the Eighth Symphony, a comparison of thematic elements in part 1 and part 2 will show not only Mahler's organic unity of structure, but also the changeability of themes and the importance of the words as inspirations for specific musical material. To begin at the beginning: after the annunciatory organ sounds promulgating the tonic key of E-flat major, we hear the "Veni Creator" theme for the first time, blazoned out by the two mixed choruses. The first two intervals of this, a falling fourth followed by a rising seventh (here, E♭–B♭–A♭), will become a critical element in all parts of the symphony—Mahler obsesses over it at climax points and varies it. This theme must have been directly inspired by the words "Veni (Veni) Creator Spiritus," making the symphony as a whole a rumination on the ideas of creativity and grace. The most emphatic expression of praise in the entire work, the "Glory be to God the father" that ends the first movement, arrives (at 21:56) with the children's chorus singing "Gloria, Gloria, Patri Domino" to a falling sixth and ascending octave. The two soprano soloists then immediately pick this up, narrowing the intervals to the fourth-seventh version of the figure, and singing it *fortissimo* and in high-flying unison. Shortly thereafter, the timpanists pick up the fourth-seventh "Veni Creator" figure from the voices and the brass, beating it out *forte* (at 22:51) and once again in unison—thereby turning the drums into an emphatic solo instrument. Jumping ahead to part 2, the very last idea we hear at the end of the symphony, ringing out *fortissimo* from offstage trumpets and trombones, is the same "Veni Creator" figure—here with the rising seventh expanded out exultantly to an ascending octave.

In the tightly packed first movement of the Eighth Symphony, Mahler makes something eventful out of the arrivals of the three major theme areas, and he closely roots those shifts of mood and dramatic intent in details of the text. The very simplicity of the opening—two introductory blasts in the organ, statement of the first phrase in the chorus, answer in the brass, concluding phrase in the chorus combined with orchestra—signals the work's almost pedantic directness. It's really only the odd shift of pulse already in the third and fourth measures—the music shunting from its usual four beats to five over the words "Veni Creator," at 0:03–0:05—that hurls the music forward and promises future intrigues. The first obvious change arrives with the "Imple superna gratia" theme ("Fill with celestial grace / Those hearts which you created"), which starts (at 1:27) in the distant key of D-flat major. This is the traditional contrasting second theme, and there are many points of contrast with the first theme: where the "Veni Creator" theme was all striving and emphatic leaps, the "Imple superna" theme is mostly stepwise motion; where "Veni Creator" was voiced by both choirs *fortissimo* and mostly in unisons and octaves, "Imple superna" is intoned by single voices, starting with the first soprano soloist, under the direction *dolce espressivo* ("sweetly and expressively"). This is followed (at 4:22) by the return of the "Veni Creator" theme, reemphasizing the urgency of the prayer, and then by an orchestral passage that pulls us for the first time in a somber direction, toward the key of D minor.

What happens here (starting at 5:17) to cast such a pall over the symphony and its message of "great joy"? The answer is the word "infirma," meaning fragility and infirmity. We realize that while the spirit is eager to embrace the Holy Ghost, the flesh is weak: as the hymn phrases it, "the weaknesses of our body" ("Infirma nostri corporis") stand in need of the Holy Spirit's "strengthening with lasting vigor" ("Virtute firmans perpeti"). "Infirma" literally means "weakness," though it could also connote mortality or, as de la Grange interpreted it, cynicism in a cynical age, by which he must have meant the inability or unwillingness to believe. Clearly, fear follows frailty—or at least does so in the absence of divine guidance. Making the arrival of this "Infirma nostri corporis" theme all the more poignant is the knowledge that the third or closing theme of a sonata movement is supposed to be a point of stabilization and entrenchment, while here the whole praise project is called into question. The "Infirma nostri" material dovetails with loose and fleeting violin figures, including an eight-bar solo. A serene cadence is set up in anticipation of the tonic E-flat major, but is interrupted (at 7:32) by a sudden hush and a scampering orchestral passage (marking the start of the development section). This music pits high against low, the tolling bell against variants of the "Veni Creator" theme, piercing flutes and oboes against scurrying cello and double bass figures. The effect is manic, discharging the rhythmic energy that has been building up over the hymnlike aspect of the movement to this point. The music turns (at 8:55) to a minor key—C-sharp minor—and the vocal soloists enter, obsessing over "infirma" yet again.

We then come across the event that Mahler himself thought key to the whole symphony, and especially to the relationship between the two parts. This is the breakthrough to the bright key of E major (as introduced by the horns at 11:59) and the jubilant double chorus pronouncement of "Accende lumen sensibus" ("Light the light of our senses," with the musicians instructed to perform "with sudden impetus"). This is the text's most fervent plea for absolution, and the key of E major offers the same kind of sudden, transfigurative transposition up by a half step that we heard in the Fifth Symphony and elsewhere: the keys of B-flat or A-flat would have been premeditated and decisive, whereas the motion from E-flat to E (or, for that matter, the movement from E-flat to D-flat, as we heard at "Imple superna gratia") is more like sidestepping impulsively into unknown territory, an exercise of spirit rather than mind. The harmonic shift and the new material at "Accende lumen sensibus" set the movement off in a dash of optimism and lead into a wild fugue on two themes. This just as quickly turns dark (at 13:06), arriving at an apprehensive E minor at "Hostem repellas longius" ("May You drive the enemy far from us," a savage episode that caught the ear of Igor Stravinsky), and then suddenly turning bright yet again. A long dominant pedal is followed by crashed cymbals, and then (at the recapitulation, beginning at 16:48) we've arrived back at the familiar ground of "Veni Creator Spiritus" with its harmonic stability and pealing brass. The theme is given complete, but the recap is shortened compared with the exposition. The concluding doxology of praise begins—the children's chorus first intoning "Gloria Patri Domino" at 21:56, in the key of D-flat major. The music steps finally back to the tonic of E-flat major, and the movement concludes with insistent, bell-like repetitions of "In saeculorum secula" ("forever and ever," starting at 23:15) before the last, sustained invocation of "Gloria Patri." Because of all the movement's sidesteps away from the tonic toward out-of-the-way keys like D-flat and E, not to mention the several grand cadences that were set up only to be conspicuously evaded, the final A♭–E♭ cadence sounds massively conclusive. In each and every performance, it is so grandly definitive yet somehow so abrupt that the ensuing silence seems even more thunderous than the music that preceded it.

EXPRESSING THE INEXPRESSIBLE IN GOETHE

The second part of the Eighth Symphony, Mahler's setting of the final scene from Goethe's great drama *Faust*, stands as the longest uninterrupted span of music he ever penned, longer in itself than any symphony before Beethoven's Ninth and longer even than Mahler's own First and Fourth Symphonies. Those who call this protracted section operatic ignore the fact that Goethe's text is so heavily allegorical—symbolic and ritualistic rather than narrative or lyric—that it's clearly a work to be read from the page and entertained in the mind's eye rather than realized in a theater. *Faust* poses insurmountable challenges for any stage director crazy enough to take it on, and Mahler doesn't try to make it theatrical. Consider Pater Profundus's soliloquy:

> As the rocky chasm at my feet
> On the deep abyss weighs at rest,
> As a thousand gleaming streams flow
> To the terrible plunge of the flood's foam,
> As with its own great strength
> The trunk is born up into the air –
> So is almighty Love
> That forms all, preserves all.

Goethe meant this as a spur to the individual imagination and not to anyone's concrete visual sense. Therefore, no one could write opera to such stuff—at least opera that's meant to function onstage. (When Charles Gounod wrote his opera *Faust*, the most popular musical-theater adaptation of the story, he and his librettist did the opposite of

Mahler and restricted themselves entirely to the dramatic narrative of Goethe's part 1.)

Goethe's *Faust* is a drama in verse about striving and grace and redemption, but the summary conclusions stop there. The overall narrative is largely irrelevant to this final scene, but I'll summarize it here because we should understand what Mahler elected to omit and where he begins. Faust is a scholar who finds himself unfulfilled in his insatiable desire for knowledge and makes a pact with Satan's helper Mephistopheles, who then confronts him with many temptations. Faust promises in a blood-drawn wager that he will die and surrender his soul if Mephisto can produce an enticement that makes him wish time to stand still. (Goethe was deeply troubled by the acceleration of human affairs that had started with the Industrial Revolution.) Mephisto presents Faust with drink, youth, riches, and ultimately the selfless and virginal love of Margarete. The young woman inadvertently kills her mother with a sleeping draught, introduced so she can spend the night with Faust; she then becomes pregnant with his child before seeing her brother killed by Faust in a duel. Driven to despair, she loses her reason, drowns her child, is imprisoned, and then is condemned to death on the gallows. At the end of *Faust*, part 1, Margarete refuses Faust's offer of freedom and thus seals his guilt.

The five acts of part 2 leave Faust's romance with Margarete behind and follow his adventures across nations, millennia, lovers, and phantasmatic scenarios. Here he leaves behind domestic drama for involvement in warfare, governmental collusion, and dubious business dealings. He advises the monarch of the Holy Roman Empire in reforms that save the nation's economy. In Goethe's act 4, Mephisto's demons help the emperor fend off an attack from a rival, and Faust is further endeared to the power and administration of the kingdom. In act 5, we find the aging Faust performing a land reclamation project with property given him by the emperor. When his administrative impatience leads to the death of a peasant couple—Mephisto, entrusted with the task of getting them to vacate their land, simply burns their house down—Faust ponders the impact of his relentless strivings, and he then promptly dies. Mephisto gloatingly comes to claim his prize. But he is pedophilically distracted by the angels who have also arrived for Faust's soul and, further intoxicated by the rose petals they've strewn, he loses his quarry—it is the angels who finally take Faust away, proclaiming, "He who strives on and lives to strive / Can earn redemption still."

Mahler dealt with none of these events, limiting himself instead to the redemption parable at the very end of Goethe's drama. Tellingly, he restricts himself to the part of the drama where Faust isn't mentioned: he enters *Faust* just after the denouement involving Faust's death and Mephisto's failure. Among the huge challenges of staging *Faust* is the question of how the main character should be represented in this final scene, a culmination of a drama that bears his name but a tableau where Faust is neither alive, nor a spirit in the Christian sense, nor a set of mortal remains in the atheistic sense. In this final scene Faust is only referenced as "he." He no longer has a name, and therefore ceases to be an individuality, as indeed is true of his moral foil Margarete: "Una Poenitentium (once called Gretchen)" speaks of her lover's return with the plain but tender words "The one I early loved, / No more troubled, / Comes back." Faust in this final scene has become a nameless "entelechy," or the actualization of potential, the kind of individual life force that Aristotle theorized centuries before Christ in his treatise *On the Soul* (*De anima*). Faust has become pure spirit, and his passage heavenward is negotiated by a host of penitents and saints as they perform a kind of dialogue of soliloquies while ascending. The lower regions are inhabited by male voices, and as we go higher the women's and children's voices dominate. The exception is Doctor Marianus, residing "in the highest, purest cell"—the tenor penitent, devoted to the Holy Mother as his name indicates, who delivers the last prayer to the Mater Gloriosa before the final edifying chorus.

Mahler himself contrasted his own setting of Goethe's final scene with "all the sugary, weak ways it has so far been done"—by which he must have meant the settings by Schumann and Liszt, and a rendering by the Belgian composer Eduard Lassen that he conducted in the later 1880s. Besides the overall sense of crescendo and climax, Mahler's suffusive thematic representations prevent his part 2 from being merely "sugary" or "weak." Representative leitmotifs are shared across the two parts of the symphony, thus straddling sacred and profane, churchly and theatrical, classical and vernacular. In one example among many, at the first appearance of the Mater Gloriosa in part 2 ("Mater Gloriosa hovers into view," Mahler writes in the score), he brings back the "Accende lumen sensibus" music from part 1 ("Kindle the light of our senses, infuse love in our hearts"); the implication, thematically and musically instilled, being that the figure who bestows grace (in part 2) is the same one who heals and rejuvenates (in part 1). The point is underlined later when the "Imple superna gratia" theme from part 1 ("Fill with celestial grace / Those hearts which you created") returns in part 2 at the transfigured Margarete's line, describing Faust as he ascends, "Scarcely perceiving the fresh life within him, / He already resembles the holy troop"; the implication is that fresh life ("das frische Leben") is a gift of grace, and indeed something granted by the *creator spiritus*. In short: divine grace is synonymous with creation, rejuvenation, and rebirth. Creation is equated even more directly with re-creation when the "Veni Creator" theme from part 1 comes back (at 41:01) in answer to Margarete's account of how her former lover now "breaks his way out of / All earthly bonds of his old husk" ("Sieh, wie er jedem Erdenbande / Der alten Hülle sich entrafft").

Mahler's part 2 jolts us out of silence with a quiet brush on the cymbal paired with a *sforzato* stroke on tremolo violins. What follows is an abstract, instrumental presentiment of place rather than description of action, a mise-en-scène using neither pictures nor words. This music has an act 2 quality to it, an anticipatory quietness after all the forceful and expository act 1 types of things we heard in part 1. As Mahler's score describes the scene, we are presented here with "Mountain Gorges, Forest, Cliff, Desert" as inhabited by "Holy Anchorites, scattered up the mountain-side, living in clefts of the rocks." These are saintly hermits, living—and waiting—midway between earth and heaven.

The ten-minute orchestral opening of part 2 counts as Mahler's strongest refutation of his own earlier idea, as he recounted it to Richard Sprecht, that "the human voice" has it over instruments as "a factor of atmosphere . . . with the terse accuracy which words alone make possible." Here orchestral instruments mime the vocal, texted music we will hear later. The opening measures are concisely evocative: violin tremolos give a backdrop to hesitant, sketched-in pizzicato figures in the lower strings and the plangent woodwind lines that prefigure the chorus's line "ehren geweihten Ort" ("Honor the hallowed spot"). Here at the start the cellos and basses mimic, with some elaboration, the chorus's opening line that will follow ten minutes later (starting at 10:03): "Forest, that sways here, / Rocks that weigh down on it, / Roots that cling, / Trunks dense on trunks." It's worth considering the very first word ("Waldung") for a moment, since it sets the rhythm and the tone for Mahler's opening of part 2. "Waldung" is actually a stilted, formal, and unexpected choice of word for "forest"—the plural "Wälder" would have been more conventional.

What does Mahler do with this intractable text, at the very opening of part 2 and when the chorus enters later with the actual words "Waldung, sie schwankt heran" ("Forest, that sways here")? He focuses on abstractions: rhythm, atmosphere, and the expectant quiet that hovers over this strange rock-hewn place. At the same time, he focuses on the weight and rhythm of the word "Waldung"—not illuminating its literal meaning but doting insistently on the hesitations, emphasizing and isolating the powerful and elemental nouns in Goethe's natural landscape: "Waldung," "Felsen," "Wurzeln," "Höhle," "Löwen" (forest, rocks, roots, cave, lions). And that backdrop plays out, even more abstractly, against a milieu of the classical four elements of earth, air, fire, and water. Mahler translates all this elementality—the creaking of weathered trees, the crash of waves against rock, the silent push of gravity, the muted footfalls of powerful creatures—into a severe and basic rhythmic language, and maintains it for four minutes against his backdrop of violin tremolos. And then, after one passionate "geweihte Ort" (at 4:08), the hushed and drawn-out expectation is suddenly over: the first violins furiously jump up a diminished ninth (at 6:33) and the orchestra prefigures Pater Profundus's impassioned line "As the rocky abyss at my feet / Reposes its weight on a deeper abyss" ("Wie Felsenabgrund mir zu Füssen / Auf tieferm Abgrund lastend ruht").

The ten-minute orchestral prelude to part 2 is a well-formed and complete musical statement unto itself. It seems a direct offshoot of the development in the first movement of the Seventh Symphony, with the same kind of extended violin tremolos, divided string section writing, and doubled melodic lines that keep reaching up to fulfillment in higher registers. It closes off by returning to the same atmosphere and material with which it opened, such that when the tenors and basses of chorus 1 finally do come in with the heavily prefigured "Waldung, sie schwankt heran," their entry (at 10:03) almost seems an afterthought—so there are singers after all? And then the chorus actually dispatches its material in less time than the orchestra had taken to anticipate it, which of course serves to make the listener eagerly anticipate anything and everything that follows.

While Mahler's orchestral introduction had been polarized between the insensible extremes of forested crags and assertive male penitents, the chorus keeps anticipating and prefiguring a place of deep serenity, namely Goethe's "hallowed spot, / Refuge of sacred love" ("geweihte Ort, / Heiligen Liebeshort"). The orchestra has already been anticipating this quietly ecstatic cadence many times up to the appearance of the penitents' music, as cloaked with the beautifully burnished sound of divided cellos, violas, and bassoons (clearly stated for the first time starting at 1:38)—every cadence of the opening to part 2 had in fact been looking forward to Goethe's "hallowed spot." When the altos, tenors, and basses do finally sing about the spot "of sacred love" about three and a half minutes after they start and one minute after the orchestra has given its last account of it, the spot is perfectly placed (at 13:10) before modulations and brighter tone colors pull us into Pater Ecstaticus's "ewige Wonnebrand" (starting at 13:58).

We join company with the men as we start our gradual ascent through the penitents. Among these, Pater Ecstaticus is the image of martyrdom, both wounded and ecstatic. He cries out (at 14:33), "Arrows, pierce me! / Lances, subdue me! / Clubs, shatter me! / Lightning, shoot through me! / So that everything trivial / May pass off in vapor / And the constant star may shine, / Nucleus of eternal Love!" Ecstaticus yearns for pain and death as ways of ridding himself of triviality; he desires escape from *das Nichtige*, a term belonging to theological history that might be better translated as "nothingness," or even "chaos" as a manifestation of evil and disbelief. So Ecstaticus's lines anticipate Goethe's conclusion at the very end of part 2, that "all that is transitory, is merely a likeness" ("Alles vergängliche, Ist nur ein Gleichnis"). And, indeed, his opening "ewige Wonnebrand" music will return at the chorus's final "Alles vergängliche" text. Following Ecstaticus, Pater Profundus appears (at 15:28) as the grandiloquent aspirer to motion, action, and tumult. He is the hammy dramatist who yearns for release and action, crying out in impulsive leaps of tenths, ninths, and octaves. He takes the "wild tumult" of the desolate, rocky penitents' landscape as "Love's messengers, who make known / The shaping force that ever flows around us. / May that force kindle my heart, as well, / Where now my spirit, confused and chilled, / Languishes in the confines of my dull senses / And the pain of tightly fastened fetters!"

Just who are these two people, with proper names and individual musical voices? Ecstaticus and Profundus are baritone and bass voices, figures who passionately desire enlightenment and redemption. Goethe introduces these two figures, review-like, as aspects of Faust's own personality as witnessed in *Faust*, part 1. Profundus is able to see and hear beyond the "wild tumult" of restive nature that surrounds him, surely a metaphor for all the preceding tragedies and tribulations. For example, he recalls Faust's massive project of reclaiming land from the sea when he hears (at 16:47) how "lovely in its rushing noise, / The mass of water leaps into the gulf, / As though ordained to irrigate the valley," and reperceives the torrent as an example of "Love's messengers, who make known / The shaping force that ever flows around us."

Profundus finishes his declaration, broadening emphatically at each mention of love ("Thus it is almighty Love," "These are Love's messengers"), before the orchestra rounds things off with reminders of Pater Ecstaticus's material (starting at 18:57). Mahler then begins our heavenward ascent in earnest by introducing the host of angels. As if answering Profundus's plea for God to "illumine my needy heart," the angelic altos and sopranos (choirs 1 and 2) enter Allegro deciso (at 19:37), "carrying Faust's immortal soul" and declaring victory with the words "Whoever constantly aspires and toils, / That man we can redeem!" This is the first time we hear the soprano voice in part 2, after spending some twenty minutes with the orchestra and the lower voices. The angels sing the all-important "Accende lumen sensibus" theme from part 1 as they explain the triumph of love over everything and pull the music up to B major, moving from a dark key to a brighter one. Trumpet tattoos celebrate the breakthrough. And then, in answer to the low-voiced and self-tormenting penitents, the boys' chorus enters, "circling around the loftiest peaks" (the Chorus of Blessed Boys, entering at 20:39, and sounding more like urchins than angels). The boys then start an accelerando with a round dance: "Clasp one another's hands / In a happy round-dance; / Bestir yourselves and add your song / Of sacred feelings." Sopranos and altos continue the dance as a "choir of younger angels." They recall (starting at 21:18) their teasing enticement of Mephisto: "Instead of the accustomed punishments of Hell / The spirits felt the pangs of love; / Even the old master of the Satans himself / Was pierced by sharp pain. / Shout for joy! We have succeeded." Here the reference to "evil ones" (*Böse*, 21:07) is remarkable for being quiet and suddenly in the minor: though victorious, these angels seem more empathetic than proud or spiteful, though teasing and streetwise cheekiness do seem in their repertoire. They are telling their story, and little four-note roulades help illustrate their mentions of deflecting and scattering: "wichen," "streuten," "flohen," and "trafen" (yielded, strewn, fled, encountered). The cries of "Shout for joy!" (at 21:48) help wave these shadows away, followed by exultant *fortissimo* brass.

The darkest moment of all arrives, confession-like, when "the More Perfect Angels" remind celebrants (starting at 21:38) of the sorrowful burden that is the human body: "There remains with us an earthly residue [*Erdenrest*] / Painful to bear, / And even if it were of asbestos, / It is not completely pure." (*Erdenrest* could also be translated as mortal "scraps," "remainders," or "relics"; it is a cousin to the burdensome triviality resented by Pater Ecstaticus.) The music suddenly hints at disillusionment, shifting downward to D minor (the same key heard in part 1 at "Infirma nostri corporis," "the weaknesses of our body"), the halting second chorus trailed by the solo violin. The somberness is fleeting: the Chorus of Blessed Boys dismisses the "earthly residue" as mere "tufts" (*Flocken*) when it accepts Faust's remains, exclaiming (at 25:18), "Happily we receive / This man in chrysalis form; / Thus we are assured / He will become an angel."

THE ETERNAL FEMININE

We reach the final male penitent, Doctor Marianus, sung by a tenor. He is the first mortal to have a view of heaven as opposed to a downward perspective on earth, rocks, trees, and mortality. From his station in "the loftiest, purest cell," Marianus has a clear vision of the Mater Gloriosa, "the Queen of Heaven," "Highest Mistress of the World." He enters in quasi-operatic fashion, intoning his first lines when the chorus of the Younger Angels and the Chorus of Blessed Boys are already underway. He quickly moves from theater to church, beginning a solo strophic hymn to the Mater Gloriosa. This has three strophes, their respective first lines being "Highest Mistress of the World" ("Höchste Herrscherin der Welt," 25:46), "That which a man's breast" ("Billige, was des Mannes Brust," 26:23), and "Indomitable is our courage" ("Unbezwinglich unser Mut," 26:58). The service continues with Marianus and choral altos, tenors, and basses all in half notes, in congregational hymn style. They now sing (starting at 28:19) in praise of "Virgin, pure in the finest sense, / Mother, worthy of honors, / Chosen Queen over us, / Equal to gods." The orchestra completes the prayer with the "Accende lumen sensibus" theme (starting at 29:25), followed by a flourish from the piano and two harps.

The supreme Mater Gloriosa then glides gently into view (at 29:57) just as we reach Goethe's highest and most rarefied feminine stratosphere. Her harmonic domain is a beatific E major, which we now arrive at by moving up a half step (a motion that Mahler habitually uses to suggest redemption or transfiguration). We've come to know E major as the key of the "Accende lumen sensibus" theme, and it's now home for the Mater Gloriosa's languid melody in lyrical unison violins (marked *schwebend*, "floating"). Mahler portrays the penitents' loving adoration for the Mater Gloriosa with a musical idiom that lies somewhere between caressing and prayerful. Some commentators, among them Theodor Adorno and the composer and author Robert Simpson, heard this section as kitsch. They were no doubt disheartened by both the instrumentation and the character of the theme. At this initial slow tempo, the Mater Gloriosa material has a supplicating rather than striving quality, and this very lack of pathos and aspiration can make it sound uncharacteristic.

The Mater Gloriosa is greeted by the men in chorus 2, who make a gentle plea for forgiving sinners (starting at 31:13, "You who can know no stain," "Dir, der Unberührbaren"). She is also hailed by the Chorus of Penitent Women ("Du schwebst zu Höhen"). Before she can appear vocally and announce Faust's salvation, we are diverted by a trio of three sanctified women—former lustful sinners who think back (starting at 33:11) to their individual salvations, and thereby shed light on Margarete's own tragic past. First is the Pharisee woman (the *Magna peccatrix*, the "great sinner") who came to wash Jesus's feet with her tears and then dry them with her hair, entering here in an innocent-sounding B major with a slightly faster version of the Mater Gloriosa theme. Next, appearing at 34:05, is the Samaritan woman who refreshed Jesus with water from the well and was then herself changed by his lesson on spiritual replenishment, cloaked here at first in the dark key of E-flat minor. She closes with a reference to the well's "pure and generous stream" flowing "superabundant, eternally bright" ("Überflüssig, ewig helle"), and Mahler links this water with the Holy Spirit by citing the "Accende lumen sensibus" theme (in the orchestra, starting at 35:14). Third and last, we hear from the once-lustful Mary of Egypt (entering at 35:27). Another mezzo, she enters in a supplicating minor key that brightens symbolically as she thinks back to her conversion.

After their individual turns, the three penitent women then come together at 36:34 in a final trio, singing a canon in three parts. This short but remarkable trio of women is the closest Mahler ever came to writing opera, insofar as he presents three distinct characters who interrelate within an ensemble. Their tone becomes conversational, different from the various grandiose supplications we've heard thus far. Conductor Michael Tilson Thomas (as quoted by Michael McManus) hears this trio as a saintly coffee klatsch, a vocal get-together that verges on the trivial but ends up being the quiet climax of the Eighth Symphony as a human drama. "Suddenly we are up a mountain," Tilson Thomas says, "at a tea party with these three martyr ladies . . . It's so charming and they are so enjoying one another's company." What is especially captivating here is Mahler's ability to fill the three women's songs with conversational nuance and local details of character, even though the texts tend to be obscure. After reminiscing, the three women jointly petition for Faust's salvation (starting at 37:08), a plea that is lovingly taken up by the former Margarete (at 38:08, in D major). Here she quickens the Mater Gloriosa theme until it becomes a playfully affectionate idea: but then Mahler's theme must have actually originated here, as a setting of Margarete's words "Neige, neige, / Du Ohnegleiche" ("Turn, turn, Oh unequaled one"). The Blessed Boys continue the rising plea on Faust's behalf (at 39:01), escorting us further upward in our heavenward ascent, chiming in with voices that are not only consecrated but also sexless.

After so much expectation and adoration, the Mater Gloriosa finally enters from a distance at 42:17. She advises the former Margarete: "Come! Raise yourself to higher spheres; When he becomes aware of you, he will follow" ("Komm! Hebe dich zu höhern Sphären! Wenn er dich ahnet, folgt er nach"). With permission now granted for Faust to be saved, Marianus reenters (at 43:38): speaking as the last individual voice in the Eighth Symphony, he urges all the penitents in commemoration to "Lift your eyes to the gaze of salvation, . . . So that in gratitude you can transform yourselves / And attain a blessed destiny!" ("Blicket auf zum Retterblick, . . . Euch zu seligem Geschick / Dankend umzuarten!" and again at 44:07 to a recollection of Ecstaticus's "ewige Wonnebrand" music). The penitents repeat his words, and at the prayerful exhortation "Göttin, bleibe gnädig" ("Goddess, be merciful") join Gloriosa in her key of E major.

After a short instrumental wind-down (harps, celesta, and pianos glimmering like the gentle wave crests on a receding tide before the tide turns and the deluge arrives), Mahler's inexorable crescendo from *pianississimo* to *fortississimo* presents the final moral of Goethe's *chorus mysticus*. The voices enter *pianississimo* and "like a breath" ("wie ein Hauch"), beginning (at 49:24) with the words "All that is transitory / Is merely a likeness" ("Alles Vergängliche / Ist nur ein Gleichnis") and ending with the promise that "The Eternal Feminine / Leads us aloft" ("*Das Ewig-Weibliche* / zieht uns hinan," starting at 51:04). This summational text is set to Ecstaticus's "ewige Wonnebrand" music and then to the quicker rendition of the Mater Gloriosa's theme (now closest to Marianus's "Göttin, bleibe gnädig"—"Goddess, be merciful"—heard back at 44:55). The chorus sings through this final text twice, tracing a huge cadential progression through to the symphony's last, utterly emphatic re-anchoring in the tonic of E-flat major. The orchestra largely disappears at the start of the second iteration of this text (at 52:58, the organ now emerging with great splendor), so that the power of human voices and words can be fully heard. The two choruses are joined here by the children's choir and all vocal soloists except the Mater Gloriosa, as supported only by the organ and its low pedals. The vocalists deliver the final, decisive descent from the dominant B-flat to the tonic E-flat at 53:45—tracing a homecoming rather than a voyage "aloft." With the final harmonic anchor reached, the instruments are free to give the last word. An offstage consort of four trumpets and three trombones enters at 53:45, expanding the symphony's sonic reach at this most dramatic moment. (A similar offstage group had sounded the Last Trump in the Second Symphony; here a set of repositioned brass provides a send-off rather than a summons.) Piano, timpani, and trombones re-emblazon the E♭–B♭–C motive as if it were a moral in itself, joined eventually by the trumpets, horns, tuba, and violins. The earthshaking last page of the symphony is driven home by the three-note motive in the offstage brass interleaved with *fortissimo* crashes on bass drum and tam-tam.

Did Mahler misrepresent Goethe in this final *chorus mysticus*? Though the non-Christian Goethe spent 265 lines of text ushering the former Faust upward, he didn't bother to give a single line indicating an arrival. But Mahler did nothing less than depict Faust's deliverance in his monumental, wordless postscript. Though the last scene of *Faust* can read like Catholic kitsch, when Mahler set it in the Eighth Symphony he did something uncharacteristic and utterly avoided parody. But then he considered Goethe a blessedly naïve thinker, incapable of irony. In a 1904 conversation recalled by family friend Erica Conrat, the composer described Goethe as a "beginner" in the best sense: "A beginner in a sphere which I shall never live to attain." But only an unspoiled soul could have elided Goethe's gaps and swept away his uncertainties, as Mahler did here. He even skimmed over the most basic ambiguity: the question of what Goethe really meant with his terse "Alles Vergängliche / Ist nur ein Gleichnis" ("All that is transitory / Is merely a likeness"). *Gleichnis* could be translated as "likeness," or quite differently as "parable" or "allegory." So Goethe's line could be a statement on the terrible trivialities of daily existence, the marginal things saints leave behind when they're absolved of their sins, or it could be an ironic comment on how ephemeral and thus futile all this stage-drama stuff is anyway. But then Mahler's answer to this question is so emphatic, posed as such a simplistic escalation from "transitory image" to "occurrence" (*Ereignis*), that the original question no longer matters.

In an oblique way, then, the Eighth Symphony tells us more about Mahler the person than do any of the ostensibly autobiographical symphonies. In her 1992 book *Faust: Theater of the World*, Jane K. Brown describes the end of Goethe's drama as a mirror that reflects the reader: "Whether we accept the triumphant tone of the final scene and affirm the natural order or whether we read it as an ironic and cynical assertion of the illusoriness of order depends on whether the Faustian or the Mephistophelean soul is stronger in us." By this account, Gustav Mahler was a Faustian through and through.

10

DAS LIED VON DER ERDE

Songs of Seclusion and Wandering

According to Mahler himself, his Eighth Symphony represented a "gift to the whole nation" and was the closest he came to writing a Mass. His next piece, by contrast, involves no such magnanimity or praise. *Das Lied von der Erde* (*The Song of the Earth*), the song-symphony for two singers and orchestra that he conceived in the summer of 1908, marks a sharp turn inward. It's an essay in introversion, an Asia-influenced study in loneliness and transience. *Das Lied* hovers at times between sound and silence, between sentience and oblivion, especially in the second and sixth movements. Its bittersweet melancholy is more subterranean than apparent, yet it imbues just about every phrase even when the lyric hints at brighter moods. It will hardly do to call this music "haunting." A better word would be "insinuative," in that *Das Lied von der Erde* implies more than it expresses, and doesn't communicate with listeners so much as it infuses them with sentiment. As musicologist Michael Kennedy has said, people don't exactly appreciate or come around to the piece in the usual sense—rather, they find that it "becomes part of one's metabolism."

Mahler wasn't a musical autobiographer in any strict sense, but there were certainly connections between his life and his works. Life's troubles gave his art impetus and at other times reined it in. At the same time, art also infiltrated and motivated daily living. Taken aback by the difficult reactions to the Sixth Symphony in May 1906, possibly including his own, Mahler was compelled the following month to set the texts on praise, creativity, and redemption that became the Eighth Symphony. But a more ruinous crisis was still around the corner: Maria Anna Mahler, the apple of her father's eye, died of diphtheria and scarlet fever the following summer. The loss of four-year-old "Putzi" in July 1907 left a deep mark on her father's musical and spiritual makeup. Mahler's friend and collaborator Alfred Roller said the tragedy even transformed Gustav's speaking voice: while his basic baritone range remained intact, that summer he lost his usual excursions into higher, brighter registers. For a habitually creative and expressive figure like Mahler, making music is much like speaking; and so it's to be expected that such a trauma would impact his compositional "voice" as much as it did his speaking voice.

Whatever happened in the summer of 1907 in biographical terms, it's Mahler's musical shift that is most pressing and real: the painful intimacy of *Das Lied* reveals those months to have been a crucible of the soul. And *Das Lied von der Erde* is all the more heartrending considering what came before. To listen to *Das Lied* after hearing the Eighth Symphony, even if you don't know the composer's biographical details, is to plunge from the heights of public affirmation to the depths of spiritual isolation. The "earth" in the title is a countermanding of "the blue, extended tract of Heaven" that Doctor Marianus sights toward the end of the Eighth Symphony. While the Eighth almost literally storms the heavens with its rhetorical power, *Das Lied von der Erde* can steal one's breath away with an understated—even banal—statement like "My heart is weary" ("Mein Herz ist müde," at 4:59 in the second movement). While the Eighth marshals a thousand musicians to accompany Faust's remains heavenward, *Das Lied* ultimately finds comfort in the earth's silent fertility.

As so often with Mahler, everything comes down to belief. To trace the successive creations of the Eighth and *Das Lied* is to hear a brusque rise and fall of faith—of the ability to believe, if not necessarily in God, then in *something*. This was a sharp juxtaposition of affirmation and negation that could only have been precipitated by spiritual collapse. The Putzi tragedy blighted Mahler's belief in deliverance through love, as he had enshrined it in the Eighth Symphony. Personal suffering pushed aside any such abstractions of guilt and salvation. Severed from his earlier systems of belief, Mahler was now open to themes of isolation and seeking. The spiritual impulses seen in every symphony except the Sixth and Seventh, they all involved motion upward: from the grave up toward life, upward from the earth toward heaven, or—as encapsulated in lines from Goethe's *Faust*—ascendant from "earthly residue" to a being "freed from every earthly bond . . . like the heavenly host." But upward passage was no longer feasible for Gustav Mahler in 1908, and some other avenue of deliverance had to be found.

It was an Eastern, non-Judeo-Christian source that offered a way out of the impasse. In spring 1908, less than a year after Putzi's death, a friend gave him *Die Chinesische Flöte* (*The Chinese Flute*), Hans Bethge's book of paraphrased Tang dynasty poetry. These writings are several times removed from their original Chinese sources: contemporary library records describe the volume as "a reworking of Chinese poetry based on prose translations in various languages." Whatever their provenance, the volume gave Mahler an alternative to Western notions of salvation and heaven, and thematicized diverse spiritual yearnings within a particular geographical and spiritual landscape. Mahler selected, adapted, and at the end conjoined two poems, and from these fashioned six movements:

1. "Das Trinklied vom Jammer der Erde" ("The Drinking Song of Earthly Woe") (9 minutes)
2. "Der Einsame im Herbst" ("The Lonely One in Autumn") (10 minutes)
3. "Von der Jugend" ("On Youth") (3 minutes)
4. "Von der Schönheit" ("On Beauty") (8 minutes)
5. "Der Trunkene im Frühling" ("The Drunkard in Spring") (4 minutes)
6. "Der Abschied" ("The Farewell") (30 minutes)

This overall plan for *Das Lied von der Erde* shows how Mahler, working after his daughter's death, had traded redemption for journeying. He had believed in transcendence until this point, and modeled it in his music as a vertical motion—the child of the Fourth Symphony glimpsing "the heavenly life," for instance, or in the Eighth Symphony the faithful bearing Faust aloft. But his practical rationalist streak had disallowed divine revelation—as a humanist, he believed in knowledge as something learned rather than revealed. Mahler's pantheism had coexisted with a kind of deist thinking—a profound love of nature mingling with the belief that while an all-powerful God designed the earth, he or she doesn't teach through wondrous actions. One can see Mahler's rationalist humanism at work in the ways he demystified redemption: he closed the two big choral symphonies, the Second and Eighth, with vaguely Christian scenarios where divine judgment is feared, then made moot. In the Second, the dead are raised and summoned to judgment, only to learn that eternal life is granted unconditionally; in the Eighth, the character of Faust commits his soul to a pact with the devil and, after living a life of moral failure and losing his bet, is redeemed on a technicality. In involving himself with these "loophole redemptions" in the Second and Eighth Symphonies, Mahler expressed faith but chose not to fall in line with doctrinaire ideologies of damnation.

Mahler arranged and tweaked two Hans Bethge texts for his last movement, fashioning "Der Abschied" as a half-hour scenario similar to that of the second part of the Eighth Symphony. In the concluding movements of both the Eighth and *Das Lied*, a certain figure is ardently sought—a figure known to have an answer to a question. After the figure is found and entreated in what becomes a pivotal moment about three-fourths of the way through, he or she makes a pronouncement about the need to journey in search of salvation. That figure in the second part of the Eighth Symphony is the Mater Gloriosa, who tells the former Margarete that the former Faust will follow her to heaven if she shows him the way: "Come, rise up to higher spheres! / If he is aware of you, he will follow." The figure in "Der Abschied" is the friend who announces his departure for remote and nebulous areas beyond the horizon, and eventually home: "Where do I go? I go, I wander in the mountains. / I seek peace for my lonely heart." The Eighth Symphony and *Das Lied von der Erde* both effectively end with these pronouncements and devote their remaining moments to expressions of praise—grandiose praise in the first case, and peaceful adoration in the other.

None of Mahler's redemptions involve mystic visions, here or elsewhere. In some of the works before *Das Lied von der Erde*, he had sought God but failed. But then it would be hard to imagine such an inveterate seeker meeting up with the Almighty, as Edward Elgar did in his choral work *The Dream of Gerontius* (1900), or imagine him even describing a particular vision of God, as Mendelssohn did in his oratorio

Elijah (1846). (In the "Urlicht" movement of Mahler's Second Symphony, the pilgrim finds his path to God blocked by an angel. And Mahler did say he might have titled the last movement of the Third Symphony "What God Tells Me," but any such "telling" involves neither words nor any kind of direct encounter: in this case, God's love would be the thing communicated.) The closest Mahler gets to divine revelation is the vision of heavenly plenty at the end of the Fourth Symphony and the Mater Gloriosa's appearance in part 2 of the Eighth Symphony, the highest vocal part to that point. As Mahler arranges it, this entrance of "the Queen of Heaven" leaves the men of the chorus so dumbstruck all they can do is echo her exhortation "Come, come . . ." ("Komm, komm . . ." at 43:27, an addition that Mahler made to Goethe's text). And then the fact that so many of Mahler's listeners are disappointed by his music for the Mater Gloriosa herself, dissatisfied with this one divine revelation in his output, speaks to his inability or unwillingness to represent actual godliness in musical terms. The friend appears in "Der Abschied" as anything but a mystic vision: indeed, Mahler changed Bethge's pronouns so as to make it unclear just when "my friend" ("mein Freund") materializes.

The usual explicit Mahlerian themes of death, life, and salvation do put in an appearance in the opening song of *Das Lied von der Erde*, but then absent themselves from the remaining five. At that point of disappearance, *Das Lied* becomes an article of natural theology, a surveying of nature's face in an attempt to discern God's plan. The piece is imbued with flora and fauna imagery—lotus blossoms, reflective pools, singing birds, setting suns, autumn frosts, dark pines, partial moons, soft winds. Though Mahler's love of nature had previously come through in the imagery of the *Lieder eines fahrenden Gesellen* and *Kindertotenlieder*, nature there sympathized with human emotion or symbolized transcendence: the meadow in "Ging heut' Morgen übers Feld" represents life's possibilities on a fine morning, and the distant green hills in "In diesem Wetter, in diesem Braus" symbolize the peace that lies beyond mortal suffering. In *Das Lied von der Erde*, natural beauty signifies transience, the jewel-like embellishments of a life that ends before we know it. Nature is seen in its cycles of life and death, the second poem set against an autumnal backdrop and the sixth ending with the hope that comes with the arrival of spring. Alongside the wanings and waxings of nature, we witness—in Mahler's own ordering and retitling of the poems—scenes depicting loneliness, youth, unfulfilled love, and, finally, wandering and departure. The ancient origins of the poems make these postcards of life all the more poignant and distant—affairs of the heart on the parts of drunkards, virgins, and pilgrims who have been dead for thirteen hundred years.

If *Das Lied von der Erde* is a new kind of Mahler work, how much of this difference stems from its basis in Chinese texts, or from any broader musical exoticism it might possess? Certainly, the texts have to be taken into account when we try to understand Mahler's shift from the emotional rhetoric of the Eighth Symphony to the elusive, barely sketched-in sentiments of *Das Lied*. At the same time, there is nothing consistently exotic about the music of *Das Lied*, at least as we might compare it to more or less contemporary orientalist pieces like Debussy's gamelan-imbued "Pagodes" for piano or Puccini's opera *Turandot*. One imagines Mahler was too intent on saying something very personal in *Das Lied* to sound anything other than himself. The third movement, "Von der Jugend" ("Of Youth"), is the most clearly pentatonic and timbrally glittering of the six—the one movement that sounds obviously Chinese. Rather, Mahler used the exotic premise as a way to reach the simplicity of style that he gravitated toward through much of his life. Listening to the vocal part of "Der Einsame im Herbst," we hear in the first line ("Herbstrebel wallen bläulich überm See, vom Reif bezogen stehen alle Gräser," "Autumn mists float blue over the lake, covered with frost are all the grasses") a rhythmic and intervallic makeup that is so simple as to be almost primitive. Cast almost entirely in quarter notes and scalewise motion, the line is set in a kind of pidgin German. Rather than sounding condescending, this style serves to heighten poignancy by adding yet another layer of distance, giving the impression that the emotions lie deeper than the singer is able to express.

Das Lied von der Erde is also different in being the least cohesively symphonic of any of Mahler's longer works. There is the intriguing question of how the six movements function in relation to each other, and this bears on what genre we might choose to call this piece. *Das Lied von der Erde* was listed as a symphony when it was published in 1912, after Mahler's death, and—according to the oft-repeated story—the composer thought not numbering the symphony he wrote after the Eighth would allow him to outwit the forces of fate that had prevented

Beethoven and Bruckner from getting beyond their own ninth symphonies. Since Mahler has two soloists but no chorus, the work stands apart from the so-called choral symphony, a genre that conjoins the theater with the concert hall—starting with Beethoven's Ninth and going via Berlioz's *Romeo and Juliet* and Liszt's *Faust Symphony* and *Dante Symphony* to Mahler's own Eighth. And the six movements of *Das Lied von der Erde* are self-contained, with none of the clear intra-movemental references that Mahler habitually used, especially as thematic recollections in his finales: this makes the designation "symphony" less appropriate than with any other Mahler work of this length. But then neither can these movements really be called songs. Since the orchestra has more to say in *Das Lied von der Erde* than in the *Rückert Lieder* or even the *Kindertotenlieder*, such that a performance of the piano-vocal reduction couldn't be considered a substitute for the full score, the six movements sound more like symphonic movements with voice parts. (As musicologist Stephen Hefling has shown, Mahler apparently thought his piano-vocal score for *Das Lied* a viable entity in its own right, but hearing the piano and the orchestral versions side by side surely presents us with a case of separate but unequal.) Mahler's symphonic orientation is especially audible in the half-hour "Der Abschied," with its evocative orchestral colorations and long instrumental interludes. The "O Mensch, gib acht!" Nietzsche setting in the Third Symphony, a movement that emphasizes atmosphere at least as much as it emphasizes any textual message, would be the closest predecessor to these six vocal-instrumental essays.

Instead of erecting some version of the four-movement symphony, Mahler creates cohesiveness in *Das Lied von der Erde* by strategically ordering songs and emotions. His six movements don't trace a dramatic progression, even though the work does begin with a call to action (the drinking song) and ends with an action (the departure to unnamed lands). Beyond this, we can say that Mahler alternates high voice (tenor) in the odd-numbered songs with lower voice (alto or baritone) in the even ones, and that the two voices don't have any kind of sequential dialogue with each other so much as their high-low contrasts serve to heighten the emotions. The odd-numbered songs are more extrovert statements, while the even ones turn inward. This contrast is amplified when performances use the tenor and alto that the composer indicated, rather than the tenor and baritone voices that he mentioned as a possibility if a lower female voice is unavailable. The basic shifts between male and female vocal color from one movement to another do accentuate the polarities of celebration (of drink, of the fullness of youth, of drink again) and looking inward. (Advocates of the tenor-baritone pairing would reply that all the texts, especially the backdrop of male companionship in "Der Abschied," are more appropriate to a man's point of view.)

SONGS ONE THROUGH FOUR: DARK IS LIFE, AS IS DEATH

The first of Mahler's six songs, "The Drinking Song of Earthly Woe" ("Das Trinklied vom Jammer der Erde"), is both announcement and pronouncement: a forceful call to raise our glasses in defiance of mortality. Mahler realizes the simple tavern-song aspect with repetitious and narrowly lyrical music, as at "Wenn der Kummer naht, liegen wüst die Gärten der Seele" ("When trouble nears, the gardens of the soul lie barren," starting at 1:07, with Mahler setting the last four words of the line almost awkwardly) and then at the toast itself, "Ein voller Becher Weins zur rechten Zeit / Ist mehr wert, als alle Reiche dieser Erde!" ("A full cup of wine at the right time is worth more than all the kingdoms of this earth!"), starting at 3:08. This tavern style is marked by simple melodic patterns, dancelike repetition, and quivering tracery in the strings and winds. But it soon becomes evident that "The Drinking Song of Earthly Woe" encompasses both celebration of life and the necessity of acknowledging death. A tone of angry defiance is already suggested at the start by frantic lashings in lower strings and woodwinds and clarion, annunciatory octave doublings in the melody. The key line in this unsettling duality, made all the more accusatory by Mahler's setting, is "But you, man, how long do you live? / Not a hundred years may you delight / In all the fragile trifles of this earth!" (starting at 6:11). Drinking songs have refrains, and the one for this song is the three-fold proclamation of "Dunkle ist das Leben, ist der Tod" ("Dark is life, as is death"), the first and third of these drawing an angry orchestral response (starting at 1:40 and at 7:59), and the second inciting a rhapsodic, lyrical reply (starting at 3:43).

At the song's climax, repetition is separated from revelry and lyricism gives way to horror. In a terrifying vision, our toast-giver—his death-mindfulness heightened by too much drink—sees and hears an ape shrieking from the graveyard: "Ein Aff' ist! Hört ihr, wie sein Heulen / Hinausgestellt in den süßen Duft des Lebens!" ("It is an ape! Hear how its howls / Shrill out into the sweet fragrance of life!"), starting at 7:09. This "wild, ghostly form" isn't some simian invasion, but rather the subconscious rearing its ugly head when faced with the inevitability of death. (As Sigmund Freud summarized this particular deeply buried fear in 1919: "It is true that the statement 'All men are mortal' is paraded in the text books of logic as an example of a general proposition; but no human being really grasps it, and our unconscious has as little use now as it ever had for the idea of its own mortality.") Transformed by this subliminal vision, the singer's melodic repetitions change from simplicity to fixation, from songfulness to pathology. The nightmarish episode climaxes at the word "Lebens!" with a high B-flat (at 7:21) followed by a long slide down a ninth. But it is gone as quickly as it came, and by the end of the song the ape's accusatory memory—our fears proving just as fleeting as our joys—becomes just another reason to raise our glasses while we still live.

The tensions in this first song are heightened by two things: a level of dissonance that increases directly with the singer's intensity of expression (most intensely where our toastmaster hears the screaming ape), and the almost combative relation between voice and orchestra. Mahler was writing for a nearly impossible combination of Wagnerian *Heldentenor* and *Lied singer*—demanding a heroic singer with a strong upper range who can be heard over the biggest orchestral passages, and at the same time summon a beautiful tone and color individual words with the subtlety common to domestic music-making. In short, he was writing unrealistically for a tenor who would be just as at home with Wagner's Siegfried as with Schubert's *Die schöne Müllerin*. But most tenors who have sung the huge, opera house–filling role of Siegfried would founder on the simplicity of Mahler's third and fifth songs. The role of Lohengrin, who isn't a warrior in Siegfried's manner but as the son of the blessed fool Parsifal embodies knightly chivalry, has been a better measure of suitability; and some of the more beautifully powerful *Das Lied von der Erde* singers—for example, James King, Jon Vickers, René Kollo, Plácido Domingo, and Ben Heppner—have won high praise in the title role of that Wagner opera. A stunning tenor in *Das Lied*, the great Fritz Wunderlich, was being pestered by Wieland Wagner to sing the role of Lohengrin at the Bayreuth Festival, but died before taking it on. None of these tenors excelled as a *Lieder* singer, but Wunderlich and his honeyed tone would certainly have matured into that role if he'd been given more time.

The sound of *Das Lied von der Erde* changes dramatically when we move from the first song to the second. If it is in music's power to illuminate the statement that a person exits life the same way he or she enters, naked and alone, Mahler's "Der Einsame im Herbst" ("The Lonely One in Autumn") fulfills that challenge. The song describes the plight of a soul whose heartsickness is only increased by the seasonal withering of the natural landscape. Chilled by the cold, she "weep[s] much in my times of loneliness" (starting at 7:08). She desires death, expressed metaphorically as the need for rest when weariness sets in and the evening lamp sputters out. The mood is immediately darkened by the descent from the highest register of the tenor voice, as we heard at the end of the first song, to this lower register of the mezzo range. The orchestration effects a similar change: we've moved outdoors, from the warmth of the tavern to some dim, damp, and isolated place. The autumn sun has set and, in the failing light, the colors range narrowly from the slate gray of low violas and bassoons to the somber blue of horns in open fifths.

In an important shift, the phrase structure of "Einsame im Herbst" proves more fluid than in "Trinklied vom Jammer." This singing character, in contrast to the one preceding, is also too shadowy and depleted to express herself through dissonance. She has a loosened grip on life, and the apparent lack of a specific reason for her melancholy only makes it all the more oppressive. We start this second song with a repetitious scalewise accompaniment figure in muted first violins, before the oboe enters with a melody that is somehow both repetitious and ever-shifting, ever-changing. The first interval in the oboe is a descending second (D–C), which sounds like Mahler is beginning with a cadence—beginning with an ending—except that the C is an unstable harmonic dissonance, not a point of rest. This opening D–C anomaly puts the whole line in motion, sets the oboe melody wandering in its own lonely journey. This descending D–C is then embellished with a lower A, which muddles the harmonic waters even further. The line also plays with the listener's sense of strong beats and weak beats: the opening D initially sounds emphasized, but then the C supplants it metrically before it disappears entirely in measure five. The two horns come in on a ghostly open fifth interval (at 0:22), finally making the downbeat clear before the melodic line starts trying to come to some kind of cadence.

All this lonely melodic wandering, set against a quiet scale figure in the violins that refuses to commit to any clear-cut harmonic resolution, closes with a noncommittal harmonic motion from G minor to D minor. When this grudging point of rest reoccurs, the motion is accompanied by descending chromatic voice leading that sends a chill down the spine: three chords follow one another (at 0:58, 1:02, and 1:07), each one sounding initially like a point of rest before it gives way to a sonority that's even darker and more forlorn than the one before. There's something cruel and existentially corrosive to this sequence: it bars the possibility of consolation for "the lonely one in autumn," though solace does peek through briefly at several points where the music shifts to duple meter and takes on a dancelike character (for instance, at "I am put in mind of sleep," 5:37; "es gemahnt mich an den Schlaf").

At the climax of this song, the forlorn person suddenly resists the pull toward loneliness, sleep, and death and summons the energy to make a plea: "The autumn in my heart persists too long. / Sun of love, will you shine no longer, / To gently dry my bitter tears?" ("Der Herbst in meinem Herzen währt zu lange . . . ," starting at 7:48). The full orchestra rises for the first time to a *fortissimo* in E-flat major, marked "with great drive," and the singer goes into a higher register (at 8:11). At first it seems this is not a rhetorical question. But the energy doesn't last: the lonely one's pleas are smothered by pathetic descending four- and three-note figures in the violins, which finally drag the music down to a hollow plucked open fifth in the cellos. The rocking triplet motion returns us to a state of fatigue, and the last vocal phrase—the culmination of the plea, emerging with the words "to gently dry my bitter tears?" (at 8:43, "mild aufzutrocknen?")—emerges "expressionless," barely uttered. This is the same melodic phrase we had heard earlier at "My heart is weary" ("Mein Herz ist müde"), and again it's answered by a strange rising scale in quarter notes in the upper strings set against a contrary descent in the bassoons, a grimly methodical circumscription of a gaping emptiness. We hear nothing more from the singer for the remainder of the song. In her absence, the opening oboe material returns, the violins go vacantly back to their quiet "wandering" figuration, and lastly the horns punctuate the song on a dark and dispiriting open fifth.

The third song, "Von der Jugend" ("On Youth"), is the shortest and simplest of the six. Here the composer's expressiveness finds voice in articulation, tone color, and melodic character. The simple foursquare rhythms, the clocklike keeping of time in the horn and triangle, the pentatonic (five-note) scale, the piquant splashes of color from flutes and trumpet and cymbals—this all suggests a charming if surfacey orientalism. The text calls for such, with its picture-postcard reference to a pavilion of porcelain, connected to land by a jade bridge, where people socialize and write poetry in their silken garb. But then in the fifth and sixth of the seven stanzas of text, something remarkable happens: the scene of unconcerned and unencumbered living among the young is seen reflected in the water, an image where everything is "standing on its head" ("auf dem Kopfe stehend"). And the music suggests an upside-down life (starting at 1:25) by slowing down, moving to the minor, and then bringing the strings to the foreground with a chromatic, sustained, almost overexpressive display of gravity. The composer seems to say that youthful life on reflection becomes something queerer and more vacant than its participants might realize. But then the youths resume their tick-tock affairs (starting at 2:25) without a second thought, and the song stops absentmindedly without even bothering to conclude.

The fourth song, "Von der Schönheit" ("On Beauty") is a cameo portrayal of life as a play of half-hidden, gamelike sensuality. Here death and solitary loneliness are gone from view, and the earth's life force surfaces as lust between the sexes; at the same time, there is a yearning for lost youth. Accompanied by dancelike rhythms, young maidens with "charming eyes" ("süßen Augen") pick flowers on the riverbanks before "handsome youths" arrive on horseback. The vocal writing shows us Mahler at his most uncomplicatedly lyrical. But trumpet fanfares and upward sweeps on the harp (starting at 2:33) intensify this formulaic fairy tale. One of the horses becomes excited in a poetic metaphor for human sexual engagement, and starting at 3:49 the story's agitated passion causes the vocalist to run out of breath: "Ah! How its mane waves in frenzy, / Its nostrils steam hotly!" ("Hei! Wie flattern im Taumel seine Mähnen, / Dampfen heiß die Nüstern!"). This climax is the first and last time in *Das Lied von der Erde* that we hear Mahler's orchestra playing all together, while elsewhere it is used as a set of chamber orchestras with varied colorations. The most beautiful of the virgins, at once desirous and proud and agitated, is quietly devastated by this display of passion. Mahler turns her coquettishness into a lovely slow waltz idea (at 4:37) that we hear sung through two strophes of text, but this ends up fragmenting and fading away: perhaps there's no partner to be had, and the dance goes unanswered.

SONGS FIVE AND SIX: OBLIVION AND DEPARTURE

The fifth song, "Der Trunkene im Frühling" ("The Drunkard in Spring"), is a bright counterpart to the second song and its melancholy: "the lonely one in autumn" and "the drunkard in spring" are quasi-operatic first-person character portraits, glances into opposing psyches. These songs portray two sufferers who practice different forms of oblivion, each of them finding a season that encourages them in their chosen manners of escape. The fifth movement is the comic relief of *Das Lied von der Erde*: the style would be at home in a comic opera, especially given the puttering, clucking, and occasionally swooning orchestral part. But this *betrunken* character is no bumbling fool: we find more layers the more we listen to him. If he were in a comic *Singspiel*, sung obtusely and in German as the local language, he would be less interesting and would be sung by a bass-baritone rather than a tenor. Traditionally, the tenor voice has heroic associations in opera, and sure enough the tenor part in "Der Trunkene im Frühling" has touches of gallantry and daring that help make him the most rounded and human character in *Das Lied von der Erde*. (We shouldn't forget that original poet Li Bai's famous love of the bottle wasn't a depravity, but ultimately a source of poetic insight.) Our tenor ends every other line of text with a leap to a high A, several times jumping up from a seventh or octave below (at 0:16, 0:35, 0:49, and 1:08). And each time the singer is called to sit on that A, meaning the note has to not only sound beautiful, but also be approached and left beautifully. It's at these leaps that one really appreciates Latinate tenors who have recorded this music—for example, Plácido Domingo and Francisco Araiza—while any of the Germans who aren't named Fritz Wunderlich or Jonas Kaufmann tend to give us a dryer and more strained sound. (Whether for reasons of language or vocal style, French and Italian tenors have tended to avoid *Das Lied von der Erde*.)

Our drunkard is more involved with his drink than with the arrival of spring: he has to ask the bird in the tree what the season is, and the bird ridicules him (at 2:56). At two points the tempo slows, the orchestral timbres become hazier, and we enter an altered state of consciousness where both drink and world are momentarily forgotten. The first is after the bird is consulted and the singer remarks, "It is like a dream to me" ("Mir ist als wie im Traum," at 1:52); the second is where the singer confesses that "I listen in deep wonderment" ("Aus tiefstem Schauen lauscht' ich auf," at 2:33). The song enters these altered states by shifting harmonically through the interval of a third, a shift that has the effect of quickly changing the coloration of the music: "It is like a dream to me" (moving from A major to F major), followed by "spring has arrived" (F major to D-flat major), followed by a fifth movement at "I listen in deep wonderment" (D-flat major to A-flat major). But the dream is short, the wine calls again ("I fill my cup again and empty it to the dregs," at 3:04), and with the line "in the black heavens!" (at 3:23) the song returns to the tonic of A major via C major. Mahler aligns these harmonic shifts with changes of texture, dynamics, and orchestral coloration to produce an absorbing miniature psychological voyage.

The sixth and last song, "Der Abschied" ("The Farewell"), is one of Mahler's most astonishing creations, an unprecedented, seamless fusion of storytelling, sound, and sensibility. I have already addressed the roles of finale movements within this composer's various ever-changing, multimovement symphonic designs. In the case of *Das Lied von der Erde*, a work with a half-hour last movement that is almost as long as the five preceding movements put together, the term "finale" will no longer suffice. I have mentioned the notion of Mahler's finales as arrivals or returns, coming to a place that the work has prepared us to expect in terms of emotions, key structure, and thematic retrievals. The Third and Fourth Symphonies give two contrasting examples of that dynamic: the finale of the Third ties the whole work off with theme restatements and a return to the climax of the first movement; and the Fourth leads to its short *Wunderhorn* song-finale as a kind of thematic lynchpin for the whole work, a centralizing piece of the puzzle that quietly slides into place as the piece comes to a close. So, while all of Mahler's previous large-scale works ended with some manner of returning or arriving, *Das Lied von der Erde* ends on a note of spiritual and musical departure. Oxymoronically, the final chord—a C major triad with added sixth—could be heard either as an unstable consonance or a stable dissonance. With its gently questioning sound, such a sixth chord can give very different impressions depending on how the composer presents and orchestrates it: at the end of Mahler's "Der Abschied," the C6 chord simultaneously suggests both departure and coming to rest.

Mahler had used half-hour stretches of music before to create a new kind of musical theater in the concert hall, most prominently in the last movement of the Second Symphony and the first of the Third—movements where feelings are so tangibly rendered in sound that they almost become visible. But those earlier movements were dramatic or even stage-worthy displays, while "Der Abschied" is inner and private—a drama of one. Given its length, its variety, its psychology of character, and the critical role of the orchestra, "Der Abschied" sounds as if it came from an early twentieth-century genre of opera, namely the psychological monodrama. An isolated and questing person narrates while navigating a natural setting that seems more an inner landscape than a real one. Described in such terms, the movement starts to resemble Arnold Schoenberg's monodrama *Erwartung* (a work written at the same time Mahler composed *Das Lied von der Erde*, but premiered after his death) or possibly those moments where we enter into the mind of the lustful, distracted Judean princess in Strauss's *Salome* (the 1905 opera that Mahler studied and hugely admired).

In the text that became the final "Abschied" movement, the poet seeks peace for "my lonely heart" out beyond "the mountains." Instead of transcendence beyond earthly life, a rite of passage that Mahler had re-created in earlier works, here the poet seeks the reconciliation of home, the *Heimat*. Rather than rising up to meet his god in an act of divine revelation, instead of moving toward a summoning presence, the poet here seeks solitude and hopes to be made whole "over there." It is difficult not to conclude that Mahler, reading Bethge's renderings of these ancient Chinese poems at this difficult time in his life, had reached a more personal and perhaps realistic understanding of redemption as a lone project:

> He dismounted and handed him the drink
> of Farewells. He asked him where
> he would go and why must it be.

He spoke, his voice was quiet. Ah my friend,
Fortune was not kind to me in this world!
Where do I go? I go, I wander in the mountains.
I seek peace for my lonely heart.
I wander homeward, to my abode!
I'll never wander far.
Still is my heart, awaiting its hour.

This state of peace beyond the "fortune" of "this world" is a solitary state, presumably just as lonely as the life that precedes it: no dramatic *chorus mysticus* appears here to guide and affirm the protagonist. And the journey toward peace is also a lonely pursuit: the earlier communal hopes for salvation, couched in terms of choral writing and an implied community of human beings, are now replaced by two single vocal soloists who are separated into movements that alternate high voice and low. These notions of peace and home also differ from the redemption invoked in Mahler's earlier works in that they are different as forms of conclusion. The theme of "Der Abschied" is leave-taking rather than death as such, and there's nothing of the death-battling heroism that we find in the Second, Sixth, and Ninth Symphonies. But then death is neither friend nor foe in *Das Lied von der Erde*: it is an implicit presence, and transcendence no longer a clear or absolute concept.

"Der Abschied" acts out much of its inner, psychological theater through instrumental coloration and timbral shifts. We begin with the stirring, shimmering, dark bronze hues of the opening chords: the lowest notes of cellos and contrabasses paired with sepulchral tam-tam strokes and half-note tollings in the harps, horns, and contrabassoon. These chords combine different kinds of resonance, and for this reason they sound different in each performance: metal is struck, strings are plucked, air columns resonate within wood and brass enclosures, all in their lowest registers, creating a sound that peals and laments. If it weren't for the added buzz of Mahler's double reed instruments, this could be an orchestral imitation of bells—bringing to mind the start of the tragic Tsar's coronation in Mussorgsky's opera *Boris Godunov*. And Mahler's opening chords could be functioning here in the various interrelated ways that church bells function when rung slowly: as a summons, as an expression of grief, or as a marking of time. These chords, demonstrating a defiant coloristic imagination, are as much experiments in acoustic space as they are with resonance—here the beautifully "irrational" noise of the tam-tam is significant. But then these chords are symptomatic of "Der Abschied" as a whole: the movement is marked by such somber colors in low registers, fine-grained and divided textures, ever-shifting phrase structures that keep the sense of time in flux, and poignant pauses that suggest existential seclusion. After the mezzo-soprano paints the opening scene ("Into all the valleys the evening descends with its shadows, which are full of coolness"), we hear at 4:34 the wintry combination of flutes, violas, and contrabasses all playing their lowest notes in a *pianissimo* chord that is held before "dying off" (*morendo*) into silence.

The tone of the music changes at 4:41. Here the underlying rhythm shifts to continuous triplets in clarinet, harp, and viola while the oboe sings a nonrepetitious, asymmetrical line that Schoenberg thought exemplified the kind of forward-looking metric freedom that he called "musical prose." In "Der Abschied," Mahler is setting a text with a variety of nature sounds, ones that he musically reflects rather than imitates: a kind of subjective impressionism. In this new section, it's easy to hear the oboe and flute solos as demonstrations of how "The brook sings, full of pleasant sound, through the dark" ("Der Bach singt voller Wohllaut durch das Dunkel") and "The earth breathes, full of quiet and sleep" ("Die Erde atmet voll von Ruh' und Schlaf," starting at 6:38). The earth is abandoning consciousness in the face of evening sleep, and "all longing now wants to dream" ("Alle Sehnsucht will nun träumen"). We hear the diminishing calls of birds and soft flutterings of feathers ("The birds perch quietly in their branches," "Die Vögel hocken still in ihren Zweigen," starting at 8:27). The world falls asleep at 8:52 ("Die Welt schläft ein!") to the sonic undergrowth of tolling harps and rustling clarinets. But the poet-protagonist remains awake: he returns to the opening music (at 9:44, "I feel a soft wind blowing / Behind the dark spruces"; "Ich spüre eines feinen Windes Weh'n / Hinter den dunklen Fichten!") and now inhabits this dormant landscape in anxious expectation of his friend for "the last farewell" ("Ich harre sein zum letzten Lebewohl").

At 10:55, just as we seem destined to survey the desolate musical topography once again, the mood is transformed. We shift to B-flat major, the meter changes to a dancelike 3/4, and we hear a mandolin—one of the most cheerful-sounding instruments in existence. Most importantly, at this moment the violins introduce an improvisatory, upward-reaching, long-limbed line (marked "with the most heartfelt feeling") that the singer repeats to the words "Ich sehne mich, o Freund, an deiner Seite" ("Oh friend, I long to be at your side"), but that will return in its fullest form toward the end of the movement with the words "Die liebe Erde allüberall blüht auf im Lenz und grünt aufs neu!" ("The beloved earth everywhere blossoms and greens in springtime anew!"). This hesitantly ascending line recalls an idea from the start of Mahler's career as a symphonist: I'm speaking of the A-flat major violin line leading into the second theme group in the finale of the First Symphony, starting at 3:07; the similarity shows how his musical representations of rapt expectation hadn't changed much in the intervening twenty years. The waiting poet expresses ever-stronger yearning for the friend's company, climaxing in the exclamation "O Schönheit! O ewigen Liebens – Lebens – trunk'ne Welt!" ("O beauty! O world drunk with eternal love and life!") But the outcry only elicits the reply of various nocturnal murmurings, and the music sinks downward yet again to the insensible tollings of harps, contrabassoon, and contrabasses.

It becomes evident that Mahler is structuring "Der Abschied" as a confrontation between two very different kinds of musical gestures: first, the mournful, subterranean, downbeat-heavy knells that open the movement; and second, the dancelike, graceful, levitating style that surfaces in the triplets at 4:41 still tinged with melancholy, only to sink back down at 6:21 and then again at 8:26 (right before "the world falls asleep"), and that then, between passionate acclamations over love and natural beauty, manages an elegant serenity at "I walk up and down with my lute" ("Ich wandle auf und nieder mit meiner Laute," starting at 12:58). Denying, or indeed defying that dancelike elegance, the heavy, tolling knells that opened "Der Abschied" return at 14:51, and then most decisively from 18:58 to perform a final melodic "burial" at 19:37. In the kind of dualistic face-off of moods and styles that we've heard various times in Mahler's work, the question remains open as to whether the negative or the positive impetus will win out.

These tolling knells stand out as a prime example of how Mahler can seem to create such blistering intensity of meaning in momentary instrumental sounds that the gestures positively demand an interpretation in terms of imagery or narrative. It just isn't enough to hear these tolling, deeply burrowing knells as thematic returns or reaffirmations of the tonic key: they must be moments of death, or bells, or funeral processions setting out. At the return of the tolling knells at 14:51, the contrabasses now emphasize the terrifying blackness of the sonority by sustaining them with accented tremolos. A dark and hesitant instrumental procession ensues, perhaps Mahler's funeral march for Putzi, punctuated by dotted rhythms and bitter downward drops starting at 18:58. At this point of deepest descent, at 20:03, we return yet again to the opening music of the movement and the poet's long-sought friend finally appears: "He alighted from his horse . . ." ("Er stieg vom Pferd . . ."). At the fateful question of "why it had to be" ("warum es müßte sein," 20:35), the procession begins anew, though now slightly faster. Then, starting at 23:02, the roving friend answers the questions that have been asked of him, accompanied by a poignant wavering between major and minor keys: "Where do I go? I go, I wander in the mountains. / I seek peace for my lonely heart." At the mention of heading homeward ("Ich wandle nach der Heimat!," at 25:06), the music returns to the rocking triplet rhythms.

Then at 26:04, a remarkable set of unisons and octaves on the pitch E clears the air of melancholy and anxiety, finally steering the piece into a restful C major that glows with no suggestion of the ironic or the saccharine. This is Mahler at his most simple, forgiving, and sincere. The tolling knells have been banished, "the earth" as a subterranean realm of physical demise vanquished. Forgotten and forgiven are the anxious tavern song of the first movement, the Chinese *bon vivants*, even the earlier springtime drunk—all banished from memory as *Das Lied von der Erde* effects its final transfiguration to Mahler's own lines (added to Bethge's text) of "Die liebe Erde allüberall blüht auf im Lenz und grünt aufs neu!" ("The beloved earth everywhere blossoms and greens in springtime anew!," starting at 26:36). The implication is that all human partings and troubles, indeed all the "sorrows of the earth," are forgotten and forgiven when nature is seen to renew itself. Life concludes with departure and absence, which then cycle back into life and its fullest and most verdant sense of promise. The flutes and oboes start to linger over the sixth note of the tonic C major chord, the gently persistent A, at 27:44. The cellos enhance the sense of unstable consonance or stable dissonance by sitting on the pitch D (starting at 28:58), thus gently clouding the harmony with a ninth interval. As mentioned, this final, blissful C sixth and ninth chord is the perfect illustration of closing a circle between eternity and evanescence: *Das Lied von der*

Erde closes in a way that still leaves itself open to the possibility of beginning.

11

SYMPHONY NO. 9

The Most Painful Lust for Life

Just as a person's last words promise revelation, the Ninth Symphony holds special meaning as Mahler's final completed work. He sketched the piece while writing *Das Lied von der Erde* in 1908, and then set most of it down on paper the following summer. His protégé Bruno Walter conducted the premiere three years later, some thirteen months after the composer's death. The Ninth's progression from conflict in the first movement to simple radiance in the last, heard in light of its posthumous appearance, can suggest the composer was settling accounts with life. ("Four Ways to Say Farewell" was Leonard Bernstein's account of this four-movement work; "It is music coming from another world, it is coming from eternity" was conductor Herbert von Karajan's description; "Not just *his* last symphony, but a last symphony in general," composer Friedrich Saathen summarized it in his preface for the Universal Edition study score.) More than a century on, listeners still hear this music as a valediction—even though Mahler was making plans for his future and had two more productive and busy years ahead of him, time he devoted to completing a draft of his Tenth Symphony.

Last words hold special meaning, but not necessarily clear meaning. The first movement of the Ninth Symphony might or might not broach the topic of death—death of the composer, or impending death of the Viennese symphonic tradition more broadly—but the music does have a hugely conflicted, earth-shattering sound. It conflates rage with nostalgia, desolation with loving gentleness. Catastrophe gives way to sweet lullabies, and vice versa. Performers are confronted with as many emotional challenges as executive ones. The piece's extraordinary discontinuity and complex texture make it Mahler's most difficult to conduct, to bring together into a musical argument and an emotional whole. To do it justice, one imagines a conductor would have to have among their life experiences climbing Mount Everest, surviving at least one all-consuming love affair, cradling a dead child in their arms, and leading a battalion into war. These impossible juxtapositions are in themselves expressive. The young Viennese composer Alban Berg, jotting down some diaristic thoughts on the piece shortly after Mahler's passing, described the movement in terms of an irresolvable conflict between a love for life and the necessity of death:

> It is the expression of an extraordinary love for this earth—a yearning to live on it in peace, to enjoy nature to the utmost before death arrives. Because it approaches relentlessly. This whole movement has a premonition of death. Again and again it is signaled. All *earthly* dreams culminate in it (thus the erupting intensifications whose upsurges keep returning after the most tender passages). It is of course at its strongest in the monstrous passage where the presentiment of death becomes a *certainty*, where, amid the most painful lust for life, "höchste Kraft," ["with the utmost strength," at 18:26] death is announced "mit höchster Gewalt" ["with the utmost violence," at 18:44].

The Ninth Symphony is a purely instrumental work, involving neither voices nor texts, nor even any of the "sound effects" percussion, mandolins, retuned instruments, climactic section doublings, or offstage tactics that he had used in every previous symphony except the Fifth. Mahler's return here to purely instrumental composition—and indeed to something closer to a Brahms orchestra, with a reduced array of four horns and three trumpets—heightens our suspicions that the Ninth Symphony asks more questions than it answers. Throughout this book, I have often mentioned Mahler's forceful invocation of meaning through instrumental means, to the point where his symphonic music no longer seems satisfied simply to paint—or more specifically to tone-paint, in the time-honored tradition of instrumental *Tonmalerei*. Mahler instead seems on the verge of acting out or even speaking through his instruments. An example in the first movement of the Ninth is his use of stopped horns, a technique where the players insert their right hands in the bell of the instrument to create a curdled sound of less definite pitch. Mahler had certainly used stopped notes before, but now the shift in timbre gives a palpable sense of dejection and defeat. The first such stopped horn note announces the return of the restless second theme (at 5:27) before the music turns to the new key of B-flat major. A more insistent occurrence begins at 14:12, where the descending second interval that started the movement returns, each of its six recurrences now marked by suffocated stopped-horn rasps that suggest a voice under duress, a petulant plea for mercy.

And then, as if in contradiction to this movement's intense expressiveness, there are its classical pretenses. In addition to some streamlining of his orchestral resources, Mahler returned here to more traditional symphonic models. The Ninth Symphony is in four movements, setting up a tension between the classical Brahmsian symphonic layout and the highly fluid, word-based style of rhythmic and thematic working-out he had developed in his two previous compositions. Mahler's layout of movements and basic tempos is as follows:

1. *Andante comodo* (At a leisurely walking pace) (28 minutes)
2. *Im Tempo eines gemächlichen Ländlers. Etwas täppisch und sehr derb* (In the tempo of a leisurely *Ländler*. Somewhat clumsy and very crude) (16 minutes)
3. *Rondo-Burleske: Allegro assai. Sehr trotzig* (Rondo-Burlesque: Very fast. Very defiantly) (12 minutes)
4. *Adagio. Sehr langsam und noch zurückhaltend* (Slow movement. Very slow and withdrawn) (23 minutes)

With this plan, Mahler upended the basic symphonic teleology that had held sway since Beethoven's Fifth. With a slow-tempo final movement, the symphony has in effect been turned inside out: it includes both a dance movement as second and a scherzo as third, and the lengthy concluding Adagio displaces the expected structural capstone. Instead of a fast-tempo finale, the listener is sent off with spare, head-in-the-clouds music that seems to dissipate even as we're listening to it.

Mahler insistently defies structural conventions and expectations in his Ninth Symphony. The Andante comodo in particular inspires conflicting formal analyses. Just when it seems to be sorting out its oppositions and reaching a consensus toward one direction, any sense of progression collapses. In the first movement of the Ninth—for the first time in a Mahler first movement, except perhaps that of the Third Symphony—not only is the expected sonata-form proportion of exposition-development-recapitulation lopsided, but the major musical events and dramatic climaxes fail to align with the expected formal events. Along with a challenge to conventional formal thinking comes a resistance to interpretation. Even if the listener chooses to hear the music as a confrontation with death, this interpretation proves difficult to pursue: the rationale for the ever-changing dynamic of dramatic tension and actualization remains obscure.

FIRST MOVEMENT: HEROISM AND CALAMITY

Always questing, always in conflict with itself, the roughly half-hour first movement seems modern in the way it models the tensions of the Freudian subconscious: as Theodor Adorno said of Schoenberg's opera *Erwartung*, this music shows the "scars" that disclose "the heralds of the id against the compositional will." The first movement of the Ninth Symphony is Mahler's most extreme example of adapting, in purely instrumental form, the dramatic, mythic, and psychological undercurrents of the Wagnerian music drama. Its structural struggle becomes inseparable from its emotional battle. Abandoning the stop-start, numbers-opera layout of Italian opera for a continuous—and long!—stream of ever-shifting experience, Wagner came to rely on techniques of setting up and then undercutting expectation, on original methods of intertwining continuity within discontinuity. When these methods are used in the service of a sung stage drama, we have *Die Walküre* or *Tristan und Isolde*; when they are divorced from singers and the theater, we have the finale of Mahler's Sixth (1904), the first movement of Mahler's Ninth (1909), or Schoenberg's huge symphonic poem *Pelleas und Melisande* (1903).

To give one example of undercutting expectation in the first movement of Mahler's Ninth: toward the end of the exposition section, only a minute or so after the first chapter of the musical argument has sunk beneath the weight of its own pessimism, the music changes course and prepares for a climax straight out of Wagner's cycle of *Ring* operas. Horn and trumpet parts come to the fore in grand doublings (starting at 6:16), the orchestra expands, majestic ascensions reach up in the harps, and then—stepping up to an allegro tempo at 6:30—the movement turns heroic and starts to march forward with an ostentatious sense of occasion. Underscored by a tremendous crescendo on cymbals and timpani and capped by the flutes and clarinets trilling in expectation, the music readies for battle, sure of victory. But right where the payoff should occur (at 6:43), this climax quickly dissolves: the ensemble drops away, and we're left with skeletal iterations of the motto rhythm on quiet horns accompanied by indignant repetitions of the ascending fourth–descending second motive on the timpani. With a few tweaks, Mahler's climax could serve as a lead-in to the majestic, full-brass version of Siegfried's horn call after that character's ignoble death in *Götterdämmerung*—one of Wagner's grandest, most heroic moments (in E-flat major about six minutes into the orchestral excerpt called "Siegfried's Funeral Music"). But then, at the listener's most expectant and vulnerable moment, Mahler pulls the rug out from under our feet. Mahler has summoned the full Wagnerian instrumental resources suggesting heroism, only to answer it with pitch-black nihilism.

The opening of the first movement is deceptively calm, or even pastoral in character given the drone-like insistence on the note A in all instruments. We are given the motivic building blocks from which this massive, half-hour movement will be erected—beginning with a quietly stuttering thematic rhythm in the cellos that will recur at climactic points, moments that gave Berg the impression of death announcing itself "again and again." The primary theme then steals in (at 0:22) with a descending second in the violins, the interval immediately repeated and then habitually returned to as the melody questions and replies, unfolds and expands, then contracts (progressing from two notes to two notes, three notes, five notes, three notes, three notes, then eight, then five, then two, and lastly three). But just as this first theme reaches a quiet conclusion, the D major key twists downward to the darkness of D minor (at 1:50), forecasting conflict. The second theme enters in that new key (at 2:05), leaping indignantly and veering between repetition and unpredictability. This music recalls the distressed Pater Profundus in part 2 of the Eighth Symphony, the character who sings, "Where now my spirit, confused and chilled, / Languishes in the confines of my dull senses / And the pain of tightly fastened fetters!" Structurally, the idea sounds more transitional than thematic. (I was unable to grasp Mahler's first movement until I identified this seemingly transitional idea as an actual theme and paid full attention to its comings and goings. Unless one recognizes and listens for it, the last seven minutes of the movement can seem simply incoherent.)

Rather than hearing the first movement of the Ninth as a sonata form, I would call it a double-variations structure and say the movement takes its conflicted character from the two contradictory musical ideas that battle each other over the soul of the movement. The songlike first theme returns in expanded form (at 3:20), followed by an antiphonal exchange between different sections of the orchestra representing an extension of this theme's conversational character. The "struggling" second theme returns (at 5:32) with the addition of new counterlines and trills, and this then leads into the aborted near-quote from Wagner's *Götterdämmerung* (as described above) and the start of the development section. This music, shadowy and fragmented, is given continuity only by the tolling motive on the harp and the overall sense of the music tentatively feeling its way back to D major. The songlike first theme then steals its way back in at the movement's opening tempo (starting at 9:02)—the sense of thematic and temporal return is strong enough here that this could have been our recapitulation in a sonata form, if we were in the hands of a less ambitious and inquisitive musical planner.

But it soon becomes clear that any sense of resolution is a false hope, as the songlike theme not only fails to console, but leads (at 12:19) into the most precipitous failure so far. The struggling second theme, now marked "passionately" (*Leidenschaftlich*), steps yet again (starting in earnest at 12:45) into the vacuum following collapse. But the writhing character of this theme leads to another protracted section of unrest and confusion, manifest in the most linear, uneven, multilayered, and uncoordinated orchestral textures Mahler had yet created. Starting at 14:12, as part of a reduced ensemble, the horns and bassoons and trombones present three fateful, descending repetitions of the falling second interval that opened the movement—now punctuated each time by that stinging, denatured sound of stopped horns. After a stern cautioning from the trombones (at 14:38), the three-fold protestations repeat (starting at 14:49) and are again answered by the trombones. The musical argument reaches such a state of dejectedness that it stops altogether at 15:26. It slowly picks up again "shadowy" (*Schattenhaft*) in E-flat minor, finding voice in ghostly gestural fragments, before the all-determining falling second interval starts to take over the argument yet again, finally leading back into the first songful theme (starting at 16:16)—begun by the horn but presented in large part through the violins.

This return still seems too easily won, and so it proves: the descending horn intervals that reintroduced the theme now pull it into a greater conflict, and we are once again preparing for a heroic Wagnerian climax, much like the one that ended the exposition. While at that earlier point the elevation of a dragon-slaying hero had been rudely aborted, here the march (now in B major) becomes more obviously cataclysmic, like Faust's ride to the abyss of hell. This climax ends (at 18:44) with a furious bass drum and tam-tam stroke ("with the utmost violence," Mahler indicates), then punctuated by the trombones and tuba with the decentered fateful rhythmic motto, first heard in the opening bars of the movement. This new tragedy is followed by a gawky funeral march in B major/minor (marked "like a slow funeral cortege"), punctuated by trumpet tattoos and more strokes on tam-tam and timpani. The music here is deeply ambivalent, at the same time despondent and energetic, droll and sinister.

The two basic themes return (marking the recapitulation, for those who do choose to hear the movement as a sonata form), but they've been tainted by all that's happened over the course of the movement. At its final reappearance (starting at 20:29), the songful theme in D major has been infected by all the shambling, processional clumsiness of the "slow funeral cortege" music. Two more climaxes of a sort occur before the movement ends, both of them short and suppressed—they are less climaxes than intensely regretful afterthoughts. The first of them (starting at 22:10) allows a short, four-measure peek-through of the second, struggling theme before a mercurial and inventive discursion pushes it aside. This highly contrapuntal section starts by showcasing in turn the oboe, then flute, solo violin, piccolo, and horn before leading into an astonishing, nearly atonal three-part invention for flute, horn, and cellos doubling contrabasses. This music has a cool, mercurial, metrically fluid, prose-like quality to it—perhaps the first music of the symphony that could be called otherworldly and impassive.

The second, even more diminished climax (starting at 23:28) returns us to the continuation of the second, struggling theme before its slow expiration ushers in the long coda section. This concluding music has the orchestra reduced mostly to solo horn (starting at 24:43), clarinet, flute, harp, and lastly solo violin. A final, lullaby-like reminiscence of the first songful theme leads to a preoccupation with the original falling second interval. The music becomes a congregation of descents. The horns pick up this nostalgic fragment, and then turn it into a falling fifth, the larger interval suggestive of someone regaining their breath. After the breathless fragmentation of so much that has preceded, a steadier and more restful tempo (starting at 24:33) provides a haven for restorative, long-breathed solos on clarinet, flute, and then violin. Bringing a deep sense of oxygenated release, the lungs can finally fully inflate (starting at 27:18). In his commentary on Mahler's Ninth, Alban Berg talks about the first movement largely in terms of mortality and landscape, but ends with respiration in the Austrian mountains. He hears the coda as a representation of how "[Mahler] wants to make a home for himself, far from all adversity, in the free, thin air of Semmering." Berg then hears the concluding horn fifth as the need "to draw in this air, this most pure of earthly air, with ever deeper breaths—gulping it down ever more deeply."

I give these specific remarks on the music with the caveat that there are in fact so many ways to hear the first movement of the Ninth Symphony. One listens differently with each audition. The listener is both challenged and gripped by the chaotic sequence of moods, ranging from triumph to petulance: as Berg heard them, these encompass intimations of love, peace, death, rage, chivalric battle readiness (those proud figures in the trumpets), and finally equanimity. The listener loses count of how many times light gives way to shadow—stopped horns and trumpets curdling the music as if it were rancid milk—and shadow to light; but then that points to the painful aspect of "the most painful lust for life," as Berg put it. For the structurally minded, I've already suggested Mahler's alternation and free development of the two very different themes, the first songful and the second anxiously frantic. Alternatively, more along lines of a narrative hearing, one can follow the half-hour first movement as a series of dynamic waves that grow to tremendous heights and are then dashed on the rocks: the two highest points of development fall into precipitous collapse (at 12:19 and then at 18:44). These two passages demonstrate Theodor Adorno's assertion in his book *Mahler: A Musical Physiognomy* that this composer's works are oriented to emotional and textural extremes: "As in novels, happiness flourishes in Mahler on the brink of catastrophe." Taking a more micro-level approach to the first movement of the Ninth, you can trace the reappearance, recombination, and development of the motives introduced in the opening bars, including the thematic rhythm heard right away, the four-note tolling figure first heard in the harp, and of course the all-important falling second interval that helps give the whole movement its air of resignation, regret, and finally release. And lastly, of course, there's the ever-shifting sequence of orchestral colors and textures, one measure hardly sounding like any other.

SECOND AND THIRD MOVEMENTS: ABSURDITY, LEARNEDNESS, AND RAGE

Alban Berg was an ardent Mahler enthusiast, and went so far in his diary entry on the work as to call the first movement of the Ninth Symphony "the most glorious thing Mahler wrote." This movement is so lengthy and all-encompassing and—at least in the eyes of Berg and other members of the Schoenberg circle—so progressive in its compositional thinking as to be a self-sufficient emotional and musical statement. Because of its length, complexity, and expressive range, the first movement poses problems for the formal strategy of the symphony as a whole. What could possibly follow this music? Mahler opted for a second movement of buoyant dance rhythms, offsetting the weight of the Andante comodo with an obsessive catalog of the dance: if the first movement of the Ninth came to involve a momentous process of thematic-motivic variation and return, the second movement goes over the top as a profusion of dance types.

Mahler verges on self-parody in the way he throws together fatuousness, high spirits, and fleeting melancholy in this movement. The orchestral instruments take turns trilling like Alpine yodelers, the horns warbling more brazenly than the rest: Mahler marks their first entrance "keck" ("cocky," at 0:21). The mania later infects the strings, who start to voice their own exuberance with furious downward slides (starting at 11:07). But the surface of exaggeratedly boastful dancing veils a deeper sadness—much as Johann Strauss's waltzes ("Künstlerleben," for instance) can combine elegance and melancholy in a seamless, quintessentially Viennese mix. Mahler had of course written earlier dance-style music, often with rustic, threatening, or feverish overtones; but the second movement of the Ninth is his first dance movement to suggest sorrow. That layer initially comes through at 5:47, in a short passage where the strings eke out a dirgelike tune in B-flat minor beneath trilling flutes and oboes. Symptomatic of the melancholy are amnesiac passages that slow down and start to wander off absentmindedly, as if forgetting the dance floor entirely. Already at 1:13 into the movement, the strutting lower strings grow quiet and meander briefly off-topic. The most conspicuous of these absentminded passages starts at 8:15, where a series of slowdowns and drooping chord changes look back to the previous movement and suggest we'll never make our way back to the heel-kicking triple meter.

This movement juxtaposes three types and tempos of dance, including two country *Ländler* and a waltz. Their convoluted, almost obsessive combinings can be summarized as follows:

(1) a leisurely *Ländler* (*ein gemächlich Ländler*, in C major, marked Tempo I), ceding to
(2) a hectic waltz (marked Tempo II, E major, starting at 2:25), moving into
(3) a slow *Ländler* (*ganz langsam*, marked Tempo III, F major, starting at 4:55), before
(4) a return to the waltz (at 6:28),
(5) a return to the slow *Ländler* (at 7:45),
(6) the leisurely *Ländler* (at 9:39),
(7) the waltz again (at 11:33), and lastly
(8) an extended version of the leisurely *Ländler* (at 12:35), interpolated with bits of the waltz and the slow *Ländler* as a summing-up of the whole movement.

In Adorno's view, the "quotation" quality of these various themes and the quick cuts between different styles make this second movement a kind of montage. Just as important as the cutting back and forth is the fact that the three dance types have different characters as well as different tempos, giving the movement a slightly frantic, schizoid quality. The two *Ländler* are easily distracted and tend to slow down, while the quick waltz music becomes manic and often leads to fast sequential repetition. This polarity is interesting, in that the *Ländler* should by definition be the rustic dance, while the waltz should offer urban gracefulness—but here Mahler has it the other way around, the boorish waltz even lapsing into garish oom-pah-pah bass figures, decked out not just with the timpani but at one point also with the cymbals, triangle, and glockenspiel.

Like all movements of the Ninth, the second movement begins—almost pedantically—with a single line of music stated as an opening proposition, something to be countered and then pursued in detail. This opening *Ländler* (marked "in the tempo of a leisurely *Ländler*; somewhat clumsy and very crude") will return in fragmented form throughout the movement, almost as a refrain. Similarly, the movement will return to the opening's coarse opposition between strings and woodwinds. The movement ends with a layering of the three dance types (starting at 12:35), vertically juxtaposing different instruments in suggestive and grotesque tone-color combinations. This concluding section begins with the trombones and tuba re-creating the emphatic downbeats of the waltz, and goes on to a surreal pairing of horn and contrabassoon (starting at 14:38), cajoling bassoon duets, and a hole-in-the-middle texture centering on piccolo and double bass. The last word is had by the leisurely *Ländler* that opened the movement, more specifically the cheeky pickup figure heard right at the start.

In titling his third movement "Rondo-Burleske," Mahler suggested a new kind of genre where structure is linked with temperament. As a musical type, the burlesque involved grotesqueness, exaggeration, and satire. Rondo form was a recurring, repetitive structure that opened the door to parody—the opening material coming back four times or more over the course of the piece. Marked by such obsessive thematic returns, the classical rondo provided an opportunity for mimicking in instrumental terms the farcical characters of comic opera—for instance, bumbling basses who barge in on boudoirs and other delicate domestic situations. Haydn had ended his Symphony no. 88 with a chattering rondo movement that mimics the second-act ending in an *opera buffa*, while Mozart imitates his own comic opera *The Abduction from the Seraglio* in the famous "Rondo alla Turca" movement concluding his Piano Sonata in A Major, op. 331/300i. Mahler confines his parodistic aspect to the subsidiary passages where he imitates the vocal patter of operetta: Franz Lehár's *The Merry Widow* (*Die lustige Witwe*) had become inescapable toward the end of Mahler's tenure in Vienna, starting its runaway success a few blocks down the street from the Court Opera, and when he moved to New York and also heard it there, he must have feared it was following him westward. But as befits his genre conflation, this Rondo-Burleske isn't just a farce, it's a strangely bitter farce. Mahler had never written music so rageful as one finds in this movement. And at first this emotion, this particular tone of voice, seems as foreign to him as it does to the form. There was ferocity in the earlier symphonies, but there the emotion had a context: it was either the tone of voice of all-powerful nature, as in the Third, or it was a resisting of fate, as in the Fifth and Sixth. But the Ninth's Rondo-Burleske sounds rageful for rage's sake.

We begin and end the movement with fierce imitative counterpoint that manages to sound both learned and indignant: the opening music is marked *sehr trotzig*, "very defiant." Contrasting with this compositional exercise is a satirical operetta style representing the Viennese popular music of the day, the sorts of tunes one would hear sung in a wine tavern in Grinzing or played by organ grinders in the Prater. Contrasting yet again are the spare, withdrawn, and otherworldly passages that look ahead to the transfigured tone of the last movement. As Constantin Floros summarizes this movement's mix of styles, the burlesque aspect resides with "the contrast between three basically different levels of expression, between the reality of a trivial surround and a dreamed-of, beautiful world, which (so far) remains unattainable." And yet Mahler somehow finds musical parallels between these three different styles. For instance, the rhythmic gawkiness that marks a fugue subject—resulting from contrapuntal restrictions enabling the subject to work later on with various combinations of itself—can sound, strangely enough, like the farcical chatter of some light music styles. To juxtapose "high" and "low" styles is a feat of compositional irony, the composer would seem to be saying, but finding common ground between them demonstrates a new kind of absurdity.

Largely on account of its stylistic mix, the Rondo-Burleske becomes a lynchpin—looking back as well as forward—within the symphony as a whole. It has tranquil oases in D major that point ahead to the style and key of the fourth movement, and at the same time ratchets up the rhythmic tension of the first two movements. The tension is aggrandized by Mahler's heavy scoring in this movement, such that the ear finds the textures difficult to parse in many performances. (Had he lived long enough to tweak the scoring yet again, as he did repeatedly with his symphonies, Mahler would surely have simplified the sound of the Rondo-Burleske.) The colorations constantly shift between strings in single lines and in multiple stops, muted brass, mottoes on the horn and trombones, and strident high-register mixtures of flutes, oboes, and clarinets. In later statements, the austere A minor fugue material gains the added insistence of percussion: bass drum, snare drum, cymbals, and glockenspiel. Without the mediations Mahler performs in the Rondo-Burleske, feats of transition and emotional reconciliation that must have been facilitated by his theatrical experience, he never could have squared the four-movement format of the Ninth with its length and expressive range. And all this reconciliation takes place in just twelve to thirteen minutes, making the Rondo-Burleske the most eventfully compact movement of the Ninth Symphony.

The Rondo-Burleske begins and ends with a stern rhetorical flourish, a three-note figure (short-short-long) carved out in octaves and unisons. The fugue theme here is energized halfway through by a daring leap up of a seventh (at 0:13), the higher note struck twice as a forceful emphasis. The first extended fugal section begins at 1:25, with a short-short-long-long-long figure initially in trombones and tuba. At 1:45, the theme recurs in the first violins and then (starting at 1:56) leads into the first of several sardonic operetta parodies. Mahler is here suggesting, more in rhythm than in terms of pitch, the "Ach, die Weiber" march-septet from act 2 of Lehár's *Merry Widow*: the seven male revelers good-naturedly complaining of how "women make a difficult study, one to which we men are condemned." The Lehár imitation continues, with snatches of violin solos and shrill clarinet figures up above. With a cymbal crash (at 3:08), we're back in the gangly opening fugue material, at first in A-flat minor and then in A minor. At 3:38, the second fugue-like section begins, now starting with the trombones in a version of the very opening figure, but pursued largely by the strings. The frolicking operetta style returns (at 4:33), this time with the added silvery glint of glockenspiel and triangle. The fugue subject reappears in a *fortissimo* entrance in the horns (starting at 5:22), marking the movement's point of greatest tension. Here the subject moves more convolutedly through entrances in fifths: D-flat in the horns, A-flat on clarinets and bassoons, E-flat on oboe and English horn and trumpet, and finally B-flat on the same combination.

This arrival far afield on B-flat facilitates a simple motion to D major and the most stable music heard so far (ushered in at 5:59 by a cymbal crash and tremolos on high flutes and violins). It's as if the symphony's mortal conflict has suddenly dispersed, to allow a reassuring glimpse ahead to transcendence. This duality between raging counterpoint and fluid tranquility becomes the Rondo-Burleske's main structural premise, such that one can hear the movement alternating between "outward" and "inward" characters. The main shuntings between these two styles are announced by cymbal crashes, the first (at 3:08, mentioned above) declaring a shift from operetta frivolity back "out" to agitated counterpoint, and the second cymbal crash (at 5:59) pulling us even farther back "in," to the peaceful glimpse of the finale. This peaceful episode in D major, sustained through held notes and quiet single-pitch tremolos, brings forth a new kind of musical idea: a balanced and steady scalewise turn figure, first heard in the trumpet (at 6:07) as G–F#–E#–F#, that suggests a new tone of simplicity and equilibrium. This turn figure will saturate this new D major musical topos from top to bottom and go on to become the basic, starting idea for the next movement. It is juxtaposed with some contrasting gestures, including preludial upward sweeps in the harp. At 7:08, the finale's Elysian fields come more clearly into view when the turn figure passes from the trumpet to the violins (now marked *molto espressivo* and *mit grosser Empfindung*, "with great feeling"). Mahler strategically disallows this new idea any clear resolution, instead interspersing the four-note turn figure with quiet high A tremolos on the violins before belaboring it with a certain restless obsessiveness.

A shift to D-flat minor (at 8:34) brings in a *fortissimo* statement of the first five notes of the fugue subject in the winds, framed by a sneering caricature of the turn figure on the E-flat clarinet (at 8:27 and 8:38, described by Deryck Cooke as a "lewd grimace"), a graceless and strident descent in the flutes, and another sweep upward on the harp. A three-measure pause above violin D tremolos (at 8:43) forecasts the acres of stillness and long-held string pedal notes that will close the finale. The solo oboe takes two stabs at the turn figure, interspersed with growing references to the fugue material heard earlier in the Rondo-Burleske. At 9:11, the solo trumpet and solo viola give the clearest foretaste of the finale so far by presenting the turn figure *molto espressivo* and in regular phrasing, and closing with a curative gesture: a peaceful seventh drop, perhaps the restorative breath that Berg heard in the first movement, now with the lungs filling with even more fresh mountain air. But the returning imitative counterpoint and its sense of indignation prevents any such arrival of peace and restoration, pushing the conclusion evasively through a variety of keys as it works up to a final climax. Shoving aside any newfound sense of peace, the fugue starts up again (with a clear theme entrance in the contrabassoon at 9:56). The movement's swift and furious coda generates a desperate percussive clatter (beginning at 11:39). Richard Osborne hears these last pages as an exercise in pure anxiety, a "mere panic, a Gadarene flight into emptiness."

FOURTH MOVEMENT: A DELICATE RECONCILIATION, A NEW SENSE OF PLACE

Peace, restoration, redemption—these spiritual states, only hinted at in the first three movements of the Ninth Symphony, arrive finally with the Adagio. This movement begins and ends in the unexpected key of D-flat major, a half step lower than the expected home key of D major. If Mahler had typically used a half-step harmonic motion upward to suggest transfiguration—moving in the Fifth Symphony from C-sharp minor to an exultant finale in D major, for instance—a semitone descent implies acquiescence.

The finale opens with a motion in first and second violins doubled at the unison, an intensely hopeful signal flung out over some vast abyss. Mahler's gesture recalls the start of the third movement of Bruckner's Ninth, a movement where that ailing composer saw fit to quote his own compositional life's work. After his far-reaching initial gesture, Mahler gives us a four-note turn figure (at 0:05–0:06): A–A♭–G–A♭, an undulating group of four pitches that centralizes the main note A-flat between its upper and lower neighbors. Reintroduced here in grand fashion from the third movement, this pivoting four-note turn will suffuse Mahler's finale, perhaps looking back to similar gestures in Wagner's *Parsifal* and Wagnerian leitmotifs of suffering, empathy, and healing. Acquiescent yet tentative in its own way, the turn figure is neither an ascent nor a descent: composed of repeated seconds, it lends much of the movement an aura of restful uncertainty (or tentative repose). In this way it functions like the touched-in sixths and ninths that gently cloud any sense of purpose or conclusion that otherwise might have transpired at the end of *Das Lied von der Erde*.

The finale's unaccompanied violins descend upon the first theme in the strings (starting at 0:17), a hymnlike, *molto espressivo* idea that seems to move along in rhymed couplets. As Leonard Bernstein and others have remarked, this theme might suggest "Abide with Me" to English-speaking Christians. It's doubtful Mahler ever heard this hymn, but the imploring last stanza of its text seems apropos: "Hold Thou Thy cross before my closing eyes; / Shine through the gloom and point me to the skies. / Heaven's morning breaks, and earth's vain shadows flee; / In life, in death, O Lord, abide with me." The hymnlike aspect isn't restricted to the melody but also characterizes the texture: Mahler imitates sacred music with all parts blended and closely voiced as if they were an impassioned hymn setting, the main melodic emphasis on the top voice while the lower voices help propel the tune forward. The movement traces a single span of sentiment across the kind of two-themed, quasi-improvisational structure he had used in the first movement. The second theme is a spare and serpentine slither up through the depths. This dark and disquieting idea, introducing a purgatorial chill at a point where God seems no longer abiding, first emerges on the solo bassoon (at 1:43) and is then stated more fully in contrabassoon doubling cellos (starting at 4:04). Mahler marks the line "without emotion" and "without feeling." However, the solo viola and violin (starting at 4:41) give warm-toned, *espressivo* commentaries on the melody.

The Adagio movement unfolds like a fantasia, an extravagant and persistently digressing set of elaborations on the first theme. The first of these starts (at 6:04) with the solo horn, leading into a chromatically restless passage that belabors the all-important turn figure as it modulates, and making reference (starting at 7:42) to the opening of the movement. Mahler strategically returns at several places to the kind of full-throated doubling between first and second violins that we heard at the start of the movement: at such points, the finale's hymn adopts an emphatic tone of voice, and entreaties become insistences. Mahler first brings back the doubled-violin rhetoric at 8:14, at a point where the main, hymnlike theme strongly reasserts itself. A climax supported by a bass drum roll resolves (at 9:30) with sudden quiet and a quotation in D-flat major from the third movement, imbued yet again with the turn figure but without the intense doubling. The slithering, purgatorial second theme enters for the last time (at 11:54), now in C-sharp minor and beginning with an oscillation in harp and clarinet that makes it sound like a tragic lullaby. (We're not far away here from the *Kindertotenlieder*, and perhaps from memories of the late, lamented Putzi.) The melody continues in a rarefied pointillist texture, supported by the serpentine rising figure in the basses. A return to the turn figure leads into the decisive, do-or-die climax of the movement (beginning at 14:25): here the turn figure is announced in longer note values in the horns and trumpet, and punctuated by a *fortissimo* cymbal crash.

As if to recapitulate, the music then recalls the start of the movement, complete with the grappling, preludial single line in unison doubled violins (starting at 14:50, the line now played *Viel Bogen*, "with lots of bow strokes," to get the biggest sound possible). Interspersed with the restless harmonic migrations are brief and increasingly simple points of rest that hold out the promise of a final peaceful arrival for the Ninth Symphony. These include the quiet, one-measure excursion into B-flat major (starting at 16:15), and then another bar where the music shuns all harmonic complication and alights on a single, serene pitch (the high C in violins and piccolo at 18:13), exited via the kind of downward slide that notioned bliss in the Rückert song "I Have Become Lost to the World" ("Ich bin der Welt abhanden gekommen") and the Adagietto movement of the Fifth Symphony. The finale of the Ninth had started with emphatic doubled violins, but now the symphonic textures begin to evaporate just as the movement starts to give up any sense of argument. With their tenuous, barely sketched-in lines, the solo cello (starting at 18:21 and again at 19:18) and English horn (starting at 18:45) give a contrasting rejoinder to the doubled violins that had opened the movement. These melodic descents create expectancy by denying the omnipresent turn figure, and by lingering over the dominant of the original D major tonic.

They also set the stage for the figure that rises quietly in the second violins (starting at 19:58) as a lead-in to the luminous last paragraph of the movement (marked *Adagissimo*). We hear an almost verbatim return of the climactic turn-ridden passage (as we encountered it back at 14:25), music that was previously overwhelming and decisive but is now muted, *pianissimo*, and riddled with gaps as if it were losing its ability to speak. Mahler briefly quotes the fourth of the *Kindertotenlieder* (starting at 20:43, the violins hinting at the song's text on how, in the midst of mortal strife, "the day is fair on yonder hills"—"der Tag ist schön auf jenen Höhn"). A series of isolated, hesitant, beautifully touched-in brushstrokes fills out the registral space, lastly reaching down (starting at 21:41) to the violas. They give last reminders of the turn figure before the symphony comes to rest in the long-anticipated key of D-flat major and then dies away (*esterbend*) from *pianississimo* into a restful quietude. In performance, the listener should be left unsure where the music stops and the final silence begins—applause comes as both an interruption and an intrusion.

If the finale of the Ninth in all its simplicity can seem insufficient as a counterweight to the convoluted and all-important first movement, or at least can seem so with performers who don't give themselves over to it two hundred percent, then we might better consider it an answer to a different symphonic question. Mahler's Fifth Symphony had progressed up a half step to allow itself unbridled optimism; the Seventh had motioned from E minor to the fairly distant key of C major as a metaphor for moving from night to day; the Eighth Symphony had remained in E-flat major but in its second part motioned heavenward in register as an enactment of Faust's redemption; *Das Lied von der Erde* had moved from A minor to C major while casting its sights to the horizon as a place where home is. And now in the Ninth Symphony, we have an overall harmonic movement from D major to D-flat major. This movement not up but downward indicates a different kind of passage: Richard Osborne sees such a large-scale harmonic turn as connoting a change in the music's "sense of moral well-being," and he hears the Ninth's concluding arrival in D-flat major as "a chastening shift." Said in other terms: the finale of the Ninth is different because it posits an argument less than it connotes and comes to inhabit a different sense of place. And that space is no longer a place for concluding aspiration and transcendence; rather, it is a position of submission, acceptance, and consent.

12

SYMPHONY NO. 10

Music from the Hereafter?

Mahler died in a Vienna sanatorium on May 18, 1911, aged fifty. A formidable type-A personality who liked to "work off" his illnesses, he was ultimately done in by a streptococcal infection that turned into heart disease. Left on his desk were drafts and sketches for a Tenth Symphony in five movements. Only the brief third movement and the long Adagio first movement were more or less complete and more or less orchestrated, while the others were variably incomplete in texture and had only scattered indications of instrumentation. In the early 1920s, Alma had composer Ernst Krenek make a fair copy of the first and third movements for performance—and these became the basis for the Tenth's first partial concert presentations, in Vienna and Amsterdam in 1924.

For those early audiences trying to fathom the majestic and disconsolate first movement, Mahler's Tenth Symphony must have seemed—from both temporal and musical perspectives—to be music from beyond the grave. Here was a key piece from a major composer, made public more than a decade after his passing. Bruno Walter had premiered the Ninth Symphony and *Das Lied von der Erde* some months after Mahler's death, but those pieces were already considered finished in the sense of being fully orchestrated and ready for concert performance—even if, as was his practice, he would have made many additional changes and revisions up to and after the work's premiere. The

Tenth, by contrast, was said at first to be simply unperformable: in his authoritative 1913 book on Mahler, Richard Specht told his readers that the Tenth "will never be brought to sounding form" from the manuscripts; "it is entirely impossible for another person to arrange the score from [these] mute signs." So it is sad to observe that when the impossible was (partially) achieved and two continuous and gripping movements of the Tenth were finally performed in 1924, comprising some thirty minutes of previously unheard music, they left little impression.

Publication soon followed, in increments and in different formats. First to appear were some of Mahler's drafts, which Alma published in facsimile in 1924. This volume allowed musicians to see the extent of the Tenth Symphony for themselves—among them the British musicologist Deryck Cooke (1919–1976), who ended up publishing the first performing edition of the work in 1976. The main autograph source for the Tenth Symphony is in four staves, like a piano duet. Mahler's priority at this point was continuity: he worked up his composition by pushing relentlessly forward day by day through the longest possible trains of thought. What this meant was writing down something—anything—at all points in the piece, whether that meant setting down part of the melody, a secondary line in the texture, a bass line, or even just a rhythm. Having thereby come to an understanding of what the symphony consisted of and where it wanted to go, Mahler in his next pass-through would have filled out the texture, adding lines of music, filling out harmonies, developing the instrumentation, and possibly adding and dropping some material. He didn't get very far into that stage of work before he was called away by conducting duties in New York, the impulse to refine parts of his Ninth Symphony, and lastly the troubles of his final illness.

The first public airing of the Tenth as a five-movement composition took place in London in 1960, when Berthold Goldschmidt conducted Cooke's as-yet-unpublished version. A broader public got to know the piece when Eugene Ormandy recorded Cooke's revised edition with the Philadelphia Orchestra in 1964, for Columbia Records. Cooke's second performing edition, published in 1976 and then again in 1989 with a few emendations, has since come to prevail as the standard version of Mahler's Tenth Symphony. The composition that emerged—reaching print more than sixty years after the fact—is a five-movement layout similar to the Seventh Symphony insofar as it follows a symmetrical order. The roughly half-hour first and fifth movements mirror one another in terms of length and tone. They enclose two turbulent scherzos of similar length, and then at the center we have a short third movement that seems to have been transplanted in from elsewhere. The Tenth ends with a long Adagio movement that closes quietly, thereby recalling the Ninth Symphony.

1. Adagio (Slowly) (26 minutes)
2. Scherzo. *Schnelle Viertel* (Scherzo. Measured in quick quarter notes) (12 minutes)
3. "Purgatorio." *Allegretto moderato* ("Purgatory." Moderately fast) (4 minutes)
4. Scherzo. *Allegro pesante. Nicht zu schnell* (Scherzo. Quickly and heavily. Not too fast) (11 minutes)
5. Finale. *Langsam, schwer* (Finale. Slowly, heavily) (25 minutes)

I go into all these historical and textual details because they help in understanding the complex character of the Tenth Symphony, or even grasping just what the Tenth Symphony *is*. The piece will never be finished. It will always have a hypothetical aspect, no matter who edits or performs it. In fact, as of this writing nine editors have produced five-movement versions, with Deryck Cooke involved in three successive editions:

Clinton Carpenter (1949, revised 1966)
Joe Wheeler (1953, revised 1965)
Hans Wollschläger (1962, withdrawn)
Deryck Cooke (first version, 1964; second performing version, 1972; small revisions by Berthold Goldschmidt and David and Colin Matthews, 1989)
Remo Mazzetti Jr. (1989)
Rudolf Barshai (2000)
Nicola Samale and Giuseppe Mazzuca (2001)
Yoel Gamzou (2010)
Michelle Castelletti (2012)

From the start, Cooke shunned any idea of completing the Tenth and limited himself to "making a performing version of the work as far as Mahler had got with it (which was really somewhere!)." He quickly realized the Tenth Symphony is much more complete in terms of horizontal argument than vertical texture. This helps explain why the various performing editions have the music sounding either gaunt (the 1951 edition of the first and third movements, Cooke's three editions, Wheeler's even more hands-off performing version), or distinctly un-Mahlerian (the more interventionist, sometimes even muddled editions by Carpenter, Barshai, Mazzetti Jr., and Samale and Mazzuca). The latter versions have curiosity value, but in aiming for a fuller symphonic experience, those editors have ended up sounding intrusive and unidiomatic. Cooke, by contrast, realized that no matter how complex and unsettled Mahler's orchestral textures may get, they never sound clotted, ugly, or over-scored; it was perhaps the lack of a consistent textual basis for what Cooke called Mahler's "incomparable orchestration" that discouraged him from doing anything more comprehensive or assertive as an editor of the Tenth. Castelletti's version, which presents Mahler's composition as "completed and arranged for chamber orchestra," sidesteps these issues by going in the opposite direction and not trying for a full orchestrational realization at all.

It's easy to be appalled at the idea of nine editors having their way with a piece by a long-deceased composer, some of them with clear intentions and others not. But one thing we can't argue is that any of Mahler's pieces are pristine, set-in-stone masterworks that shouldn't be touched. He was in the habit of changing his own music well after the fact—with those symphonies already published as well as those yet to be published—and thereby contrasted with his colleague Richard Strauss, who rarely revisited earlier scores. Mahler's changes were so habitual that one could even say he was accustomed to creating and re-creating different "performing versions" of his own compositions. He would commonly make such changes when preparing to conduct an earlier piece, and these tweaks could go on for decades: he was still changing the instrumentation of the First Symphony, for instance, when he conducted that work for the last time in New York in 1909, and the Fifth Symphony was in a continual state of textural revision.

One tantalizing mystery with the Tenth is the long, winding, desolate viola line with which the first movement begins. At the indicated andante tempo, the violas play alone for more than a minute before they're joined (at 1:16, and at the new adagio tempo) by three trombones and the rest of the strings. The viola melody is frighteningly lean and haggard, and for that reason an unusual way to start an eighty-minute symphony: couched in the dusky and lonely sound of these low string instruments, the theme lurches along fitfully and ventures far enough from tonal clarity that its first eight notes include seven of the twelve chromatic pitches (only D is repeated before the melody ascends to a high B). This modern-sounding chromaticism could be a sign that Mahler was taking Arnold Schoenberg's recent freely atonal music to heart; we do know he was a staunch supporter of the younger composer and his associates, even when it created political difficulties for him and even when he found their music hard to understand. Or, rather than demonstrating an "advanced" compositional style, the line might just be incomplete. Mahler had never before written such an extended and uninterrupted line for one kind of instrument, and that makes the viola theme sound uncharacteristic and undeveloped as it stands (in all editions). But this long viola line is just one of many gaunt, alienated-sounding passages in the Tenth Symphony, and the disaffected tone of any of these sections could be attributed to Mahler's time limitations at the drafting stage.

It's tempting to hear in the desolate tone of the viola melody an expression of the composer's pressing sense of mortality. But Mahler was not ill when he sketched the Tenth at his summer retreat at Toblach in the South Tyrol. The summer of 1910 was a busy and productive one for him: while working on the Tenth and preparing to conduct the premiere of his epic Eighth Symphony in Munich, he was stoking an appetite and taking his usual long walks. In telegrams to Alma that July, he reported feeling "in excellent health," "cheerful," and "constantly well." But that's not to say it was a peaceful time. Two contrasting emotional events towered over those four months from June through September: Gustav's discovery that Alma was having an affair with genius architect-in-the-making Walter Gropius, followed by the predictable accusations and marital ultimatums, and then Gustav's touching expressions of love, guilt, and tenderness of heart; and on September 12 his first performance of the Eighth Symphony, a task that consumed much of his time and energy.

Mahler's Tenth, at least in the first and third movements, is unusual in that it reapportions to the small scale the large-scale chordal changes that we'd expect to hear in sonata forms. Instead of departing from grounded thematic areas through clear modulations and transitions, the music deviates and then returns within a single bar, or from one bar to the next, or even by having single chords function as harmonic departures. Instead of the dominant key being broached as its one big harmonic excursion, the movement gives way to a sudden climactic passage I've mentioned: the unexpected eruption of A-flat minor before the music piles up layers of dissonance to form the nine-note "scream" (at 18:58). This shocking detonation of A-flat minor—the clear climax of the movement, but harmonically inexplicable within its overall context of F-sharp minor—seems to discharge the half-hour movement's pent-up harmonic tensions in a mere minute and a half. Before that, the only point where the movement really tries to leave the key of F-sharp is partway into the sort-of development section (starting at 10:30), where A minor serves as a point of departure. This movement doesn't really sound like it's able to get away from F-sharp as a key center, and that undermines any sense of primary and secondary themes that would support hearing a sonata structure. But then there's also the long, chromatic first theme on violas at the opening, an idea that questions the possibility of an F-sharp basis before it even occurs—and gives a sense of departure before there's anything to depart from. In short, the first theme of the movement somehow sounds at the same time like an initiation and an arrival.

FIRST, SECOND, AND THIRD MOVEMENTS: CIRCULARITY, PROPHECY, PURGATORY

Before the A-flat minor outburst, Mahler's first movement expends considerable time and energy without going far either musically or emotionally; it has a circular, returning-to-where-we-were quality. Across statements of second and third themes, the movement continues to gravitate inevitably back to its earlier sounds. Clearly, this music redefines traditional ideas of symphonic tonal motion, tried-and-trusted coordinations between short-term and long-term in lengthy musical spans. Going along with that in the first movement are melodic arcs that tend to be circular, going round and round, rising and falling, not getting far; and journeys between soft and loud that seem short-breathed and uncoordinated. (All this makes the A-flat minor–based scream seem almost inevitable in retrospect, shocking as it may be when it arrives.) In a 1961 article cited by Constantin Floros, analyst Eberhardt

Klemm presented the first movement of the Tenth as "the image of frozen space," a situation where "the dynamics of the movement move in a constant up and down, an 'on the way' without ever getting there." The last notes of the opening viola theme give one example. The line struggles (starting at 0:44) to reach some kind of cadence, a real task after all the chromatic wandering, and the search for rest and resolution becomes a circular effort. When the full orchestral theme (the second theme) finally comes in at 1:16, it's firmly in F-sharp major—a key center that we've arrived at through chromatic pitch circling rather than any real harmonic motion. (Talking about the start of this theme, a theorist might say what starts as "on" a wistfully suggested F-sharp pitch somehow becomes "in" a resolute F-sharp major. This jump, along with the sheer oddness of these closing viola pitches, is another reason to think Mahler intended to go back and fill out the movement's initial textures.)

This second theme, lyrical and static but also striving in character, soon starts to move upward; but when it reaches its apparent point of arrival (at 2:10), we are simply back where the theme had started, in F-sharp major. This unrushed music is interrupted by a more dancelike theme (the third theme, starting at 2:36), which—shifting again by half step rather than through any real harmonic movement—begins in G major. After a short divergence in flutes and oboes that centers on G-sharp, the music becomes more predictably tonal and actually gives us our first proper authentic cadence of the movement—to F-sharp minor. Especially with the violin solo and string pizzicatos, this section sounds like the sinister yet coquettish *Totentanz* (dance of death) style that Mahler had hinted at in earlier symphonies. But then, just as quickly as it started, we're back (starting at 3:35) in the heavily chromatic viola first theme—though this time with some rhythmic touches from the F-sharp major second theme. After only fifty seconds of that (starting at 4:23), we're back again in the F-sharp major music, which in this instance is extended and spurred on to new emotional heights. This is followed (starting at 7:51) by the longest version yet of the dancelike third theme material, this time offered in the dominant key of C-sharp major and filled out with more elaborate woodwind contributions. An overabundance of trills adds to the sarcastic feel of the passage.

Mahler's first movement is a moment-to-moment, freeform structure, but one that ends up being largely symmetrical. It intermingles and varies the three contrasting themes, with their statements as brief as four measures and as long as thirty. As we go through this movement, the third "dance of death" theme becomes ever more diabolical, while the first and second remain stoic and implacable. When the chromatic first theme comes back shortened to only seven bars (at 9:47), it leads into a segment that sounds like a development in the way it expands on and puzzles out material from all three themes. Clocking in at two minutes, this development section also turns out to be strangely short. Matters of length aside, this becomes the most conventional part of the movement. It is peppered with solos and, as one would expect in a development section, the writing has a more consistent contrapuntal-imitative character. As this development section comes to a close, it hews even closer to the old sonata-form rules by presenting a retransition—the traditional closing off of the development where the music prepares a clear return to the first theme and the tonic key. For the first time in the Tenth Symphony, the harmonies move regularly through fifths: starting in E-flat (at 12:06) and then moving to A-flat, C-sharp, and finally—at the movement's recapitulation, starting at 12:53—the tonic F-sharp major. What returns here isn't the expected first theme, but the questing second theme, its string lines now passionately stretching up and under through wide intervals, often larger than an octave. The cynical and dancelike third theme follows (starting at 14:03), and after working up to a dead-end climax, the theme quietly starts over again.

What follows could hardly be expected, and indeed stands as unique in Mahler's output. The "questing" second theme comes back (at 16:22), but after just six measures gives way (at 17:00) to an elaborated version of the first theme that tentatively sets the stage for the distant key of A-flat. When A-flat minor arrives (at 17:58), it is a powerful *fortississimo*, and with brass and winds in an organ-like texture backed by sweeps on the harp and up-down figuration on the strings. This music has an austere and archaic sound—most analysts call it a chorale. (If this is a chorale, its tone suggests a fire-and-brimstone, Old Testament message rather than a Protestant lesson in faith and grace.) This chorale-like passage aims for a high point that doesn't arrive; instead of concluding, it trails into a thirty-second rendition of the dancelike third theme, complete with the pizzicato strings. All this foreshortening and unsettledness is tacitly preparing us for the nine-note scream that will become the climax of the movement. The preparation begins in earnest when the violins latch on to a quiet A-natural (at 18:44), the note that underpins a crescendo and forceful accrual of the climactic dissonance. The piercingly dissonant scream piles up as layered blocks of sound, suggesting separate manuals on the organ that we've been hearing in the would-be chorale passage. The nine-note dissonance begins with the A, then adds in the block of horns and higher winds playing *forte*; followed by the block combination of trombones, lower winds, and the rest of the strings playing *fortissimo*; and lastly by the bass tuba, the block of trumpets, and the higher winds kicking up to a higher register. At 19:02, the solo trumpet takes over the clarion A from the violins, and then the whole nine-note dissonance is repeated en masse—unlayered and *fortissimo*, its godly wrath reiterated and unappeased. (Cooke chose to mix religion and cosmology when he likened the chord to "some awe-inspiring cosmic revelation." This is Mahler referencing the earsplitting climax of the third movement of Bruckner's Ninth, and possibly recalling that devout composer's fear of sin and his belief in Old Testament prophecies.)

The nine-note scream's apocalyptic prophecy is quickly dispersed: coming out of it, we take only four bars to reach back to the tonic F-sharp major and a long, lyrical coda section (starting at 19:30) that is less contrite than gently regretful—or maybe just evasive. A descending three-note figure leads into this coda, where it generates a gentle theme in the first violins. Parts of the movement's three themes all return in this closing section, with tensions momentarily reintroduced by chromatic elements from the opening first theme (starting at 20:16). An excursion into E-flat major in the violins and violas (at 22:44), a brief reference to the radiant string writing in Wagner's *Lohengrin*, hints at transcendence and renewal. The expressive pauses and the slow dovetailings between isolated notes suggest the end of the last movement of the Ninth Symphony, while the quiet and methodical construal of longing recalls the end of the first movement of that same work. There is a return of the opening single-line desolation and the second theme, and an oboe solo is followed by one last threat of anxious chromaticism in doubled strings and winds. The strings then descend lower and lower, until the double basses land on a low C-sharp (at 25:00) and there begins another sonorous piling-up: this time quietly and slowly gathering up a C-sharp dominant seventh chord, as a gentle and assured reply to (or perhaps resolution of) the unrequited nine-note scream that had also been built over a C-sharp in the bass, but left hanging. At the close of the movement, the authentic cadence and F-sharp major tonic pizzicato chord sound too simple and maybe trivial to avert memories of all that's come before.

The cogent and incisive second movement of the Tenth—music that wasn't aired publicly until more than half a century after it was composed—makes a strong contrast with the purgatorial first movement. (At one time Mahler thought of this second movement as the finale, and so the Tenth could have ended very differently than it now does: with the joyous, whooping music at the end of what is now the second movement. With its basis in F-sharp major/minor, the scherzo movement would certainly have closed the Tenth in an appropriate key.) This music is all about rhythmic clarity and emotional conciseness, meaning the movement's precarious balance between anger and joy is honed to razor thinness. The metric shifts in the opening section are difficult to coordinate: conductor Riccardo Chailly, interviewed by Michael McManus after he'd been performing Cooke's edition for a quarter of a century, described the second movement as "impossibly complicated to play and to conduct," at least as much a technical challenge as the notorious "Danse sacrale" in Stravinsky's *Rite of Spring*. (Mahler's recurring patterns are like Stravinsky's in having "one too many notes," meaning the strong beats soon become weak beats, the downs become ups, and vice versa.) Mahler's manic scherzo manner, which is here lightened in texture by imitative polyphony and lightened in tone by rhythmically steady dancelike trio sections, harks back to the Ninth Symphony—more specifically, to the defiant Rondo-Burleske movement in that work. While the textures of the two movements are both contrapuntal, the second movement of the Tenth ultimately resembles the big, central scherzo of the Fifth Symphony in the way it promises to steer the whole musical journey from dark to light. Its energy becomes more dancelike than diabolical.

The form of the movement becomes almost simplistic in its broad outlines, making a contrast with the first movement, yet both A and B sections become more variable and impulsive as the movement goes on. The B trio section sounds all the more quaint for having its own woodwind-dominated central section in G minor (starting at 3:50), complete with written-out repeats. The shifting A material returns at 5:19, after which the B sounds less traditional than before when it comes back at 6:25. This material also starts to wander harmonically, moving fleetingly to B major and F major, among other keys. The A material also becomes more erratic at its final return (starting at 7:48). The coda section (starting at 8:50) marks a sudden departure, beginning quietly at a slower tempo and in the key of F-sharp major (having shifted from the A-minor close of the preceding section). The instrumentation is for solo trumpet over lower brass: this melody sounded a bit vulgar when it first growled its way into the earlier B section; now, played more slowly on a high brass instrument, it sounds rather boozy—a considerable stylistic and emotional digression so close to the end of the movement. The tempo then pulls back even more, and at 9:33 we hear faint and fleeting allusions to the A-flat apocalypse of the first movement, but of course without the climactic dissonance. There's a final reference (at 10:40) to the *Ländler* music we heard in the B section, and one last questioning digression to an unstable key area. At 11:14, the harmony sidesteps to the tonic F-sharp major, and the trumpets and horns throw their hats in the air with a jubilant, ascending line that propels the movement to its close.

Mahler's tiny third movement is the only one he gave a title to in the manuscript. "Purgatorio" could refer here either to the second part of Dante's *Divine Comedy* or, as is more likely, to the "Purgatorio" poems by Mahler's old university friend Siegfried Lipiner. As his jumping-off point for this four-minute essay in perpetual motion, Mahler took a repeating figure from his *Knaben Wunderhorn* song "The Earthly Life" ("Das irdische Leben"). In this song, a child begs his mother for food while she hurriedly harvests the grain and threshes it, only to see him die of starvation when she finally pulls the bread from the oven. The song depicts life as a path of drudgery, deprivation, futility, and ultimately death. Henry-Louis de la Grange was the first to suggest (in 1986), on the basis of dates and manuscript evidence, that the "Purgatorio" movement in the Tenth was Mahler's immediate musical reaction to Alma's affair. In the heated discussion that followed that revelation, she claimed Mahler had become distant and was forcing her into a life of emotional deprivation—an unapologetic declaration that could have made Mahler think back both to Lipiner's text and "The Earthly Life."

Chailly calls the "Purgatorio" movement "a treasure," a word that could describe the way Mahler manages here to contain and alchemize conflict, and then miniaturize and colorize that containment in such a way that the anguish becomes beautiful and jewel-like. The "Purgatorio" shows how conflictedness can be picturesque, even exquisite. The movement catalogs confrontational and repentant sentiments in its brief span, and it juxtaposes them in kaleidoscopic orchestral colorations. The violins and violas are all muted at the start, making the string timbres dampened and remote. The opening violin melody dangles the possibility of resolving: it settles on the second scale degree in a "proper way" three times (at 0:10, 0:13, and 0:17) before it quietly—though arbitrarily and abruptly, perhaps cruelly—ends on the home pitch in an "improper way" (at 0:19). It wouldn't be far-fetched to hear this as an allegory for life itself, as describing a grinding stretch of time that's informed and articulated by its own ending. But the movement's graceful if unpredictable shifts from minor to major (and back again) suggest these dark lessons shouldn't be taken too seriously to heart, since life just goes on—until finally it doesn't. The movement's conflictedness also finds a voice in call-and-response repetitions: the three-note figure repeated between oboe (at 0:04) and bassoon (at 0:07); the flute managing to escape the treadmill just long enough to squeak out an absurd, complaining version of the same figure (at 0:24); and the lower strings, still muted, cranking out a gruff retort (at 0:59) to the graceful woodwind statements.

The trio section (starting at 1:31) brings in the brass and wrenches the music into D minor/major. A lamenting, heavily burdened theme (starting at 1:58) shuns the breathlessness of the purgatorial treadmill: it becomes the movement's first lyrical element, and the first idea to span more than one bar. But its lyricism soon collapses into indignant discords (at 2:17), and the perpetual treadmill starts up once again. The whole movement then starts over seamlessly in a *da capo* repeat (at 3:05), demonstrating the eternity of human toil. As before, the musical representation of drudgery moves into a major key, but this time around the brightening seems a matter of necessity rather than choice. A rough swipe of trombone, horns, and harp brings everything to an abrupt and arbitrary end—double basses and tam-tam trailing in the wake.

FOURTH AND FIFTH MOVEMENTS: OPPOSITIONS RESOLVED IN REGRET

With the fourth movement, we arrive at the Tenth Symphony's second scherzo. These textures often get thin in Cooke's and Wheeler's editions. Mahler resorted to minimal shorthand in drafting his fourth and fifth movements, sometimes cutting back to one or two notes per measure, and had more or less stopped giving instrumentation cues. As if in compensation, the manuscripts of these last movements have the added detail of Mahler's despairing marginal scrawls—his pen-and-ink references to oppressive agonies, including Amfortas's unbearable wound in Wagner's *Parsifal*, and several times calling out directly to Alma herself. Following their confrontation that summer over the affair, Alma remembered her husband pacing and reading the Bible; similarly, his exclamations in the Tenth Symphony manuscript, including some recollections from scripture ("Oh God, oh God, why have you forsaken me?"), suggest encroaching madness. Mahler's diabolical inscription at the start of the fourth movement ("the devil dances with me"—"Der Teufel tanzt es mit mir") hints at some kind of mania.

The fourth movement of the Tenth alternates five statements of the "demonic scherzo" material with five renditions of the "tender, happy waltz." As in earlier rondo- or sonata-related movements of the Tenth, these sections vary in length, from a mere six-measure mention through an opening-out that takes up 130 bars. Recognition and variation of the two types becomes the structural idea, as opposed to any traditional symphonic proportioning of them. Listening to the movement in broader terms, we hear a series of five pinnacles (at 1:59, 3:52, 5:01, 8:17, and 9:20), each of them discharging through a slower, descending four-note melodic segment in a high register. These four-note statements again suggest passages in "Das Trinklied vom Jammer der Erde," though it's one three-note tag that echoes that piece most specifically: at 3:25 in the fourth movement of the Tenth, we hear an F–E–E–D in the solo cello and violas that recalls the tenor's line from "Das Trinklied" at the words "stirbt die Freude, der Gesang" ("joy and song die"), a moment of paradoxically indignant resignation. These five climaxes generally become noisier and more discordant as the fourth movement goes along: we approach the climax at 8:17 through a strange transition that borders on Schoenbergian disharmony, and then come out of it (in

Cooke's edition) to the ghostly, wooden twitch-twitch of the *Rute*; and then the last climax at 9:20 proves to be the most melodic of all but also leads us to a state of "modern" tonal-harmonic collapse (at 9:42). The movement is gradually becoming sparer and more otherworldly, less melodic, and more focused on a gloomy descending bass figure. This last climax ushers in the spectral coda, which mingles elements of both the scherzo and the waltz. Finally (at 10:38), we hear one last exhalation, a descending tremolo figure first heard in the "demonic scherzo" material (at 1:28), and now given by Cooke to the tuba and contrabasses. This leads to the vacant closing section of the movement: Mahler didn't have time to supply any melody here, and so all we get are the skeletal rattlings of drums accompanied by rising two-note splotches in some melodic instruments.

The pitch-black, startling stroke of a large muffled drum leads into the finale and initiates a succession of such beats. Writing at this point in his draft, Mahler called out to Alma in pen and ink, "You alone know what it means. Ah! Ah! Ah! Farewell my lyre!" ("Ach! Ach! Ach! Leb wohl mein Saitenspiel!"). As the famous story has it, the Mahlers witnessed a funeral procession in the street while at the Hotel Majestic during their first stay in New York. A fireman had died in the line of duty and, as Gustav and Alma leaned out their windows and wept at the sight, dampened drumbeats impelled the dismal procession down Central Park West. When Mahler inserted those real-life drumbeats into the Tenth's finale, he made simultaneous reference to Alma (whom Mahler called his "Saitenspiel," meaning his music or, more broadly yet, his muse), their joint experiences, and the fleeting nature of life itself. The drum strokes are interspersed with gaping silences, and then a dirgelike ascending scale figure in the bass (given by Cooke to the low tuba, a coloration that—though appropriately funereal—might count as more Wagnerian than Mahlerian). We are still suffering from the near-absence of manuscript detail with which Mahler ended the previous movement, and at this point we're waiting for melody—any kind of melody—to surface. The extended denial of light, focus, and songfulness makes for an agonizing wait, especially with this most irrepressibly lyric of composers. The tonal harmonies are clouded by sixths, minor sevenths, and elevenths. There are hushed tattoos in the horns (recollections of the three-note figure from the "Purgatorio" movement), and then (starting at 0:47) a gesture of tragic, hollow expiration in the winds and horn section. (Cooke's choice of tam-tam and low harp here are further signs that he associated this music with *Das Lied von der Erde*, in this case with the final "Abschied" movement of that work.) Then we encounter more rustlings, more waiting, more ascending tuba figures, and (starting at 1:31) a second expiration.

Finally, a hopeful ascending seventh in the first horn ushers in a long-breathed, seemingly limitless melody in the flute (starting at 2:11), an idea that will be taken up and expanded by the strings. (It was Mahler who specified the flute here—a sound that, in this middle register of the instrument, is both cool and warm, powered by human breath but not as colorful and forthcoming as a string instrument.) This entrance of the movement's first theme is a heart-stopping moment, a pastel color intruding on the blackness, poignant not least for the darkness from which it emerges and the listener's length of waiting. And the melody itself is transcendent—fragrant, hopeful, gently desirous, and not to be forgotten, like the early-spring lilac that blooms forth from lifeless earth at the start of T. S. Eliot's *The Waste Land*: "April is the cruellest month, breeding / Lilacs out of the dead land, mixing / Memory and desire, stirring / Dull roots with spring rain." Mahler's gradual descent in the bass—the harmonies moving from the initial D minor to an extraordinarily voiced B major chord at 2:52—reveal a farsighted line of musical sight that's new to the symphony, the thought manifesting some manner of hope in its way of looking forward, reaching melodically and harmonically far over the bar line. The sound, too, reaches forward: as the solo flute gradually ascends to a higher register, its tone becomes more vibrant and more intricate. Things become even brighter when the strings take up the melody (at 3:36), moving it to a slightly higher register and pulling the music into the brighter key of B major.

But nothing is ever easy or simple in Mahler: transformation and redemption, once promised and in some measure achieved, are revealed to be complex, fragile, or impermanent. It's never too late to withdraw a promise. Now that the finale has reached higher registers and a brighter key, the hopeful ascending seventh is able to return—but this time (starting at 6:17) it brings us back to the funeral drumbeats, bass-figure dirge, and somber expiration-cadence. The last such expiration-cadence leads not back into the first theme, but directly (at 7:24) into a faster allegro tempo and the start of the sonata form proper. Beginning on a note of immediacy and action, with its contrapuntal textures and development of motives from earlier movements, the music seems to banish any funereal memories but is not truly positive in tone. A new D major idea at 8:36 brings together the orchestra as a whole, unified ensemble—the first real tutti music for quite some time—but the mood remains ambivalent. One of the previous movement's climactic "Trinklied vom Jammer der Erde" quotes is referenced again (starting at 9:10), inserting a "demonic scherzo" element into the finale. The hopeful rising seventh interval is taken up by the horns (at 9:24), who start to sketch out the beginning of the first theme and gradually mete out more and more of it. As at the start of the movement, the first theme is pulled into B major: starting at 10:52, a variation of the melody is split between first violins, the horn, and then the trumpet, all underpinned by the harp. To round off this five-minute Allegro section, we hear (at 11:56) a short restatement of material from its opening.

With preceding movements cited, the hopeful promise of the finale's first theme kept, and some hint of structural finalization already made, it's time to return to unfinished business from the first movement. Approaching the end of the finale of the Tenth, Mahler proceeded roughly in reverse order as he recollected those earlier crises. First recalled from the opening movement are the nine-note scream and its preceding chords (the quote starting at 12:17 in the finale), the scream (at 12:59) now followed by and discharged through the unison opening theme, played here (starting at 13:09) by the horns instead of the original violas, and with solo trumpet taking over from the original violins as keeper of the high A. In later revisions, Mahler might have given a clearer purpose to the return of the A-flat music and dissonant scream. As it stands, should we hear a resemblance to the chorale returning at the close of the Fifth Symphony, or hear it more like the finale of the Third Symphony quoting from its own first movement?

The finale's hopeful first theme then returns and is restated and indulged at length, starting in B-flat major in the woodwinds and then in the horns and tuba; then it appears in the tonic F-sharp major with the strings (starting at 15:43 with the hopeful seventh leap, now finally seeing its promise kept). Starting at 16:32 the clearest restatement yet arrives, on strings and harp, followed (beginning at 18:05) by a continuation in G major (under which, given just a melodic line in the draft,

Cooke managed to construct or reconstruct an extraordinary sequence of intensely expressive harmonies).

There is plenty of wrapping up and closing off to be done at the end of a Mahler symphony. And the amount of detail the composer included toward the end of his draft of the Tenth—the short score sometimes expanding to five staves—shows he had carefully crafted ideas on its completion. As already suggested, the first theme was primary in his strategy for the finale, and it would need a suitable restatement. We hear this theme return (starting at 19:34) in an open-throated and conclusive declaration, back in the tonic F-sharp major and played *fortissimo* and with "grosser Ton" (a big tone).

With the initial promise of that melody now well and fully kept, we are free to enjoy a static and leisurely outro statement—the F-sharp major harmony strongly sustained against diminishing dynamics and thinning textures. This would seem to be some sort of repeat of the gradual and rarefied letting-go we heard at the close of the Ninth Symphony. Or the end of the Tenth could also be heard as a clarification of the enigmatic emotions at the end of *Das Lied von der Erde*. The writing is similar, but the mood toward the close of the Tenth is openly regretful—a new addition to Mahler's expressive vocabulary—while the Ninth and *Das Lied* ended in a state of gradual detachment. The finale of the Tenth has one last gambit in store: the violins, violas, and cellos muster all their remaining energy (at 24:00) and leap up a thirteenth in unison, from B-sharp to G-sharp, before descending briefly and dying back to a state of peace and collectedness. Cooke hears the gesture as "a sigh of great tenderness." This concluding signal in Mahler's last symphony, ending with a touched-in sixth in the horns as an assurance that continuation is possible, is also a decisive gesture, a display of strength and hope. And of love: at the top of his last page, Mahler wrote "für dich leben! für dich sterben!" ("To live for you! To die for you!"), and then over the final leap, his wife's nickname: "Almschi!" This final expression of life and expectation, a passage and a movement not played until a half century after the composer's death, could be a corrective to Mahler's status as the self-centered neurotic of symphonic history. Cooke was among those so convinced, writing in his introductory book on Mahler, "The Tenth Symphony reveals that the Ninth had been a phase, like the Sixth, which he had faced and overcome."

AN EMERGENT SYMPHONY

Times have changed. When the Adagio and "Purgatorio" movements of the Tenth were first played in 1924, the overall reaction was indifference—and conviction that the Tenth Symphony was at worst a flawed or irretrievable work, and at best a piece that would only be violated by completion. But Cooke's publication of his "performing version" in 1976 turned out to be a decisive moment in Mahler reception—a new fascination, a catalyst to further energize the Mahler boom that had begun in the 1960s. In the decades since, the Tenth has gone from being a derelict piece with many Mahler conductors to a calling card for some younger *maestri*. Among the old-guard devotees who rejected a five-movement Tenth out of hand were Bruno Walter, Otto Klemperer, Rafael Kubelik, Georg Solti, Leonard Bernstein, Pierre Boulez, and Claudio Abbado. But among younger conductors, Simon Rattle made a renewed cause of it when the Berlin Philharmonic named him music director in 1999, and more recently the Montreal-born Yannick Nézet-Séguin has followed Rattle's example in releasing not one, but two recorded performances, with two different orchestras.

Some fifty years ago *New York Times* music critic Harold C. Schonberg commented cynically on the devotion that Mahler inspires: "The worship of Mahler amounts to a religion . . . his admirers approach him mystically." The Mahler religion has only increased since he made that remark, and the Tenth Symphony has played a role in this upsurge. In the twenty-first century, a time when Mahler has all but overtaken repertory stalwarts like Beethoven and Tchaikovsky, the Tenth Symphony has become one of his most frequently played and recorded pieces—usually in the Cooke edition. At a time when canonic repertory pieces are being shunned on account of their fixity, authorial self-importance, and social irrelevance—their elite status as monads and as museum objects—the Tenth Symphony offers a bilateral experience as well as a good story. Part of the Tenth's increased relevance can be traced to the very aspects that were suspect back in 1924: the incompleteness, variability, and indeed open nature of the piece, where autobiography has merged with musical style and compositional structure. Mahler didn't plan on leaving his Tenth incomplete, obviously, but that very aspect has become a point of connection for us. In the words of *Gramophone* critic David Gutman, over recent decades we've gone from being skeptical of "tampering" with unfinished pieces of music to "almost seeing in their unresolved tensions some prophetic vision of the life to come."

The 1924 partial publication of Mahler's sketches, now in the public domain, means that Mahler's Tenth has even become a do-it-yourself project for an era of wikis, mash-ups, and fan fiction. Tenth Symphony completions have, in fact, become a cottage industry: Clinton Carpenter was an insurance adjuster who labored over the score after hours for more than twenty years, in his basement no less. More recently, Mahler-enthusiast mbhaub suggested in an online review of the Tenth Symphony versions that "if you're looking for a challenge, you could use [Cooke's transcribed] short score and make your own performing edition!" Given its popularity, Cooke's performing edition has helped advance recent cultures of musical archaeology: a trend in completing unfinished musical masterworks, ranging from Richard Maunder's and Robert Levin's editions of Mozart's Requiem (1988, 1991) to Brian Newbould's completion of Schubert's last symphony, no. 10 in D major (1995) and Anthony Payne's realization of Elgar's sketches for a Third Symphony (1997).

Aren't these all just instances of meddling? It's a false question, insofar as we now live in a non-hierarchical culture of communality. For two centuries, classical music, authorship, and "high culture" more broadly were based on a foundation of respect for textual authority and creative expertise. The various Mahler Tenth renderings, from Clinton Carpenter to today's bloggers, show these old ideals waning. Replacing them are ideals of consumerism, individualism, and amateurism. And collaboration: it's hard to think of another piece of classical music that demands the kind of input, the do-it-yourself decision-making, that the Tenth requires. Do you dismiss the work out of hand because its creator didn't live to approve it in any textual form (i.e., are you a strict intentionalist or originalist)? Do you choose to experience only those two movements that are more or less complete (i.e., are you a moderate pragmatist)? Do you involve yourself in the last Cooke edition, or the editions of Carpenter or Wheeler? Or do you involve yourself in the fullest textual "play" of the Tenth by engaging with all of the above, maybe depending on the day of the week, or on your attitude at the moment?

The Tenth Symphony requires us to make such choices, posing exceptional challenges at the same time it invokes unique mysteries. If the piece weren't so dramatic as music, the work of a virtuoso composer at the peak of his powers, its hypothetical basis and its insolvable enigmas would make it insupportable. But in the event, Mahler's Tenth proves just as prophetic as it is instructive, in equal measure beautiful and inscrutable.

SELECTED LISTENING

Not listed here are the entries in Leonard Bernstein's first Mahler cycle on Columbia/Sony, the set providing the time stamps for the main text of this volume.

SYMPHONY NO. 1

New York Philharmonic Orchestra, Bruno Walter. Columbia/Sony, 1954.
Chicago Symphony Orchestra, Carlo Maria Giulini. EMI/Warner, 1971.
Boston Symphony Orchestra, Seiji Ozawa. DG, 1977. (with "Blumine" movement)
Berlin Philharmonic Orchestra, Claudio Abbado. DG, 1989.
Cologne Radio Symphony Orchestra, Gary Bertini. EMI/Warner, 1991.

SYMPHONY NO. 2

Soloists; chorus. Philharmonia Orchestra, Otto Klemperer. EMI/Warner, 1962.
Soloists; chorus. Chicago Symphony Orchestra, Claudio Abbado. DG, 1977.
Soloists; chorus. Czech Philharmonic Orchestra, Ken-Ichiro Kobayashi. Exton, 1997/2004.
Soloists; chorus. London Philharmonic Orchestra, Vladimir Jurowski. LPO, 2009.

SYMPHONY NO. 3

Maureen Forrester, contralto; choruses. Concertgebouw Orchestra, Bernard Haitink. Philips/Decca, 1966.
Judith Blegen, mezzo-soprano; choruses. Chicago Symphony Orchestra, James Levine. RCA/Sony, 1975.

Jessye Norman, mezzo-soprano; choruses. Vienna Philharmonic Orchestra, Claudio Abbado. DG, 1982.
Agnes Baltsa, mezzo-soprano; choruses. Vienna Philharmonic Orchestra, Lorin Maazel. CBS/Sony, 1985.

SYMPHONY NO. 4

Edith Mathis, soprano. Berlin Philharmonic Orchestra, Herbert von Karajan. DG, 1979.
Lucia Popp, soprano. London Philharmonic Orchestra, Klaus Tennstedt. EMI/Warner, 1983.
Kathleen Battle, soprano. Vienna Philharmonic Orchestra, Lorin Maazel. CBS/Sony, 1985.
Hanna-Elisabeth Müller, soprano. Düsseldorf Symphony Orchestra, Adam Fischer. Avi Music, 2017.

SYMPHONY NO. 5

Cologne Radio Symphony Orchestra, Hans Rosbaud. ICA, 1951.
Philadelphia Orchestra, James Levine. RCA/Sony, 1978.
London Philharmonic Orchestra, Klaus Tennstedt. EMI/Warner, 1979.
Chicago Symphony Orchestra, Claudio Abbado. DG, 1980.
Seoul Philharmonic Orchestra, Myung-Whun Chung. DG, 2014.

SYMPHONY NO. 6

Berlin Philharmonic Orchestra, Herbert von Karajan. DG, 1978.
Vienna Philharmonic Orchestra, Leonard Bernstein. DG, 1988.
Concertgebouw Orchestra, Riccardo Chailly. Decca, 1995.
San Francisco Symphony, Michael Tilson Thomas. San Francisco Symphony Media, 2001.
MusicAeterna, Teodor Currentzis. Sony, 2018.

SYMPHONY NO. 7

Chicago Symphony Orchestra, Georg Solti. Decca, 1971.
Czech Philharmonic Orchestra, Vaclav Neumann. Supraphon, 1978.
London Philharmonic Orchestra, Klaus Tennstedt. EMI/Warner, 1981.
London Symphony Orchestra, Michael Tilson Thomas. RCA, 1999.
Simón Bolívar Symphony of Venezuela, Gustavo Dudamel. DG, 2014.

SYMPHONY NO. 8

Soloists; choruses. Chicago Symphony Orchestra, Georg Solti. Decca, 1971.
Soloists; choruses. Vienna Philharmonic, Leonard Bernstein. DG, 1975.

Soloists; choruses. Cologne Radio Symphony, Gary Bertini. EMI/Warner, 1991.
Soloists; choruses. Deutsches Symphonie-Orchester Berlin, Kent Nagano. Harmonia Mundi, 2004.

SYMPHONY NO. 9

Vienna Symphony Orchestra, Jascha Horenstein. Turnabout/Vox, 1952.
Berlin Philharmonic Orchestra, John Barbirolli. EMI/Warner, 1964.
Czech Philharmonic Orchestra, Karel Ančerl. Supraphon, 1966.
Berlin Philharmonic Orchestra, Claudio Abbado. DG, 2002.
Seoul Philharmonic Orchestra, Myung-Whun Chung. DG, 2014.

SYMPHONY NO. 10 (COOKE PERFORMING EDITION)

Berlin Radio Symphony Orchestra, Riccardo Chailly. Decca, 1987.
Tokyo Metropolitan Symphony Orchestra, Eliahu Inbal. Exton, 1995.
Orchestre Métropolitain, Yannick Nézet-Séguin. Atma, 2014.
Seattle Symphony Orchestra, Thomas Dausgaard. Seattle Symphony Media, 2017.

DAS KLAGENDE LIED

Soloists; chorus. Berlin Radio Symphony Orchestra, Riccardo Chailly. Decca, 1992.

DAS LIED VON DER ERDE

Murray Dickie, tenor; Dietrich Fischer-Dieskau, baritone. Philharmonia Orchestra, Paul Kletzki. EMI/Warner, 1959.
Christa Ludwig, mezzo-soprano; René Kollo, tenor. Berlin Philharmonic Orchestra, Herbert von Karajan. DG, 1973.
Janet Baker, mezzo-soprano; James King, tenor. Concertgebouw Orchestra, Bernard Haitink. Philips/Decca, 1975.
Brigitte Fassbaender, mezzo-soprano; Francisco Araiza, tenor, Berlin Philharmonic Orchestra, Carlo Maria Giulini. DG, 1984.

KINDTERTOTENLIEDER; RÜCKERT LIEDER

Christa Ludwig, mezzo-soprano. Berlin Philharmonic Orchestra, Herbert von Karajan. DG, 1975.

LIEDER EINES FAHRENDEN GESELLEN; KINDTERTOTENLIEDER; RÜCKERT LIEDER

Janet Baker, mezzo-soprano. Hallé Orchestra and New Philharmonia Orchestra, John Barbirolli. EMI/Warner, 1968 and 1970.
Thomas Hampson, baritone. Vienna Philharmonic Orchestra, Leonard Bernstein. DG, 1990.
Brigitte Fassbaender, mezzo-soprano. Berlin Radio Symphony Orchestra, Riccardo Chailly. Decca, 1994.

LIEDER EINES FAHRENDEN GESELLEN; RÜCKERT LIEDER; TWO SONGS FROM *DES KNABEN WUNDERHORN*

Frederica Von Stade, mezzo-soprano. London Philharmonic Orchestra, Andrew Davis. Columbia/Sony, 1979.

LIEDER EINES FAHRENDEN GESELLEN; RÜCKERT LIEDER; ASSORTED SONGS

Christian Gerhaher, baritone; Gerold Huber, piano. RCA/Sony, 2009.

SELECTED READING

Adorno, Theodor. *Mahler: A Musical Physiognomy*. Translated by Edmund Jephcott. Chicago and London: University of Chicago Press, 1992.

Barham, Jeremy, ed. *The Cambridge Companion to Mahler*. Cambridge and New York: Cambridge University Press, 2007.

———, ed. *Rethinking Mahler*. Oxford and New York: Oxford University Press, 2017.

Bauer-Lechner, Natalie. *Recollections of Gustav Mahler*. Edited by Peter Franklin. Translated by Dika Newlin. London: Faber, 1980.

Bekker, Paul. *Gustav Mahlers Sinfonien*. Berlin: Schuster and Loeffler, 1921. Translated by Kelly Dean Hansen as "Gustav Mahler's Symphonies (*Gustav Mahlers Sinfonien*) by Paul Bekker (1921): A Translation with Commentary." Musicology Graduate Theses and Dissertations, University of Colorado at Boulder, 2012. https://scholar.colorado.edu/muco_gradetds/4/.

Berlioz, Hector. *Berlioz's Orchestration Treatise: A Translation and Commentary*. Edited and translated by Hugh Macdonald. Cambridge, UK: Cambridge University Press, 2002.

Bernstein, Leonard. *The Little Drummer Boy: An Essay on Gustav Mahler*. Directed by Humphrey Burton. Hamburg: Deutsche Grammophon Video, 2007.

Bishop, Paul, ed. *A Companion to Goethe's* Faust. Rochester, NY, and Woodbridge, Suffolk, UK: Camden House, 2001.

Blaukopf, Kurt. *Gustav Mahler*. Translated by Inge Goodwin. New York: Praeger, 1973.

———. *Mahler: A Documentary Study*. Oxford and New York: Oxford University Press, 1976.

Blaukopf, Kurt, and Herta Blaukopf. *Mahler: His Life, Work, and World*. London: Thames and Hudson, 1991.

Brown, Jane K. *Faust: Theater of the World*. New York: Twayne, 1992.

Cooke, Deryck. *Gustav Mahler: An Introduction to His Music*. Cambridge, London, and New York: Cambridge University Press, 1980.

———. "The History of Mahler's Tenth Symphony." In *A Performing Version of the Draft for the Tenth Symphony / Gustav Mahler*. Prepared by Deryck Cooke, in collaboration with Berthold Goldschmidt, Colin Matthews, and David Matthews. London: Faber, 1989.

Coote, Alice. "Mahler's *Rückert-Lieder*: Alice Coote Talks to James Jolly about One of Gustav Mahler's Most Intense Sets of Songs." *Gramophone* 95, no. 1150 (July 2017).

Dahlhaus, Carl. *Realism in Nineteenth-Century Music*. Translated by Mary Whittall. Cambridge and London: Cambridge University Press, 1985.

Downes, Stephen C. *After Mahler: Britten, Weill, Henze, and Romantic Redemption*. Cambridge and New York: Cambridge University Press, 2013.

Draughon, Francesca, and Raymond Knapp. "Gustav Mahler and the Crisis of Jewish Identity." *Echo* 3, no. 2 (Fall 2001). http://www.echo.ucla.edu/Volume3-issue2/knapp_draughon/knapp_draughon1.html.

Feder, Stuart. *Gustav Mahler: A Life in Crisis*. New Haven: Yale University Press, 2004.

Floros, Constantin. *Gustav Mahler: The Symphonies*. Translated by Vernon and Jutta Wicker. Portland: Amadeus Press, 1993.

Franklin, Peter. *The Life of Mahler*. Cambridge and New York: Cambridge University Press, 1997.

———. *Mahler: Symphony No. 3*. Cambridge and New York: Cambridge University Press, 1991.

Greene, David B. *Mahler, Consciousness and Temporality*. New York and London: Gordon and Breach Science Publishers, 1985.

Kaplan, Gilbert. "A Dirge? No. It's a Love Song." *New York Times*, July 19, 1992. https://nyti.ms/2GHsRat.

———. "A Guide to the Resurrection Symphony." Liner notes for *Mahler: Symphony No. 2*, London Symphony Orchestra conducted by Gilbert Kaplan, MCA Classics MCAD2-11011, compact disc, 1988.

Kennedy, Michael. *Mahler*. 2nd edition. London: Dent, 1990.

La Grange, Henry-Louis de. *Gustav Mahler*. Vol. 2, *Vienna: The Years of Challenge, 1897–1904*. Oxford and New York: Oxford University Press, 1995.

———. *Gustav Mahler*. Vol. 3, *Vienna: Triumph and Disillusion, 1904–1907*. Oxford and New York: Oxford University Press, 1999.

———. *Gustav Mahler*. Vol. 4, *A New Life Cut Short, 1907–1911*. Oxford and New York: Oxford University Press, 2008.

———. *Mahler*. Garden City, NY: Doubleday, 1973.

———. "The Tenth Symphony: Purgatory or Catharsis?" In *Fragment or Completion? Proceedings of the Mahler X Symposium, Utrecht 1986*, ed. Paul Op de Coul. The Hague: Nijgh and Van Ditmar/Universitaire Pers Rotterdam, 1991.

La Grange, Henry-Louis de, and Günther Weiss, eds., in collaboration with Knud Martner. *Gustav Mahler: Letters to His Wife*. Revised and translated by Antony Beaumont. Ithaca: Cornell University Press, 2004.

Mahler, Alma. *Gustav Mahler: Memories and Letters*. Enlarged ed. Edited by Donald Mitchell. Translated by Basil Creighton. New York: Viking Press, 1969.

Mahler Broadcasts 1948–1982: Mahler in New York. New York: New York Philharmonic Special Editions, 1998.

Martner, Knud. *Mahler's Concerts*. New York: Kaplan Foundation/Overlook Press, 2010.

McManus, Michael. "Mahler by the World's Greatest Conductors." *Gramophone* online. https://www.gramophone.co.uk/features/focus/mahler-by-the-worlds-greatest-conductors.

Mitchell, Donald. *Gustav Mahler*. Vol. I, *The Early Years*. Revised and edited by Paul Banks and David Matthews. London: Faber and Faber, 1980.

———. *Gustav Mahler*. Vol. II, *The Wunderhorn Years*. Berkeley and Los Angeles: University of California Press, 1975.

———. *Gustav Mahler: Songs and Symphonies of Life and Death*. London: Faber, 1985.

Mitchell, Donald, and Andrew Nicholson, eds. *The Mahler Companion*. Oxford and New York: Oxford University Press, 1999.

Osborne, Richard. Liner note for *Mahler: Symphony No. 4*. Berlin Philharmonic Orchestra conducted by Herbert von Karajan. Deutsche Grammophon 419 863-2, compact disc, 1991.

———. Liner note for *Mahler: Symphony No. 6*. Berlin Philharmonic Orchestra conducted by Herbert von Karajan. Deutsche Grammophon 415 099-2, compact disc, 1984.

———. Liner note for *Mahler: Symphony No. 9, Kindertotenlieder, Rückert-Lieder*. Berlin Philharmonic Orchestra conducted by Herbert von Karajan. DG 453 040, compact disc, 1997.

Peattie, Thomas. *Gustav Mahler's Symphonic Landscapes*. Cambridge and New York: Cambridge University Press, 2015.

Schaufler, Wolfgang, ed. *Gustav Mahler: The Conductors' Interviews*. Vienna: Universal Edition, 2013.
Specht, Richard. *Gustav Mahler*. Berlin: Schuster and Loeffler, 1913.
Stoll Knecht, Anna. *Mahler's Seventh Symphony*. Oxford and New York: Oxford University Press, 2019.
Tovey, Donald Francis. *Essays in Musical Analysis*. Vol. 2, *Symphonies (II), Variations and Orchestral Polyphony*. Oxford, UK: Oxford University Press, 1939.
Wagner, Richard. *A Pilgrimage to Beethoven and Other Essays*. Translated by William Ashton Ellis. Lincoln and New York: University of Nebraska Press, 1994.
Walter, Bruno. *Gustav Mahler*. Translated by Lotte Walter Lindt. New York: Knopf, 1966.
Youmans, Charles. *Mahler and Strauss: In Dialogue*. Bloomington and Indianapolis: Indiana University Press, 2016.

INDEX

ABOUT THE AUTHOR

Arved Ashby is professor of music at the Ohio State University, where he specializes in 20th and 21st century art music as well as cultural history and media and communications. He has published articles on Arnold Schoenberg, Frank Zappa, and Benjamin Britten, and he has taught classes on topics as varied as ancient music, film music by Philip Glass, and 20th-century music through the prism of the Beatles.